Searching For A Sister Lost At Sea

A Family Memoir
by Christine Andreae

Cover Photo: Mary Ewing with Mercy by Joan R. Challinor

Cover Design: Pam Owens Design

978-0-9992242-0-5

Also by Christine Andreae

Non-Fiction

When Evening Comes:
The Education of a Hospice Volunteer

Seances and Spiritualists

Fiction

Smoke Eaters

Small Target

Grizzly

Trail of Murder

FOR MY GRANDCHILDREN
MERCY AND CECILIA AND BERTIE
AND THEIR MANY COUSINS

❧

THAT THE OLD GRIEF OF THIS STORY

MAY NOT CALCIFY AND SINK BELOW THE SURFACE;

THAT IN MY TELLING OF IT, THEY MAY FIND CHARTS

FOR THE EBB AND FLOW OF LIFE'S TIDES.

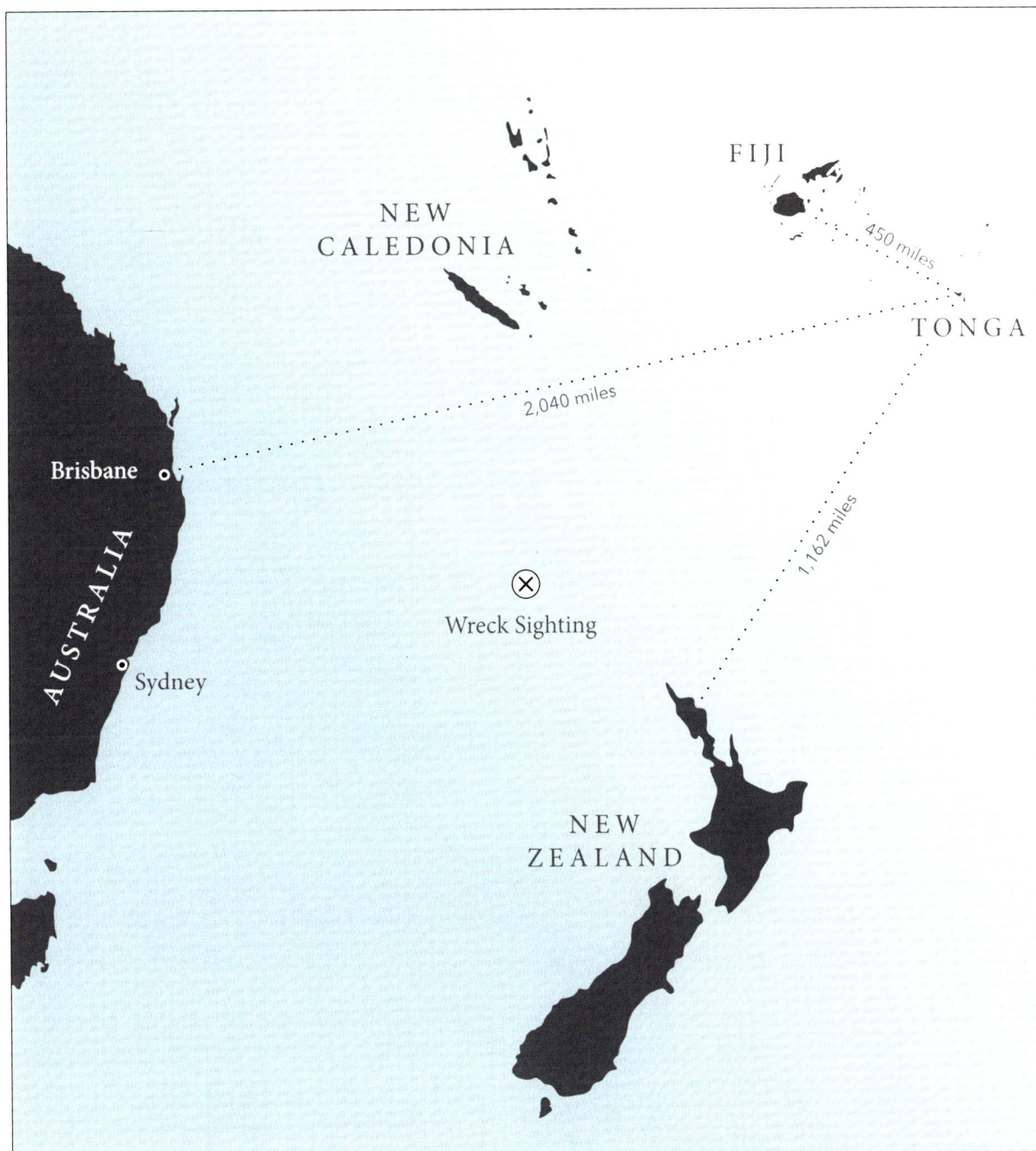

FIJI

NEW
CALEDONIA

450 miles

TONGA

2,040 miles

1,162 miles

Brisbane

AUSTRALIA

Sydney

⊗
Wreck Sighting

NEW
ZEALAND

Family

John D Crimmins
1844-1917

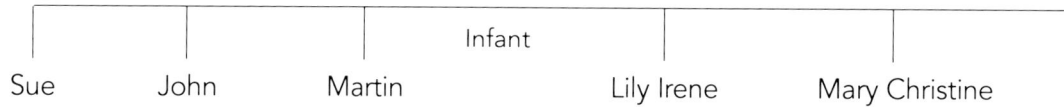

Sue   John   Martin   Infant   Lily Irene   Mary Christine

Frederick Berthold Ewing   m.   Jessie Vallé
1853 - 1897   1856-1926

Vallé   William Ewing   Frederick "Fritz"
                 "Buck Sr"
Maria Taylor   m.   1880-1965
1885-1956

William Ewing Jr   Jane   Jessie   Grace
"Buck"
1912-1996

Ewing

Mary Christine "Christie"   Sheila   William III   Frederick II   Jessie Vallé
b.1942   b.1943   "Billy"   "Fritz"   b.1950
m. Frederick "Andy" Andreae m. Thomas "Tom" Daley b.1946   b.1948

Chart

m.   Lily Lalor
            1848-1888

Thomas   Infant   Constance   Cyril   Evelyn   Clarence

David Challinor   m.   Mercedes Crimmins
1886-1962   1885-1966

David Challinor, Jr   m.   Joan Ridder   **Mary Challinor**
1920-2008   b.1927   **1922-2009**

Julia   Mary   Sarah   David "Tom"
b.1953   b.1954   b.1956   b.1960

Children

David Challinor   Patrick Crimmins   **Mercedes Crimmins**   Thomas
1952-2008   1954-1995   **"Mercy"**   Crimmins "Tom"
                                             1956 -1977   b.1960

PROLOGUE

*I'm growing...And i've got
to have lots of room.*

- Mercy

    Sometime in October or November of 1977, my sister Mercy Ewing disappeared. She was twenty years old, the youngest girl in a family of nine kids raised on the Connecticut shore of Long Island Sound, and she had taken off to see the South Pacific. After two months of backpacking in the Fiji Islands and the Kingdom of Tonga, she hitched a ride on an orange catamaran bound for New Zealand. We never heard from her again.

    For all the anguish and heartbreak my mother and my father (and my younger sisters and brothers) went through, I was somewhat removed from it. I was the first-born and Mercy was the eighth. We were both July babies, born under the sign of Cancer, but we were fourteen years apart. When I was born in 1942, my father William Ewing - nicknamed "Buck" - was wearing the uniform of an Army Air Corps officer and preparing to fight the Japanese. When Mercy was born in 1956, he was wearing a Brooks Brothers suit and commuting to Wall Street. When she was a baby and a little girl, I was away from home, first at boarding school - the Convent of the

Sacred Heart in Noroton, Connecticut - then at Manhattanville College in Purchase, New York, and after that, in graduate school at Yale in New Haven, Connecticut, where I met my husband Andy, a student at Yale School of Architecture. Mercy was eleven when we were married. I remember very little about our wedding except that it was a humid August day so hot and sweaty that congratulatory kisses slid off my cheek. In photographs of our reception, Mercy is wearing a pretty cotton shift and white anklets with her Mary Janes. Her sun-bleached hair is damp, her face flushed, her brown eyes unfocused. My teenaged brothers and their friends had thought it a great joke to get both her and our youngest brother Tom drunk on champagne.

1973: Building our tower house in the Virginia woods.

When it came Mercy's turn for boarding school, Andy and I were living in Washington, DC, where I was working as a free-lance feature writer for the old *Washington Star Evening News*. After I had the good luck to get a contract to write a young adult book called *Seances and Spiritualists*, at my mother's suggestion Mercy produced some clever, whimsical ink drawings of mediums floating out of their bodies. My editor praised the samples but opted to illustrate the book with period photographs and etchings, so the book was published without her work.

By 1977, the year she was lost, Andy and I had moved to the Shenandoah Valley of Virginia and were raising our two sons in a house he had designed and we had hand-built ourselves in the woods that adjoined the Shenandoah National Park. From time to time, usually late at night with too much wine and in the company of friends, I would relate the circumstances of Mercy's disappearance. Andy would jump in to correct me and we might argue about what had happened, but inevitably, someone would exclaim, "You should write about it!" and I would simply shake my head. The story was impossibly complex. There was no way to sort out what really had happened. It made me feel tired and it made me feel sad. Sad for the way her loss had driven a wedge between my parents, sad that I never had a real connection with her.

Gradually, I found a kind of crust forming around of the sadness of it, like a callus on the heart. The story became static, almost ritual: "My sister was lost at sea, sailing on a catamaran in the Pacific." Some times I told it one way, some times another. Her boat went down in cyclone or was run-over at night by a freighter. It was an accident of nature or a stupid human mistake. With repetition and the passing of years, the story shrank and became small enough to tuck away, an indigestible lump that I got used to. When my sons were teenagers and got their driver's licenses, I used to pull the story out and threaten them with it: "I don't care how late you stay out, but I have to know where you are. If I don't hear from you I'll call the state police and have them track you down. I'm not going to go through what my mother went through with my sister Mercy."

Still, rather than tackle the mystery of what had become of her, I began writing mysteries of my own making and, during the nineteen-nineties, I published four murder mysteries. I also wrote a book about real-life death: an account of my experiences as a patient care volunteer for hospice. But I continued to push aside the story of my lost sister. To write a satisfying mystery, you need to tidy up all the lose ends; in Mercy's case, there was nothing but loose ends. As for hospice work, along with the profound spiritual gifts that come from attending a person who is dying, there is a body at the end and the possibility of closure. There is no end to a disappearance. Why revisit it? What was there to gain by it?

However, in 2005, when my mother, Mary Challinor Ewing, was 83, she excavated a packet of letters and postcards from Mercy and gave them to me. They ranged from her school days to her last letter home from Tonga. I had never read them before and Mom had never read them since. She had no desire to read them again but as they were all she had of Mercy, she had kept them. There were postcards of killer whales or views of the snow-capped Rockies, badly misspelled ("sweeter" for sweater, "farry" for ferry) and bizarrely curt and sassy. Was she stoned when she wrote them? The letters from Fiji and Tonga were on blue airmail tissue, covered with her cramped, peculiar handwriting and sprinkled with little drawings in ballpoint. The stamps were exotic: tropical fruits and birds, a black queen on a throne.

My mother also gave me a large manila envelope she had found in Dad's desk after he died. It was worn soft as velvet in the corners and filled with flotsam from the search he had made for Mercy. There were phone numbers on the backs of envelopes, air mail letters from New Zealand, copies of cables, faded photocopies of reports, official letters on stationary bearing a US State Department seal.

I put Mercy's letters and Dad's folder safely away in a bottom drawer of my steel file cabinet. But through the metal, the actuality of them, their very tangibility worked on me. Gradually bubbles of curiosity began to perk through my resistance. I began asking my family questions. I deciphered Mercy's handwriting and, for the first time in my life, got to know her as an individual. I asked my brothers and sisters what they remembered. I arranged Dad's file in chronological order. I had strange dreams. I began to write. And to rewrite and rewrite. There were long periods of not writing, months or a full year, a kind of gestation process, perhaps. After my mother's death in 2009, I found more letters and that primed my pump again, sent me back to my drafts.

What follows is the story of my parents' search for Mercy. It is also the story of Mercy's own search for herself. But anyone who has tried to write about a family's past knows that the territory of memory is not firm underfoot. Packed paths suddenly become swampy; markers shift; reflections waver in a changing light. At times, my memories are at odds with Andy's or with those of my sisters and brothers and cousins who grew up with Mercy. Memory, I've learned, is self-serving - tinted, if not richly colored, by our own psychological needs and wants. So given the uncertain territory of the past, I have tried to ground this account with dates and facts from letters and cablegrams of that time. Still, there are guesses, leaps across dark water from one marshy hummock to another, and in the end, this is a story of my own making fashioned over ten years, a story of my own search for a sister lost at sea.

1

Firwood

It was on New Year's Eve, 1977, that I abruptly learned Mercy was missing. Andy and I and our boys, Morgan and Tim, then six and three, had driven up from Virginia for a post-Christmas visit to my parents at "Firwood" in Noroton, Connecticut. This was a hulking, four-story Victorian that my great-grandfather John D. Crimmins had built as a summer house by the sea for his thirteen children. Growing up, the massive size of the house was sometimes embarrassing.

I remember being taken aback when a schoolmate referred to it as a "mansion": its threadbare hall carpets, rusty pipes that spewed brown bath water, and cracked plaster ceilings didn't mesh with my idea of a mansion. Firwood was simply "home" - the house where our family lived and where, in a previous century, my grandmother and her brothers and sisters had spent their summers and holidays. I loved my grandmother's stories about the place. I loved the house's secret corners, the huge copper beeches on the lawn, the spectacular views of Long Island Sound, and I wanted my children to connect to the place - to love it as I did. But in reality, when we visited, Morgan and Tim often got lost in the chaos of adult siblings staying up too late, drinking too much and fighting over resurrected nursery grievances.

New Years Eve, 1977, was no exception. My sister Sheila, a year and a half younger than I, lived next door with her husband Tom Daley and their three children in "The Garden House" a shingle-style pavilion that "John D." (as we called our great-grandfather) had built for tennis parties and dances. Sheila had invited us, along with Mom and Dad and whoever else was home, for a buffet supper. In the great room, her table was laid with wedding china and crystal. High above the table, in the two-story gloom, the glassy eye of a moth-eaten moose head caught sparkles from her Christmas tree, an elegantly decorated 12-foot spruce.

I remember my mother sitting in an armchair nursing a Scotch before supper. Later, she and Dad were going on to a neighboring cousin's party and she was dressed up as much as she ever dressed up: slacks and a cashmere cardigan, calf-skin Belgian slippers that had escaped David Dog, her black lab named by my youngest brother Tom after my brother David. But that night, Mom was more part of the chair than the conversation. She sat pressed back into its cushions. Her face was drawn, her jaw tense and her blue eyes distracted.

I knew that the Christmas invasion of returning children, spouses, and grandchildren always exhausted her. Dad was sentimental about Christmas and liked to have everyone home, but it was Mom who did all the preparations: shopping for mountains of presents and groceries, bed making, tree trimming, and cooking. Usually there were twenty or twenty-five of us for Christmas dinner - a twenty-pound turkey at each end of John D.'s massive oak table. By timing my visit over New Years, I had hoped for a relaxing visit with my mother. But that hadn't happened. She had been remote, both with me and with the boys.

Later in the evening, Andy and I took the boys back to Firwood and settled them in the "baby room" next to Mom and Dad's bedroom. They had come home early from their party and offered to baby-sit, so Andy and I went back to see in the New Year with Sheila and Tom at the Garden House. Of course we all had had too much to drink: bourbon before dinner, champagne with dessert, and afterwards my brother-in-law Tommy Daley's Stingers - a lethally delicious "digestif" of brandy and white créme-de-menthe. We sat by the fire in what was originally a billiard room paneled in walnut, now a den furnished with a leather sofa, comfortable chairs, and

Mercy's ink sketch of an OBE (out of body experience)
for my book *Seances and Spiritualists*.

a TV. I was slumping in my chair, but if Sheila was tired after cooking supper and putting her kids to bed, it didn't show. As usual, she sat with her back as perfectly straight, the pleats of the long kilt she wore making a graceful fan around her ankles.

"What's the matter with Mother?" I asked.

"She's worried about Mercy," Sheila said flatly. "She hasn't heard from her. She was supposed to be in New Zealand at Thanksgiving."

My alcohol-soaked brain turned slowly. Dimly I remembered hearing that Mercy, who had been living in Jackson, Wyoming, had taken off for the Fiji Islands at the end of the summer. I felt a righteous prickle of annoyance at my freewheeling youngest sister: the least she could do was let our mother know where she was. I felt sorry for my mother, but perhaps more sorry for myself: I'd come all the way up from Virginia to visit my mother and thanks to Mercy, she was inaccessible.

The conversation turned towards Dad; a well-worn topic when we adult children got together. Buck Ewing ruled his roost with a iron hand: as an investment banker, he could not control the ups and downs of the stock market, but as a father he expected to be able to control his family. Once he got an idea of how things should be, he was immovable. This of course led to battles. As the first in a long line of sullen teenagers, I frequently clashed with him. Sometimes it was because I answered rudely when he demanded to know who had left a light on. Sometimes it was because he felt I wasn't responsible or dutiful enough: because I was buried in a book instead of helping out with the younger kids. Sometimes it would go beyond yelling and he would let lose with a hard slap to my face. One time, I remember being frightened as well as humiliated: the force of impact knocked me off my feet and I landed on my knees, blubbering at his feet as I scrambled to pick up the ice that had spilled from the glass of ginger ale I had been holding. But usually, after being hit, I would turn and flee to my room, burning with fury, and slam the door so hard that the walls would shake. Dad always felt badly after he hit. Moments later he would knock on my door and then come in shamefaced but without waiting for permission. He would apologize for losing his temper and ask for my forgiveness. Still shaking with hatred, I would force myself to utter the absolution he required - "I forgive you" - but the words came out dripping venom and often the battle would resume.

I don't remember what I said about him that night to set Sheila off. But I remember the gist of what she said to me: Mercy was missing and it was all my fault. I had poisoned her and our younger brothers and sisters against our father.

"What do you want?" she demanded of me, her voice full of anger and disgust. "Someone out of Father Knows Best? Grow up!" She jumped out of her chair and strode out of the room. I could hear her angry footsteps as she ran up the stairs to her bedroom.

We sat there stunned, as if we had just witnessed the impossible: a familiar hill in a gentle landscape suddenly erupting with the incalculable force of a volcano. I saw Andy was as shocked as I was. His family rarely argued and never fought openly. And while he enjoyed entering into the usual drunken fray of late-night sibling arguments at Firwood, this was different. It had never occurred to me that my fights with my father affected anyone else in house but me. Mercy hadn't even been born during my worst years at home; after I was sent off to the Convent at age thirteen, my encounters with him became coldly dutiful and polite. How could I be responsible for Mercy's fights with him? The accusation seemed bizarre. It was as if Sheila had accused me of having three heads. I remember thinking, "What on earth is wrong with her?"

I don't know how long the three of us sat there in the after-shock of her explosion or if we talked at all. But after a while, I went upstairs on unsteady legs. I knocked on Sheila's door, and (like my father) without waiting for permission, I went in. It was dark. From the light coming through the doorway, I saw she was buried under the covers of the king-sized bed. "Sheila?" I said.

She made a muffled noise.

"Are you alright?"

"I just had too much to drink," she said.

"But what's the matter?"

She surfaced. I heard her take a ragged breath. Then she blurted out: "I think Mercy's dead!"

Our youngest brother Tom surveying Mom's table set for New Year's Day lunch in the kitchen. Mercy in the corner smoking. Tom and Mercy were buddies.

Mom was deeply attached to Firwood and took many photos of the place. This one is a winter view of Long Island Sound from the living room.

She started to cry.

For the second time that night, I was utterly shocked. I turned on a standing lamp by a chaise on the far side of the room. It cast a soft light on the rumpled bedclothes. Sheila was wearing a pale satin nightgown and her shoulders were bare in the lamplight. Her eyes were red, her face puffy. She told me that Dad had not wanted Mercy to go to Fiji. He didn't approve of her taking off on her own. He wanted her to go to college. They fought about it, fought bitterly. He threatened to cut off her money, but she had saved enough money to buy passage on a freighter. She wrote to Mom asking for the passport she had left at home and Mom mailed it to her in Jackson.

My mother saw nothing wrong with the idea of the trip. She saw it as an adventure, a learning experience, and she refused to back Dad in his insistence that Mercy not go. Sheila, in the role of peacemaker, called Mercy in Wyoming and talked to her for over an hour. "Go if you have to," she ending up telling Mercy, "but at least come home first and say goodbye. You can't leave this way. It's the least you can do for Mother." So Mercy flew home for a short visit. Then Mom drove her to the airport and Mercy flew out to Seattle to board a freighter bound for the Fiji Islands.

Sheila started to cry again. "It's all my fault," she wailed. "I told her she could go, and now she's dead!"

I found my way downstairs and reported what I had heard. Andy and Tom decided there was only one thing to be done: to start looking for Mercy. Tom thought the last place she'd been was Tonga. Where was Tonga? We got out the National Geographic Atlas and found the Pacific Ocean. Tonga turned out to be a dot on a blue page lined with latitudes and longitudes. Impetuously, Tom picked up the phone and dialed the operator: "Get me Tonga," he ordered. The simplicity of it took my breath away. Why, if Mother had been so worried, hadn't she picked up the phone herself?

It was one o'clock in the morning on New Year's Day. Lord knows how many drunken long distance callers the operators had already dealt with, but somehow, with Andy, my husband, prompting from a National Geographic atlas, half an hour later Tommy ended up connected to an operator in American Samoa. "I want to talk to the priest," he demanded.

Several beats later: "Yeah, the Catholic Church."

"The priest?" I objected as if he were crazy. "You think she went to Mass?!"

I don't remember if we ever raised the priest. Andy remembers that they talked to someone at a police station then tried to reach the American consulate - without success.

The next day at Firwood, Mom had a New Year's Day luncheon. My brothers and their wives arrived with children in tow. We fixed ourselves Bloody Marys, straight vodka on ice for Mom. From a Polaroid photo that Dad took, I see that my sister Jessie was there and my brother Patrick who was physically and mentally handicapped - back then we all said "retarded" without shame.

Grandchildren ran around hallways. In the living room, Mom lit a fire she had laid earlier in the fireplace. We lit our cigarettes. Winter sunlight streamed in through the bay window, sparkled on a blue Long Island Sound. Sheila and Tom came in, their coats exhaling cold air. Sheila was wearing sunglasses. "Sorry," she said to me. She sounded embarrassed.

"It's okay," I said back.

As if she were at a funeral, she kept her sunglasses on in the living room.

Dear Ma, sorry 3/21 spring I don't write more often. I never really I don't ~~write~~ ... I forget, never really think about it ... or ... notice write. I write ... Like people who they're being ~~...~~ bitch ... and only realize when they're ... in ... that so.

I usually ... letters for informing you on ... long time — ever since we moved ... haven't ... this ... It's all quite comfortable ... ~~...~~ in this house ... to a nice ... and friendly people. Maybe too com... But I ~~...~~ been in a situation like this — living ... while, so I think I'll enjoy it while I can.

I feel a lit of pressure to make an ... much a pressure of finding something or someone that ... show me a path I can take ... but ... more before they're ruined ~~...~~ ... there are ... go and could go ... and even could go with no other and I wouldn't feel guilty or like I was wasting time ... a desirable way to ... up. I mean, do you think ... and keep striving + pushing even though I'll probably ... next time something exciting + new catches my eyes ... but feel like its more important for me ...

All these places, South Pacific, Alaska, Tibet, Mongolia, ... being crushed or prosperity(?), building, reassignment, people ... people with ... I don't want a ... assume so involved in earning a ... that I miss out on all the rest. I ... some kind of general goal for the ... but its so unforgettable ... now. Mostly just ... that make my ... and my ... and ... Maybe I shouldn't go by my feeling if I ... or even hold on to them long enough for a clue

March, 1977
Jackson, WY

3/21 Spring

Dear Ma, sorry I don't write more often I never realize I don't. I forget – never really think about it. I only notice when I write Like people who never realize when they're being a bitch and only realize when they're being nice. I think I'm like that too.

I usually save letters for informing you on my future plans. For a long time – ever since we moved I haven't been thinking of the future. It's all quite comfortable living in this house working, skiing, coming home to a nice fire and friendly people. Maybe too comfortable and secure? I haven't been in a situation like this – living with other people in a while, so think I'll enjoy it while I can.

I feel a lot of presure to move on and see more lands. Not so much a pressure of finding something or someone that will guide me or show me a path I can take but to see more places, lands and peoples before they're ruined. There are so many places I wanna go and could go...and even could go with no other purpose than to "see" & I wouldn't feel guilty or like I was wasting time...Do you think that is a destructive way to grow-up? I mean, do you think I should have a goal and keep striving & pushing even though I'll probably change my mind the next time something exciting and nice catches my eye?

I just feel like its more important for me now to see all I can. All these places, South Pacific, Alaska, Tibet, Mongolia, Scandinavia, Northern Scotland are being crushed by prosperity (?) & building, development, people trying to achieve, get-ahead people with goals. I don't want a goal right now. I don't want to become so involved in learning a profession, in becoming a career woman that I miss out on all the rest. I guess I do have some kind of personal goal for the near future (3-5 yrs) but it's so intangible now. Mostly just a bundle of feelings that make my decisions and give me energy.

Maybe I shouldn't go by my feeling if i can't catagorize them or even hold on to them long enough for close look...living on emotion but not logic and reason. If every one worked that way the world would be a mess. But I think I can get away with out hurting too many people, maybe worry a few, but...there's always some one that will worry.

Do you worry about me? I mean, do you think I'm totally blind, missing the whole point of living....that I need some guidance? I know how important it is for you to have me keep my mind, moving, reading, drawing, communicating... And I'm trying to...But school for me now would be useless. I know it would be...well, I feel it would be. I just don't want you to worry about me. I'm growing-up... just starting out. I'm growing...And i've got to have lots of room.

Well, as I said I haven't been making any plans for my future. I'll get to work on it --Yeah, yeah, we've heard that before --and I'll let you know what my latest dreams are...

Sorry I don't write more often...I'll try and do it more often. I like to...I just don't.

Much love Mercy

hope every thing goes well with your visit to Chicago, say hello to Sheila and Jessie

2

When Mercy was born in July 1956, Dad gave Mom a present of four South American emeralds. He had them set in a brooch designed like a flower and the liquid-looking green stones bloomed on graceful diamond-studded stems. Mom, who lived in madras shorts all summer and blue jeans all winter, could probably count on one hand the number of times she got dressed up enough to wear emeralds, but they were much admired and approved of by her mother, my grandmother Mercedes Crimmins Challinor, and her sisters, "the Aunts". They saw it not only as a romantic gesture on Dad's part, but a well-deserved reward for the hardship of bearing an eighth child. Their own mother had died after the birth of her thirteenth - a boy named Clarence.

Mercedes as a young woman.

After the death of their father in 1917, Mercedes and two of her sisters inherited the family's "country seat" as John D. referred to his summer home in his diary. The sisters divided the estate between them, and every June, they would decamp from New York apartments to spend summer "on the place." One sister, Evelyn Crimmins Patterson, moved her family into Firwood. Two other sisters, Constance Crimmins Childs, a widow, and Mary Christine Crimmins, a spinster, occupied The Stables, a three-story converted barn that had once housed their horses, carriages, and grooms. Late in June the Aunts would take up residence along with two generations of our cousins and a contingent of Irish maids. Their arrival was always an excitement for us.

My grandmother Mercedes had taken over The Garden House. I loved my grandmother and basked in her attentions. I remember the smell of her roses in the cool darkness of her great room.

My grandmother Mercedes c. 1923 with my mother Mary on her lap and her brother David Challinor, Jr.

On her porch, on a glass-topped table, she often had a bunch of the green flowers called Bells of Ireland which smelled faintly of lime. We would sit in rattan chairs with the Sound sparkling in the near distance, and she would tell me stories about the old days on the place. Sheila and I would run barefoot back and forth between her house and the Stables where we played tag and swam with our cousins or visited with the Aunts. We watched them arrange flowers cut that morning from their garden, lay out games of solitaire in the afternoon. In the evening, after baths at home, we would run down to the Stables in our pajamas to visit during cocktail hour when the Aunts, having dressed for dinner, would appear in long taffeta tea gowns.

A day after our new sister was born, I was playing backgammon at the Stables with my older cousin Sandy, later to become Dom Luke of the Dominican order. It was a hot July afternoon, and we sat in uncomfortable ladder-back chairs at a small polished game table in the long, whitewashed living room. Through a small window beside us, I could look out onto the Sound, pale and flat in the heat. More interesting than backgammon was Sandy's name game. Among other exotic names, he proposed that the baby should be called "Octavia."

"Octavia?"

"She's the eighth," he explained. "Tavia for short," he decided. The aunts, who sat needlepointing in their accustomed chairs, smiled. Was he serious? Sandy devoured history the same way I, who had just turned fourteen, devoured romantic fiction, so perhaps he was being ironic. Octavia was the name of Nero's wife - a wife whom he poisoned. Not an auspicious name. But I was ignorant of history and after saying "Tavia" out loud several times, I found I liked it. Tavia. As exotic sounding as the names in Tolstoy. Perhaps the name of an orphaned heroine in a Southern gothic novel. At home, I lobbied for Tavia but was summarily dismissed. The baby would have a traditional family name. She would be another Mercedes in honor, at last, of my grandmother.

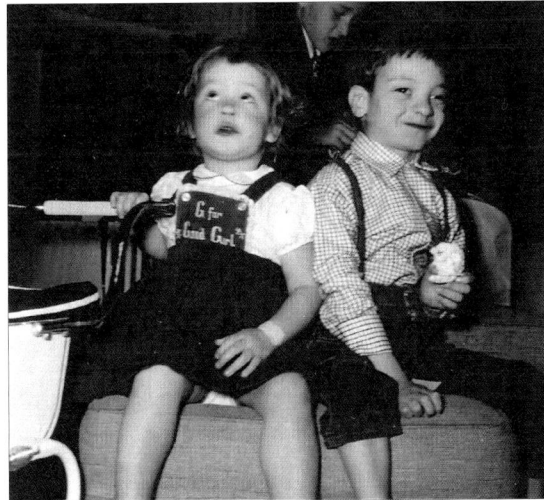

Mercy and Pat

The only one of us who did not have a family name was our brother Patrick who was born two years before Mercy. He had not been expected to live; a priest had baptized him in the hospital. This, as we knew from our Baltimore Catechism, was to prevent his soul from being stuck in Limbo, a gray area between Heaven and Hell inhabited by unbaptised babies. Dad wanted to name him after an army buddy named Patrick O'Riley who had served with him in the Pacific and whom Dad greatly admired. But Mom balked at "O'Riley." In the end, they agreed on Crimmins for a middle name. The name was less obviously Irish than O'Riley, but Irish nonetheless: John D. Crimmins had emulated the life-style of an English peer, but he was the son of an immigrant gardener from County Cork.

For Patrick, Mom had replaced all the stained baby dresses and receiving blankets with new ones in gender-neutral yellow. When she finally brought him home from the hospital and unswaddled him for us to see, we saw a listless baby with a slightly lopsided face, a thatch of black hair and yellow skin made more yellow by his new garments. We were told he had jaundice, as well as a hole in his heart.

By the time Mercy was born, two years later, it was clear that Pat was not developing normally. Mom held out hope that he would "catch up" as he grew older, but when Tommy - christened Thomas Crimmins Ewing and her last baby - was born, it was clear that Patrick, now aged four, was worse-off than "slow". It was explained to us, and we in turn explained to our friends, that due to the hole in his heart, his brain had not gotten enough oxygen at birth; consequently he was "retarded".

Eventually he learned to walk, but it was more of a lurch-and-stagger than a walk. He could understand us, and could talk after a fashion, but he sounded as if his mouth was full of marbles - wet, garbled sounds, impossible to understand if you didn't know him. Furthermore, he had a lazy eye that would roll around independently of his "good" eye, so he seemed to possess the ability to see in two directions at once. Despite these handicaps, or perhaps because of them, his lopsided grin pulled at my heart and his looks intrigued me: thick dark hair and skin was so pale you could see blue veins at his temples. When he was calm, his hands, with their delicate long-fingers, moved like as seaweed under water. He was altogether alien.

According to one doctor's label, mentally he was around the age of nine, and throughout his life, his tastes and interests were those of a young boy: he loved circuses, was an ardent admirer of Minnie Mouse and played the LP of Hello Dolly so often that he wore out the vinyl grooves. When one of us, fed up with hearing Carol Channing sing about a parade for the thirtieth time, would threaten to break the record if he didn't stop, he would let out a vehement roar that would bring Mom or Marie Burns, our Scottish nurse, running to his defense. "Ye have to make allowances for him," Marie would scold.

When he got his way, which he usually did, he had a sly, cat-like smile of satisfaction. "You are spoiled, you know that?" my sister Jessie would tease him. "Pat, look at me. You know you are spoiled?" And he would knit his eyebrows together in a dark scowl, then rumble "NO!" and she would laugh. Pat the Rat. Sneaky Pete. Sometimes he would sulk when teased, but more often he perked up. He liked to ham it up.

If his relationship with us was edgy, his love for Mom was pure, powerful, and unshakable. Whenever she came into the room, the joy on his face illuminated him. And she loved him back with the fierce maternal devotion that only a wounded child can inspire. The quickest way to Mom's smile of approval was to show Pat affection. My own infrequent and half-hearted attempts to connect with him were not a great success - I was, after all, the wicked older sister subbing for Mom. I once knitted him a sweater - without a pattern, no less. I think I was seventeen. I measured him, bought navy blue wool and ended up with a garment whose small torso and extra long arms looked like a little monkey sweater. I gave up on it.

Mercy, Patrick, and Tommy. The three little ones, we called them. From my aloof vantage point as a college student, I saw Mercy and Tommy as cute. They were sturdy toddlers, blond, rosy-cheeked, and funny. In a 2008 email, Sheila remembers Mercy as "a beautiful child, round and healthy, and a striking contrast to Pat who so spindly - all elbows and knees and awkward movement." She went on to comment:

> Mercy's robust physique must have been a tremendous relief to mother
> coming after the birth of Pat. In fact in one of the photo albums she captioned a
> picture "Mercy arrived - a healthy baby girl".

The three little ones shared the same room, the "baby room" sandwiched between Mom and Dad's room and our nurse Marie's room. In Mom's snapshots, Mercy - first as a baby, then as a toddler - was always in the same picture as Patrick. The family album shows them on Mom's bed together, Mercy sitting up, head erect and alert, Pat propped up on pillows, one eye half open.

There's a shot of them on the same rocking horse and another of them sitting on my grandmother Mercedes' lap. Mom included Patrick in all family activities and vacations. In public, his lurching gait, his moans and hums, his habits of eating Kleenex and of grabbing his crotch unfailingly attracted stares. I remember Mercy, maybe age seven or eight, staring defiantly back as if to say, "So?"

I only heard her express anger about him once. I think she would have been six at the time. During spring break, Dad took us all to the races at Belmont - a rare outing for which

In June 1965, Mom and Dad took the family to their vacation house in Bermuda. (I stayed in New York job-hunting.) Mercy, age 8, a month away from 9, was cooking bacon in the kitchen when she spilled hot bacon grease on her right hand. The burn was serious and left permanent scars.

we all dressed up. We were going to meet our grandfather, Buck Ewing, Sr., at the track and see one of his horses run. The boys drove with Dad in his black Buick. The rest of us, the girls and the little ones, piled into Mom's gray Plymouth station wagon. All except Patrick, who for once, stayed at home with Marie. Perhaps Dad was uncomfortable having Patrick around his father. Buck senior placed great faith in bloodlines, both equine and human. If a horse had been born with Patrick's defects, he would have destroyed it. Certainly he regarded Pat with a disapproving eye. Yet Mom must have missed having him along. At the end of the day when she pulled back into the courtyard between the back door and the garage, she exclaimed, "I'm so glad to get back to my Patrick!"

Mercy and Tommy had been sitting in the station wagon's back seat and as they clambered out over the middle seat, Mercy exclaimed loudly and vehemently, "I wish he were dead!"

I was shocked. Did she understand "dead"? There had been no deaths in the family since she was born. There could be no question that she wanted Pat out of her life. But did she really want him dead? I looked at Mom. She shut the car door behind her, pretending not to have heard, and kept on moving towards the back door and "her" Patrick.

Two years later, in February 1965, when Mercy was nine, Mom and Dad started Pat on an intensive, experimental physical therapy program. Dad heard about a physical therapist named Glen Doman in Philadelphia who had a clinic dedicated to treating brain damage - be it at birth or from stroke. Doman and his associate Carl Delacato, an educational psychologist, claimed that their program of physical movement could "repattern" the brain and repair the damage. Doman boasted that his program had enabled adult stroke victims to walk again and mentally retarded children to attend college. Although Dad was conservative when it came to social mores and politics, as a venture capitalist, he was always intrigued by new ideas, particularly fringe ideas - be it a cure for acne made from cow cartilage or a way to squeeze oil out of Australian shale. So Dad and Mom went to Philadelphia to hear Doman who told them, and a bunch of other hopeful parents, about his method and his miraculous successes. For two days, in an over-air-conditioned room, he sold his program. In the end, my parents bought into it. As Mom said, "He promised to cure Pat. How could we not give it a try?"

Mom and Patrick

Today Doman's theory is condemned as pseudoscience by such professional organizations as the American Academy of Pediatrics. Even in the 1960s, his claims did not stand up to scientific testing. However, once Dad had committed to something, he was extremely stubborn. He was ever loath to abandon any of the companies he backed as a venture capitalist and perhaps the same was true of his investment - both monetary and emotional - in Pat.

Doman's regime was grueling and non-stop during Pat's waking hours. It required "patterning" sessions during which Pat lay on a table. One person would hold his head. Four more people would grasp each leg and arm. Then, to a prescribed count and in unison, we would turn his head from side to side and move his limbs in a kind of swimming motion, five or six times a day. All the kids at home were all pressed into duty; friends and neighbors volunteered to help. My brother David remembered with disgust that he was stationed at Pat's head and that as he turned Pat's head back and forth, Pat drooled all over his hands. Tommy remembered that every day after school, he had to help pattern Pat. No doubt Mercy, who was older than Tom, was also drafted. When Dad came home from work, he would take off his suit jacket and take a post at Pat's table. When Pat wasn't being patterned, he was creeping and crawling up and down the upstairs hallway. The program required six hours a day of this, and Mom and Marie were strict enforcers. Under their supervision, he creeped and crawled till the carpet - a woven red runner installed by John D two generations earlier - was threadbare. To spare his knees, Mom buckled on kneepads.

All this was an operation that went on every day of the week without a break for four years - a kind of black hole that consumed the greatest share of Mom's prodigious energy. My grandmother Mercedes and the Aunts praised her strength and determination. To them, and to everyone outside the family, particularly at the outset of the program, Mom and Dad were embarked on a heroic mission. Mercedes would marvel, "Your mother is just wonderful with Pat!" and she would brag to her friends how devoted we all were to him. Granny's praise was always a balm to me, but not very far deep down I knew none of us were "devoted" to Pat - he simply was there, a fact of our lives. I don't think it occurred to her or anyone else to worry about how Pat and his handicap affected the rest of the family. The four older of us were away at boarding school or college and removed from the demands of Pat's program. As for Jessie and David, Mercy and Tommy, they were, after all, "normal" and their problems - be it dyslexia or chronic asthma, a crushed toe or a burned arm - were nothing compared to Patrick's problem.

When Pat turned thirteen, Mom and Dad finally let go of their hopes for him. It was clear that he making no progress toward the promised goal of normalcy. All the workouts made him physically strong, but as he neared puberty, he became more and more difficult to manage. Sometimes he would strike out and hit who ever happened to annoy him. Late in August of 1969, Dad and Mom decided to send Pat to the Woods Schools in Langhorne, Pennsylvania, a residential facility for the mentally handicapped.

This was an exquisitely painful decision for Mom. In a letter to me written over the Labor Day weekend, she described visiting an institution in Connecticut and pronounced it "a waste of time as they only took children with emotional problems." She then drove Pat to the Woods School in Langhorne, Pennsylvania, for testing.

He got that awful dopey look on his face and acted as if he wasn't there at all. I spent the day telling them how witty and intelligent and how well he understood everything that was said to him. . .etc, etc. . .and the testers just sat and looked at me as if it was I that should be going to their school. That night I had the most fearful case of depression. The next day was more of the same. . .Finally they told us they did have a place for Pat and we should think about it and let them know in a day or so. Well seeing that we had spent the summer thinking about it we could have told them then and there. . . Anyway he is going there and I drive him down on the eighth of September. And of all the awful first trips to boarding schools that I have made this one is going to be a real lulu. I'm sure he knows what it is all about. I have tried to talk about it normally, and continually to make references to his brothers and sisters going away to school. . .but I am not sure it will work. . .and this my dear is one of the times that nothing can help you but prayer.

3

Summer 1960: Family portrait by the seawall. I had graduated from the Convent that June. Left to right, in front, Sheila and Mercy, Mom and Tom, me, Billy and Fritz. Left to right in back, Pat and Dad, David and Jessie.

One summer afternoon when Mercy - nine or ten at the time - was changing for a swim with her Challinor cousins, Mary Challinor, who was two years older, was deeply shocked to see that Mercy was wearing Patrick's jockey underpants. Mercy was defiant. She claimed they were in her drawer - which in Mary's eyes only made it worse. Mary told her mother Joan who also was shocked. Joan was convinced the underpants were not only a sign of neglect, but also a dangerous indication of penis envy. She swooped Mercy up, drove her to Bloomingdale's and bought her a floral bedspread with girly ruffles. Sarah Challinor, who was just Mercy's age, remembers being jealous. "I had nothing like that in my room!" she declared with a laugh.

Mary and Sarah's father was David Challinor, my mother's brother, who was also my godfather. In 2007, shortly before he died at age 87, he sent me excerpts from his journal concerning Mercy's disappearance. In a follow-up conversation on the phone, he remembered Mercy as a neglected waif. "Your mother was so involved with Patrick," he said. He wondered whether Mercy would have taken off for the South Pacific if Mom had had more time for her. He believed that Mercy's trip was a fatal attention-getter, an acting-out of Mom's own suppressed desire for adventure. "What Mercy did was something your Mother had wanted to do herself," he declared.

It is true that my mother had a taste for adventure - at least armchair adventure. Her bookshelves were full of real-life survival-at-sea accounts and biographies of harrowing polar explorations. She bought duplicate copies and sent them down to me in Virginia and they were a welcome escape from the confines of my own motherhood. What mother has never been torn between the all-consuming needs of her children and her own, perhaps unformed, impulse to escape and find self-fulfillment? But would Mom as a twenty-year-old - without babies to raise or a husband to answer to - have taken off on a risky adventure of her own? She was not afraid of hardship and I've often thought she would have made a good pioneer woman. Physically, she had unusual strength and endurance. She was also unusually self-disciplined - perhaps due to her convent training. After each of her nine babies and one miscarriage, she would determinedly regain her slim figure. Still, by nature she was passive. I can imagine her signing onto adventure - certainly her wartime marriage was one - but I can't quite imagine her taking the initiative like Mercy did. So I question David's analysis. It seems a bit too neat and tidy.

My sister Sheila disputed his theory in a 2008 email:

I don't think Mercy suffered lack of attention due to the amount of care Pat needed. If any child did, it was [our brother] David who was so needy. Mercy was never needy. She always seemed quite self-contained and confidant - quite serious. As a small child, she was "adopted" by [our elderly and childless cousins] Gracie and Gould who [lived on the place in a cottage] during the summer. Mercy used to visit them on a daily basis. They lavished her with attention and started her on a collection of silver dollars that Gracie later gave to me to pass along to [my daughter] Maria. Marie Burns [our nurse] doted on her and would bring real Scottish kilts for her when she came back from her trips home to Glasgow. Mercy had quite a collection of them. That was pretty much her uniform through her grade school years. Later, when she was older and in her "hippie" mode, Gracie used to give her presents of clothing from Lord & Taylor or Saks- nothing Mercy would EVER think of wearing. But she would always be gracious and pretend that she loved it. I think she was sensitive to other people's feelings, but not at all sentimental. She wasn't exactly tough, but she had a certain edge, a bit of an attitude. Even when she was older, she always made a point of visiting Gracie when she was home. After Mercy was lost, Gracie told me that she had intended to leave Mercy her property.

Even allowing for all the time and attention Patrick demanded, Mom once confided to me that she had enjoyed Mercy and Tommy far more than she had Sheila and me. I remember being startled by her frankness. We were in the upstairs hallway where Patrick used to creep and crawl. Perhaps we had been talking about my children and my mothering - or mothering in general. She was not apologizing for the mother she had been to Sheila and me some forty years earlier. Though her tone was rueful, she was simply describing her experience - or inexperience. "I didn't know what I was doing," she said. She had barely been into her twenties, a new mother with two babies, the handsome soldier she had married after a breathless wartime romance was away in the Pacific and she was still dependent on her parents, living with them and chafing under her mother's rule. Each of these circumstances alone ranks high on the stress scale - never mind piled all together. So, as much as she loved us - and I have no question that she did - it's no wonder she didn't find us bundles of fun.

But when Mercy and Tom were little, she was older and wiser. They were the end of the line. She was done with the baby mill. There were no more pregnancies to endure, no more swollen feet and back pain, no more infants to nurse, no more diapers to wash. We older children were away at boarding school. She was healthy and still in her thirties. She had more time and energy for her two youngest. She could sit down and read to them in evenings, laugh at their antics and take pleasure in watching them develop as individuals. She relished their independence and gave them a far longer leash than we older children had had. Sarah Challinor, along with envying Mercy's new bedspread, envied her freedom. She recalls being somewhat in awe of her boldness and independence.

So even if Mercy had wished Patrick

Mercy on the bow of the *Maria*. After Dad's mother Maria (pronounced Mariah) died in 1956, he spent part of his inheritance from her on a 40-foot wooden sloop designed and built in Norway. Although he named the boat *Maria* in memory of his mother, he worried that his father would disapprove of the expense, even though his father kept a stable of racehorses.

dead when she was six, by the time she was a teenager, I think she would have dismissed the notion that her handicapped brother had any deep-seated formative influence on her. In her journal, she remarked: "Jessie, Tom and David are the only people I can consider brothers or sister." Patrick, along with the four oldest of us, didn't count. We were out of sight and out of mind. Like Dad who laughed a survivor's laugh when he recounted childhood "whippings", Mercy would have laughed - or perhaps snorted with derision - at the idea that Pat had caused her, in someway, to escape to the Pacific.

Still, Mercy in her teens was subject to the storms of adolescence, rebellious and at times she could be as obnoxious as any teenager. She fought with Dad, as I had fought with him, but she also fought with our nurse Marie. By that time, Marie had been working for us for twenty-five years - ever since Sheila was born in 1943. A short, heavy-set woman, with sharp black eyes set below heavy black eyebrows and a thin ironic mouth, she wore her hair strictly pulled back into a tight knot the size of the walnut. She smoked Pall Malls non-stop and her voice was husky and had a strong Glasgow burr. Sometimes when she was frustrated, her accent would thicken and she would swear under her breath in incomprehensible working class slang. When she was pleased, or talking to a newborn, the cadences in her voice were bright, like sunlight breaking through cloud cover. But when she was in a bad mood, she was like a glowering thunderstorm and when she was angry, she would lash out with a sardonic or cruel comment.

She also played favorites; she preferred the boys and waited on them in ways she never waited on us girls. On cold winter mornings, she would warm their underwear on the radiator while they lay in bed, then hand them their toasty undershirts and underpants, so they could begin dressing for school under the covers. Once dressed, they would lie back on their beds and lift up one leg at time for her to put on their socks and lace up their shoes - brown oxfords she had polished the night before. She also favored the younger sibling over the older. Thus she tended to favor Tommy - the youngest and a boy - over Mercy, three and a half years older and a girl.

Mom ignored these faults; Marie Burns was indispensable, a tireless worker, honest, and staunchly loyal. She washed and mended our clothes, supervised baths, quizzed us on our multiplication tables and heard our catechism. When we were sick in the night, she held our heads over a basin and cleaned up if we missed. When the younger ones had nightmares, she let them sleep with her in her bed. Sometimes by morning she would end up with three of them under her covers.

Pat, Marie Burns and Mercy at Christmas.

Without Marie, Mom could not have managed the years of Patrick's intensive patterning therapy. When he finally went off to his school, Marie was left with little to do. Mercy and Tom were at school during the day and, Mom recalled, Marie, now in her seventies, shuffled aimlessly up and down stairs between the laundry room and her own room. In the laundry she washed dust rags when she ran out of clothes and linens to wash. In her room, she sat in her easy chair by the window and smoked one Pall Mall after another, drank milky coffee sweetened with saccharin tablets, listened to the news on the radio, wrote letters on blue airmail forms, and said the rosary or muttered prayers from a little black book stuffed with holy cards.

"I think she didn't feel well," Mom remembered. "When Tommy and Mercy would come home from school, Marie would take it out on Mercy. She would come down from her room for supper and pick at Mercy through the whole meal. It was very unpleasant."

"What did she pick about?" I wondered.

39

"It was just nitpicking."

"You mean like leaving her clothes on the floor?"

"Oh, you all left your clothes on the floor," Mom said dismissively.

"So what did they fight about?

"I don't want to remember. It was very unpleasant." End of conversation.

Twenty years earlier, I had shrunk away from Marie's wrath, but not Mercy. She took nothing lying down; Marie must have felt her authority eroding with each supper. Mom solved the conflict by sidestepping it. Her solution was to have two sittings. She would call Marie down from her room to the kitchen for supper and when Marie had finished eating and was safely back in her room, Mom would call Mercy and Tommy down from their rooms and serve them. Later, when Dad got home from work, she would cook a dinner for the two of them and serve it in the dining room by candlelight.

Marie and me on my wedding day.
I was not one of her favorites.

"What was Marie's reaction?" I asked.

"She didn't like it." Her tone was grim. "But there wasn't anything else I could do." Deprived of supper with the kids, Marie's days were even lonelier. So our parents made plans to send her back to Glascow to live with her sisters supported by a generous pension from Dad. Marie, however, resisted. She wanted to remain at Firwood. She enlisted her nephew, a priest named Father Quigley, to argue her case. He came to visit and he instructed my mother that after all Marie's years of faithful service, she deserved to live out her life at Firwood under my mother's care. "You owe it to her," Mom remembered him insisting. But in the end, no doubt with Dad's backing, Mom prevailed. Marie went back to live with family. She returned to Firwood several times for summer visits until she became too sick from lung cancer to travel. She died in her eighties in Scotland some years after Mercy was lost.

If my fights with my father were always confined to home, Mercy's, on more than one occasion, were spectacularly public. Sheila recalls a family ski trip in Vermont:

> The weather was horrendous - sub-zero, blowing, snowing, just horrible - visibility zero. Everyone said, "No way!" But Daddy convinced (coerced) Mercy to take a run. He bought two lift tickets, and while everyone else was huddled in the lodge, they went out. I guess they got to the top of the mountain and Mercy took off and made a beeline for the lodge, leaving Daddy in the blizzard. About an hour later, Daddy comes stomping into the lodge, icicles hanging out of his nose, in total melt-down, yelling, "Where's Mercy?? Has anybody seen her???" Mercy had quickly disappeared into the ladies room. Somehow (did he go in after her?) he found her and they had this unbelievable screaming match in the crowded lodge. I can't even remember why he was so angry, but he called her a spoiled brat and said she could forget about a trip she had planned to go out west to ski with friends. I am pretty sure she went anyway.

My brother Tom tells another ski trip story: Over spring break in 1974, he and Mercy went along with Dad and Mom to visit Dad's sister Grace Huffman who lived in Aspen with her six children. Going through security at La Guardia, Mercy set off a metal detector alarm. Perhaps her appearance triggered suspicions as well. At the time, most women wore heels and stockings on a plane. Mercy was wearing hiking boots with a short kilt. Her hair was in its usual wild hippie frizz and she was also wearing an old Abercrombie shooting jacket that had belonged to Dad's father. The jacket had a

I was not a very loving big sister. Our Uncle David Challinor took this snapshot of me wrestling with Sheila in 1945 when he was home on leave from the Navy.

41

back pouch designed for carrying dead birds, and inside the pouch, the guard discovered a metal pipe with the residue of marijuana. The guards pulled her off the side and started grilling her about it. "Whose is this?" they demanded.

"It's mine."

"Where did you get it?"

"A friend gave it to me."

"What friend?"

"I'm not going to tell you."

She refused to tell them who gave it to her.

"It was a major scene," Tommy remembers. "The guards were yelling at her and Dad was yelling at her to tell them what they wanted to know and Mom and I moved back into the hall. Like, *Who are these people?!*" Tommy laughed. "Mercy didn't give an inch. Dad was furious! He completely lost it and he let loose and slapped her in the face. The guards hustled her off to an interrogation room. I think they were afraid he was going to kill her!"

Tommy and I both laughed - though if you were to ask what was so funny, it would be hard to say. Perhaps it was the incongruity: things like that weren't supposed to happen to "nice" families in airports. Or perhaps it was a survivor's laugh, full of relief and dark irony.

"Mercy was tough," Tommy said admiringly. "She never cried when Dad slapped her. You could see the mark of his hand coming out on her cheek, but she just stared at him. Eventually the guards let her go - without getting a name out of her."

Imagining the scene, I feel a tinge of pity - not for Mercy, but for Dad. "So what was the trip like? I wondered. "I mean after all that."

"Oh, Dad apologized for slapping her and that was the end of it. He never mentioned it again. We had an awesome time! Our cousins couldn't have been nicer, they took us skiing with them everyday. It was great trip."

Mercy's artwork

April 3, 1977
Jackson, WY

4/3

Dear Ma,

Thank for your letter. I got it at a good time. Monday ugg. I looked at the clock and it was 11:30...I promised myself I wouldn't look again until it was noon— lunch time— and went back to work for what seemed half an hour... then went to get ready for lunch...I looked at the clock and it was only 11:45. COLD SWEAT, another ciggarette, Hell, Damn, piss, etc.

Clenching my teeth & fist, back to work for another 15 min, eternity.

My days have been ruined so many times by that damn clock. My anger gets so intense & real...& its all about the way I perceive the time. THE CLOCK disagreeing with me...How dumb to waste my energy on that clock.

Well you're letter inspired me to give my boss two weeks notice...so I'm quitting April 15th Yahooo.

I don't know what quitting my job means for my future...I mean how it will effect my plans— leave

Jackson or stay. NOT HOW IT WILL EFFECT MY FUTURE OPPORTUNITIES IN THE JOB MARKET.

(I'm dropping out of that)

I'm getting so confused again...choices, choices and I can't decide what's right for me to do...What I really feel is right for me... One choice is to stay here in Jackson, Maybe even in this house, but preferably a house out of on my drawing, with that teacher I told you about, and make crafts and sell them, raise chickens & goats & geese, and get a puppy. Sound pretty domestic after all my talk of feeling rushed to see see SEE THE WORLD.

But I'm starting to think about just running off again on to new land & then from that new land on

to another new land...

I'm looking for internal growth, sharpening my sence, quickening my mind, dealing with immediate. and as my art teacher says, "learning to see"...Oh I wanna see.   I'm not directing all my growth to ART.... its not that big with me... what's more important to me is dealing-with-people situations & head situations... looking for internal growth- ETERNAL Growth and i'm not sure how to go about it. College is absolutely out for the next year... I'm sorry...but... It would just stifle me...

Travel, transience, drifting, floating, growing? Or Being

domestic with close friend, and a couple of non- threatening goals... farting around learning to draw & making craft & loving my puppy. and growing stagnant?

I could grow just as stagnant traveling...Ya know?

Just not being able to see what's there....being too involved in getting from here to there or what ever.

But I could grow stagnant in both situations. It's all in my mind... I've just gotta decide what I'm ready for... I wanna do both, but which first?

4

Mercy at boarding school

Mercy attended the Thomas School, a small private grade school in nearby Rowaton. The head mistress there was Jean Harris, who later became notorious for having shot and killed her lover Dr. Herman Tarnhower, a prominent cardiologist and author of a diet book, "The Scarsdale Diet", which enjoyed a long run on the best-seller lists. Although Tarnhower had treated her cruelly, the jury at her trial was unsympathetic - she sat ramrod straight in her pearls and conveyed a chilly hauteur rather than distress - and in the end, she was sentenced to prison.

Mom remembered Mrs. Harris as "uptight." "I didn't like her. She scolded me." There was indignation in her voice.

"Scolded you? About what?"

"Oh, I was supposed to supervise the clean-up after a dance in the gym and she didn't think it was clean enough. Mercy didn't like her either." She paused, then added magnanimously, "But she did wonderful work with all those women in prison."

After seventh grade, Mercy went to boarding school, a tradition in our family, if not always a happy one. Dad, whose mother found him too unruly to manage, at age four was sent to live with his grandmother who disciplined his tantrums with a belt. At age ten he was sent away to school at St Mark's. As for Mom, she was packed off to the Convent of the Sacred Heart at Noroton because "my mother and father wanted to take a trip around the world and didn't want to leave me home alone with the maids." She had been happy at her school in New York City and even in old age, remembered the uprooting with some bitterness.

Like Mom and Dad, we older children were given no choice in the matter. It was a parental decision, not ours. Mom decided where the girls would go and Dad decided where the boys would go. For Sheila and me, Mom chose the same convent school she had attended: it was important to her, at that point in her life, that at least we girls receive a Catholic education. The Convent, a former mansion overlooking the Sound, was familiar to me. It stood behind gates at the end of the Point we lived on and we all went to Sunday school there. Still, the place was deeply mysterious: all those nuns in black habits, the smell of floor wax, the sonorous bell in its tower ringing out times for prayer. But I was happy enough to leave home: Dad and I were locking horns. Moreover, all my friends were also going away to school.

Years later, when Mom was choosing a school for Mercy, a Catholic school was no longer an imperative. She chose the Darrow School in New Lebanon, New York. Darrow was then, and is now, a small progressive school (a hundred students, twenty-five faculty) with an emphasis on the liberal arts. Established in 1935, the original buildings were built by Shakers. I never visited

Darrow when Mercy was there, nor have I been there since, not even for a 2007 fund-raiser which featured an exhibit of Mercy's artwork that Mom had saved. But an aerial view in a recent alumni publication shows a rural setting; the campus is surrounded by the wooded hills of the Lebanon Valléy. When I logged onto the school's web site, I saw snapshots of ethnically diverse young faces, all happy and healthy-looking. The text advertises "hands-on learning", classes of eight supplemented by "one-on-one tutorials", and the "freedom to make mistakes."

In 2007, as Mom was packing up Mercy's drawings to send to the school for their exhibit, I asked her: Why Darrow?

She thought about it, then said flatly, "I don't know. It was so long ago."

"Did you go visit the place with her?"

"Oh yes. There was lots of land around it. It was an outdoorsy kind of place. It had a good art department, a good music department. It seemed Mercy-ish."

"What kind of grades did she get?"

"Some good, some bad. She was in plays. I think she was happy there. Of course she got into trouble."

"What kind of trouble?"

"She and some of her friends got caught outside a liquor store getting some man to buy her a bottle."

"Did she get suspended?"

"No, just a lot of lectures." She let out a small resigned sigh. Then her voice brightened. Fondly and with pride, she said, "Mercy always was 'agin' the government.'"

When Mercy was at Darrow, I was a young mother helping my husband hand-build a tower in the woods of rural Virginia. Our lifestyle was "alternative" in the sense that it did not meet paternal expectations, but we were still very much "on the grid". We used power tools, wired the house for electric heat, and installed conventional toilets. I remember feeling half-envious and half disapproving of Mercy's school. After the academic rigors and austere disciplines of

the Convent, Darrow struck me as indulgent hippie school where all the kids smoked dope without punishment and no one agonized over Latin declensions. Of course I judged the place only by what I saw of Mercy on our occasional visits home: she was aggressively free-spirited: braless, her hair in a brazen frizz, she would sunbathe naked by the pool when there were work men around or she would suddenly take off with Tommy, who was three and a half years younger and under the drinking age, for a boozy lunch at a fancy restaurant in Westport.

Sheila remembers taking Mercy to buy a dress for a family wedding. "We bought a long batik dress, navy and brown, with a halter top that despite her hairy armpits looked smashing on her. Some of [our brother] David's friends hit on her at the bar - she blew them off. I never heard of a boy friend, but those were different times and 'dating' was out."

At Darrow, Mercy studied the clarinet. At the time, it struck me as an original choice. Sheila and I and our brother Billy, the oldest of the boys, had taken piano lessons; the clarinet was mysterious to me. I don't remember ever hearing her play. But I remember seeing her from an upstairs window at Firwood when she was practicing on the sea wall at the bottom of the lawn: a wild-haired, androgynous figure in the distance, she conjured up the god Pan hunched over his pipe.

In her senior year, she set her sights on attending the famed summer music camp at Tanglewood, Massachusetts. Her teacher, however, refused to recommend her. In April 1975, she wrote home to mom:

I would of liked to have gone there, who wouldn't? But I know there wasn't a chance that they'd accept me. He didn't want me to apply. It was horrible. He kept saying, I don't want to break your heart Mercy, but the musicians there are way over your head, you'd feel too unconfident. And I kept saying, I know I won't get in but I'd really like to apply just for the hell of it. He kept saying that it would be useless and my heart would be broken and I kept saying that I didn't care. Finally. . . he leveled with me and told me that his reputation was at stake. He trains junior prodigies to get into the Tanglewood program on scholarship and if I went to Tanglewood and they asked me who my instructor was and I told them, and said that I've been with him for 2 years . . . . his darn reputation. That means I can't get into any Ω way decent music school around this area. That really hurt me. . .man, I almost started crying. . .I told him I'd never mention his name and he could sign my recommendation under an alias. But, no, it was no use, I couldn't spoil his reputation.   . .

I never thought I'd panic so much at the end of my school days. I always thought the thrill, excitement, adventure! would flow into my veins and erase any kind of nervousness or scaredness. I just hope I have my summer worked out before June 6th. Do you think I could leave a day early and avoid the ceremony? I'd like to and it would be easier for you.

These are two paintings I did in the fall. All of my teachers were trying to psychoanalyze my self-portrait. There's nothing to it. I didn't know how to make it any different.

Much love Mercy

I'm not really sure where me and Mike are going. We'll probably end up camping in the Pittsfield State forest. If we camp there I'll call you. . .is that all right?

On a rainy June evening at Firwood, Mom celebrated both Mercy's graduation from Darrow, and my sister Jessie's graduation from college, with a family party. (She rarely, if ever, had non-family dinner parties.) "It was supposed to be a dinner al fresco," she wrote me. "Why does that sound better than a cook out - or barbeque - a barbeque should be held in the desert with cowboys - and cookouts should be held at girls camps in Vermont. Anyhow we had chicken vermouth- not bad - with shrimp & raw vegetables with curried sauce for hors d'oeuvres. . ." Chicken Vermouth was a recipe from her culinary standby, volumes one and two of the "I Hate to Cook" books by Peg Bracken. In a PS at the end of her letter, Mom commented on a diet fad in the news:

> "Special K Roast - ugh - I think if you cut out butter and cream & cut down on beef, pork, etc.- & keep calm - & be happy you'll live a long time - that of course isn't what people really want - they just want to die without getting sick."

5

Summer 1956, at the "Garden House". Left to right, seated in front, Fritz, Billy, David on trike, Patrick on my grandmother Mercedes' lap, Julia Challinor, my grandfather David Challinor, me holding newborn Mercy. Back: seated, Mary Challinor, Joan and Sarah Challinor. Back: standing, Jessie, Sheila, Mom, Dad, and Uncle David, my godfather. Mom and I were both a little embarrassed because the photographer believed Mercy was my baby. We didn't correct him.

Mercy spent the year after graduation at home. She moved into a small room - formerly a valet's room, I think - on the third floor by the back stairs. She painted the walls cream-color, hung her pictures, added a rocking chair and her stereo. She found a day job at a school for handicapped kids and after work, caught a train into the city and rode the subway to night classes at the New York School of Visual Arts. She also started a new journal in an old leather diary she found. It had index tabs and gilt-edged pages, one for each day of Nineteen fifty-five.

Twenty-five years after she was lost, my mother was reluctant to give me the journal. Mercy's letters were one thing. But the journal - Mom was determined to burn it. Intensely private about her own feelings, after Dad's death, she had burned a laundry basket full of letters she had written to him during the war. She had written every day he was gone - years of letters - and he had saved them all. I had protested but she had ignored me. "They're nothing," she had insisted. "They're boring."

I turned the journal over in my hands. On the front cover, Mercy had Scotch-taped a black and white photograph of two naked African runners bounding gracefully over a desert. Onto the back, she had glued a card with the look of a

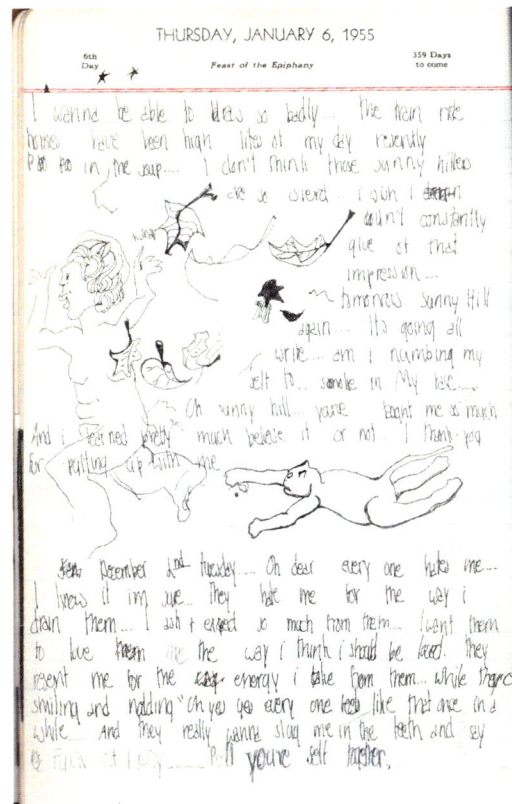

Mercy's journal

Persian painting: three tigers in a field of stylized flowers.   I couldn't believe Mom wanted to destroy it. What on earth had Mercy written in it?

"Let me have it," I pleaded.

 "It's nothing! It's nothing at all - she was just venting in it," Mom declared.

"But it's neat!" I exclaimed. "Look at it!" I flipped through the pages. Mercy's peculiar, cramped writing and her doodles wandered around a collection of photographs and pictures that had caught her fancy: nineteenth century lady gymnasts hanging upside down; an old Kodak of mom at twenty-three with Sheila and me, ages one and three, dressed up in soldier suits; a piece of dried sagebrush; a Maurice Sendak illustration from *Where the Wild Things Are*, a typed copy of " Bob" Frost's poem "Birches". The book was as much scrapbook as diary.

In the end, my mother relented and gave it to me along with Mercy's letters. Mercy's handwriting, however, was so difficult to read that after transcribing her letters, I ignored her journal for a long time. Many of the bits I did make out seem to have been written when she was high; some entries disintegrated into large, wobbling letters that drifted off the page:

"HA

HE

ha   he..."

Other entries devolved into nonsense: "black and blanched.. bladed blocked blanket black blank...blanched tee damned..."

Was this, I wondered, why Mom had wanted to destroy it?

Finally in 2008, when I did take the time to decipher it, I felt a wave of compassion. The final vestiges of my judgment dissolved and I found myself identifying with her. She wrote of feeling stifled. Was it by parental expectations? She did not elaborate. But I too had felt stifled at home. Not so much by the weight of expectation. I don't think Mom had ambitions for me; rather, she was supportive of my own ambition to write. Dad, on the other hand, had very concrete expectations for me: get your nose out of your books, lose twenty pounds, and go out and meet some 'nice boys'. Although of course I wanted to lose weight, the rest of his prescription was easy enough to walk around - they seemed as irrelevant to me as an Easter Island monument. No, what made it hard for me to get a sharp, clean breath at Firwood were the soft emanations of its past. My grandmother Mercedes' stories, her fierce love of the place, the sepia photographs of her elegant family, the sheer beauty of its lawns and gardens and views of Long Island Sound - all were deeply seductive and imbued me with a sense of place that had an almost tangible power - a power that often felt suffocating. Only after four years of college was I able to distance myself from my romance with Firwood and its ancestral ghosts.

If Mercy felt stifled at home after graduation, she also was struggling with a flesh and blood romance. She was in love with one of the boys from Darrow and he had rejected her.

> June 24: I don't understand where all this pain is coming from...Oh God I can sit and cry & cry. Is it my losing him or realizing I have no one...God it's hard to be myself.

On the next page she pasted a cutout color photograph of the dancer Baryshnikov executing a jété in black tights. Down the side of one leg she wrote:

> Well here I am on the first day of July. I finished my letter to him and mailed it today. It was a good letter I think. I talked of being not honest with him. I used examples of: not telling I was a virgin the first time we made love...and of how I never told him how much I loved him or of all the hours I spent thinking of him and missing him. Then I brought up the word "embarrassed" and I reminded him of what a horrid, inexcusable word it was. I love him more now. He's not growing farther away from me. . . he's becoming more & more a part of me...is it just that I'm horny?

Down the side of the other leg she wrote:

> I walked into my room and sat down in my good old rocking chair and wondered what I was going to do...earlier today I tried drawing but fuck nothing would work

I couldn't draw shit...so so frustrating...at times like this the thought of art school
totally depresses me...I keep on wanting to look to my right and see my reflection
in the mirror - an artist, a musician, a lover - what other fantasies am I going to try
and fulfill...? I'm feeling so totally worthless. Oh the poor dear...

If her journal was a safe place for self-doubt, she was quick to mock self-pity.

A few days after this July entry, Andy and I and the boys came up to Firwood to celebrate
the Fourth - an annual gathering of aunts and uncles and cousins, complete with baseball on the
lawn, a clan picnic by the seawall, and illegal fireworks set off with great glee by Dad. I remember
coming up stairs to bed late one night after too much to drink and too much raucous argument
with my siblings. I heard the strains of Dave Brubeck coming from Mercy's stereo and found
her standing naked at an easel, brush in one hand, a palette of oils in the other. My sister Jessie,
fully dressed, was sitting in Mercy's rocker talking to her. I felt as if I were intruding - and also
disconcerted by Mercy's nakedness. Although nudity was a convention of the Age of Aquarius
- a kind of daring "statement" - and I was more or less comfortable being naked with friends,
my sister's nakedness seemed somehow more nakedly naked. I focused on her canvass. She was
painting a stormy, navy-blue sea. My memory puts a small sailboat in the picture, but perhaps
that is an overlay from later on.   Given her fate, the painting seems ominous but in fact, at that
moment in time, it was an accurate reflection of Mercy's emotional state: she was very much "at
sea". I think I made some kind of drunken older-sister-ish compliment and she, no doubt, made a
sarcastic reply.

Perhaps because Mercy was "at sea" during that time, she discovered a new footing with Mom.
A few days later she wrote in her journal:

Mother and I had good (or at least better) communication...so good and
refreshing...Libations...yes a toast to you...hear, hear...it was just open...and I felt
like I could say anything to her...for the whole time I was with her after dinner, she
was able to step out of the Mother role & likewise with me...out of the daughter

role...I was getting to know someone...new input...new connections...I'm drunk...
well it happened with beer & screwdrivers & wine..well good nite.

Mom's ever-liberal hand with booze loosened her own reserve and allowed her to escape the Good Girl inculcated in her (and in Sheila and I) by the nuns and by society in general. After several stiff drinks, Mom relaxed and became more herself, and thus encouraged confidences from her adult children. At the same time, when we gathered, alcohol also tended to fan the embers of old nursery insecurities and rivalries. If Sheila and I had not had our drunken fight on the New Year's Eve of 1977 - the night I realized Mercy was missing - the seriousness of the situation would not have dawned on me. I'm sure that at some point, after I was back in Virginia, Mom would have clued me in by letter - she did not really like talking on the phone - but she might well have kept her fears to herself during our New Years visit. She once told me that she had planned to "raise the alarm" after she'd gotten through the holidays. For better and for worse, alcohol facilitated communication in our family.

Early in 1976, after six months at home, Mercy enrolled in a National Outdoor Leadership School (NOLS) course in Wyoming. During the first segment of the training, her group was taught basic survival skills while winter camping in Yellowstone's backcountry. The last segment was spent in the desert of Utah's Canyonlands National Park. Again, a pang of envy that still smarts: although my brothers had taken NOLS courses, it had not been an option for Sheila or me. The only "outdoors education" available to us was playing field hockey at the convent in dress-length blue tunics.

In a letter to me written in August 1978, some nine months after Mercy was lost, Mom remembered driving her to the airport for her NOLS course:

> We had gotten mixed up with the time the plane left & instead of arriving at
> the airport with an hour and ten minutes to spare - she had 10 minutes to
> spare. Anyway she made it. She never really came home after that again. . .

Still, she had not broken ties with home. After she completed the winter camping section of the course she wrote to "Dear Ma and Dad and Tom and whoever else is around." She went on describe her learning curve:

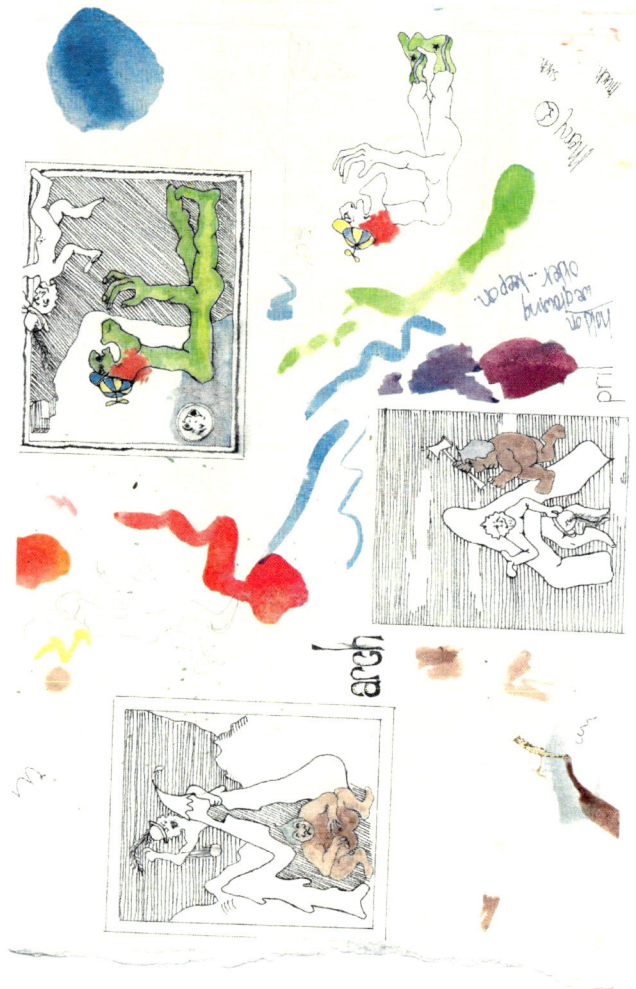

Mercy's journal

We were on cross country skis for 3 weeks and the only time we didn't have them on was when we were in our sleeping bags and then I was constantly dreaming I had them on. . .I'd have a real problem trying to turn over cuz it was so hard move in my sleeping bag with skis on...a couple times I woke up with a jerk cuz I was sliding down a hill. . .after a while they were just like long feet and came in handy around camp... reaching for things and getting people's attention. The first couple days it was horrible...I was quite the spaz...every little bump in the trail I was on my face with a 60 lb pack squashing me into the snow...I swear, every 20 ft. I'd be in the snow. Falling wasn't bad - but lifting that damn pack just wore me out completely...After the 10th time I fell I had to fight crying, screaming, swearing, asking someone to carry my pack, along with completely breaking down and asking for a warm hotel room. It wasn't that bad all the time...just sometimes in the beginning.

The first part of the course we were really pushed pretty hard. We woke up a 5:30 (dark-thirty) every morning...on the trail by 7:30 or 8:00 and didn't get into our next camp until dark...we'd get up our tent (that was my job) and my tent mate would cook dinner...we eat and then go to bed...There was time for nothing but trying to keep warm and happy. Ugg...those were the worst days...I'll never feel good about them.

After four days, they made a backcountry base camp near a hot spring and went exploring from there. She described being startled by a Bison she'd mistaken for a snow drift and how, with five feet between them, she had stared at the beast for 10 minutes, paralyzed with fear, before she backed away. ("Boy, afterwards I felt like such an ass for being so scared.") She wrote how "the Hot springs, Geysers and thermal areas are all the more magical and mystical in winter" and how she and her tent mate would get up early, "around 6:00, before anyone else", and ski off looking for wildlife. "We saw Elk...and mule deer...and one Moose...that was the best morning."

In the desert of Utah's Canyon Lands she was happy to be warm, but unhappy with her tent mate. At the end of the course, she complained in a letter home: "God, every little thing he did drove me up a wall. If any body else did most of the things he did, I wouldn't have thought twice about it. It's just his manner. He such a dense, negative, pessimistic Jerk. Well that's all over with now. Thank God."

Nonetheless, her wilderness experience was a high that she did not want to give up. She applied to take a NOLS instructor course. But she needed recommendations from all 13 of her instructors. "So far," she wrote home, "I've gotten along really well with them all and I think they like me alright. But it just seems to get all 13 of them to recommend you, you have to be some kind of super woman. Oh I don't know maybe I'm blowing it out of proportion, but I just don't wanna get my hopes up high and then have them knocked down." As a fallback, she applied for a summer job at the Teton Science School in Kelly, Wyoming, about 20 miles from Jackson Hole. The head of the school encouraged her. "Boy, he was so nice. He really made me feel good and gave me confidence in being able to find something so I can take care of myself."

After completing the NOLS course at the beginning of April 1976, she and three NOLS "buddies" hitchhiked to the West Coast. "Just the adventure I needed to leave NOLS with," she wrote in her journal. Sheila remembers hearing that after leaving her buddies in California, she thumbed her way alone up to Portland, Oregon, and was picked up by a man who drove her to a remote area and threatened her with a knife. According to Sheila, "Mercy's reaction - which was verbally aggressive - somehow intimidated him and he let her go."

When she finally arrived at a girlfriend's home in Portland, she was four days overdue. Her friend had been worried sick about her. She felt a twinge of guilt, but at the same time, she felt alienated from her friend. "She had no idea of what I was going through," Mercy wrote in her journal. "All she was interested in was her school ending...she was oh so Domestic. I crashed into the reality of houses and cars and laundromats...hitchhiking had lost all glamour and NOLS was a fairy tale. I wanted to be home with Ma cuz I knew she understood...how hard it was to come back into civilization. Tuff darts. Little baby Mercy running home."

By the end of May, she was back home at Firwood, grieving for paradise lost. I recognize this feeling: Andy and I and our boys used to spend summer vacations in Montana and we took two extended pack trips into the Bob Marshall Wilderness. The western landscape,

SATURDAY, JANUARY 8, 1955

8th Day   357 Days to come

Amen. Oh yea... so desperate. Nett where are you... I need a man to ride. He was beautifull... at least he was beautifull when I saw him at nads Xmas party... Oh no... Oh so. I wish I could fall in love right now... this very moment someone to kiss my neck... I feel rootless... with out roots hat how can I fall in love... need overed heels? with no obligations to hold me only... where... whitin no idea of the future... Oh help me hold me... Romeo Romanov... I'm sorry you won't hope I think... Gentle Madison we're celebrating my birthday tonite... true pals... Mom + Dad.

35th week.

The way Madison sees it now... Peace & love... You drive soon I'll appreciate life so. G. M.

SUNDAY, JANUARY 9, 1955

9th Day   First Sunday after Epiphany   356 Days to come

May 26th Wednesday.

Ah where you from... Well I just got back from Portland Or.... before that California. I dropped off two newly made friends there. In Sacramento and Loreto... Oh and hey before that Lander Wyoming was my mailing adress. Oh, now I cry for Lander... Have you ever heard of NOLS?

Oh Spring Semester 76... It's so frustrating trying to tell to any one about it. I'm still so good at or in letting go. I don't wanna. I hey. that I'm recomended for the instructor... lines there only a dream And I ... you'll by to the land of love and off to wild its young jagged mountains and old pine forests, its glacial lakes and alpine meadows, inspired and informed the mysteries I wrote. Every time I returned to the worn mountains of Virginia and our patch of woods, I suffered a kind of love sickness for "Big Sky" country. It was not as bad as falling painfully in love with a person. There was no rejection, only separation, and recovery was much quicker. But I understand very well the unrequited longing Mercy struggled with upon her return home.

At the same time, she was happy to be home. She went over to visit Sheila and "liked talking with her. . . I wish I was gonna be here longer so I could get into the run of things here once again. My mind is still with NOLS thinking over the every day things we [did] that would be so special here in Noroton. I'd love to take Billy & Chris & Maria [Sheila's children] out in the woods for a week."

Sheila remembers: "She returned from her trip out West looking very rugged and woodsy. In my kitchen, we had a nice conversation about her experiences. She said she loved it and found "re-entry" difficult. She used to come over and play with Billy. She taught him how to somersault."

Both Dad and Mom were concerned about her plans for the fall. Mom was encouraging her to apply to art school. If Mercy's music teacher at Darrow had discouraged her from pursuing a serious study of music, her art teachers, both at Darrow and at Thomas, recognized and fostered her talent for drawing. Art offered a possible career option, but it also was more than that for her: it seemed to be a kind of overflow valve. Her stormy sea painting was an example in oils. But she doodled constantly with pen and pencil: small devilish faces with spiky hair, malformed sprites and Bosch-like imps floated and danced around the margins of her letters and onto envelopes. She hid grimacing faces inside drawers and on closet walls at home (thirty years later we still found them) and drew roses and naked acrobats wearing sunglasses in her journal. Her doodles are whimsical and cartoonish, but when you look closer, they startle. The wings of a tiny fairy are actually three arms fused together. A jester wears a dopey grin that reminds me of our retarded brother Pat's grin - but the jester's cap is actually an arm growing out of his head. Her line is delicate and freely whimsical but she plays with the grotesque and malformed. It's as if she is doodling away a subterranean anger.

6

Mercy inherited her talent for drawing from Mom - and perhaps as well from Mom's father, David Challinor, Senior. As a child, I was in awe of a drawing my mother had done of the Archangel Michael ramming a sword down the throat of a dragon. Her model was a small clay statue, a gift that her mother Mercedes brought back from the trip that had landed Mom in the Convent. Mom's birthday was the feast of St. Michael the Archangel- September 29 - so the statue was a birthday gift as well as a souvenir cum peace offering and she always kept it on her desk. It was only twelve inches high, but her drawing of it was five times larger: a bold charcoal drawing on a long sheet of brown wrapping paper. How, I wondered, had she managed to enlarge it? And if the scale of the drawing was a striking puzzle, the realistic folds of the Archangel's robe and the dragon's coils were even more impressive.

Further evidence of Mom's talent was a series of small woodcuts that Mercedes proudly had framed and hung on the wall of her bedroom in the Garden House. One was of the Archangel's head. Another depicted a handsome bearded man, an imagined portrait of Richard the Lionhearted who had inspired romantic teenaged longings in her. From the Convent, Mom went to Manhattanville College of the Sacred Heart where she took art classes from Nina Wheeler Blake - "a real artist" as Mom put it, who became a close friend and mentor. This was in 1941, the early days of World War II. Hitler had invaded Poland, and the Luftwaffe was bombing England, but the United States refused to join the fight. The general popular feeling was that war was inevitable, that sooner or later we would jump in to support our allies, so young men were leaving school and jobs to enlist.

Mary attributed the artistic success of her woodcuts to her teacher.
"I was just a draftman," she used to say.

In December of 1940, Mom and Dad met at a debutante party. She was eighteen and he was twenty-eight. She was a couple of inches taller, wore her blond hair in a long pageboy, and red lipstick. He had flashing black eyes and black hair and wore an aura of wartime glamour: he was an artillery officer on leave from the Army's Air Corps. In a letter to his Aunt Vallé, his father's sister, Dad described their meeting:

> I saw a very tall handsome girl whom I cut in on without an introduction. I cut in on her from then on at every opportunity and was very much impressed. I asked her if she would write a lonely soldier boy down in Alabama and she laughingly said she would if I wrote first.

He went on to confide that back at Fort McClellan, "she kept popping up in my mind and I picked up my pen and wrote. She wrote me a very nice letter back and from then on I wrote her frequently." He also gave her a gift of a leather-bound volume of the poems of Robert Browning. (Mom doubted that he ever read them - Robert Service was more to his taste.) A month later, he flew home on a four-day leave and they had several dates. He proposed marriage and she told him, "she would think about it." Two months after that, he invited her to spend a ten-day leave with him and his family on Cape Cod. "The fifth day," Dad wrote to his aunt, "Mary said yes much to both our families surprise." They celebrated with champagne and Dad gave her a large, emerald-cut diamond engagement ring.

Despite the fact that she was only eighteen, her parents made no objection. In fact, Mercedes was delighted by the match. The families knew of each other. Dad's sister Grace was a classmate and friend of Mom's. Moreover, in Mercedes' eyes, the Ewings were a "good" family; Catholic (at least in name), but belonging to the wide WASPy circle of schools and clubs listed in New York's Social Register.

In August 1941, Dad was being transferred from Texarcana, Arkansas, to San Antonio, Texas, for more training. He obtained five days leave and he and Mom planned to be married at St. John's, our parish church in Noroton, Connecticut. Mercedes rose to occasion. An extrovert with a sense of adventure, during the previous war she had sailed for France with the Red Cross against her father's wishes. There she was stationed in a canteen at Orly airport and this was where she met her husband David Challinor, who ferried biplanes to the front for fighter pilots. Perhaps her own wartime romance gave her sympathy for Mom's. Never mind the fact that Mercedes was thirty four when she met David - no doubt she expected for her eighteen year old daughter the same happiness she'd found in her own marriage.

Mercedes' talents were of the organizational variety: still a volunteer for the Red Cross, now

Mom's engagement photo

during this second world war, she devoted her considerable energies to war-time fundraising. The challenge of a big, spur-of-the-moment wedding was right up her alley. She sent out two hundred invitations by telegram and took Mom on a whirlwind shopping excursion. According to a surviving packet of saved bills, the trousseau included 2 pairs of gloves from Bonwit Teller ($4.00), a lace-trimmed satin "robe and gown" from Altman's ($19.95) and a "going away" hat and dress from Saks Fifth Avenue ($45.75). Mercedes also hired a seven-piece band, a 40 foot square marquee for the lawn in front of the Garden House, and the New York caterer Louis Sherry who provided a "wedding breakfast" that included Lobster Newberg ("large pieces" specified), champagne, scotch and gin, and cigarettes ("popular brands"- another specification).

Pat Patterson, Jennifer Crimmins, Mary and Buck

Mom's favorite cousin Sheila Crimmins had just married a navy officer and Mom borrowed her satin wedding dress. Dad wore a cutaway. Mom's brother David and some of her male cousins were in uniform. She recalled a contagious urgency in the air: live now for who knows what's coming. "It was like the end of the world," she said. "It's hard to describe the excitement. It was electric. People were enlisting, getting married. Everyone was living *hard*."

Instead of a honeymoon, she followed Dad to San Antonio, Texas, where he trained as an aerial observer who would pinpoint bombing targets, radioing positions from a plane, or more

Buck Ewing Sr and Buck Jr playing with a bull whip on the Garden
House lawn the day before the wedding. A fatherly gag-gift to help the
groom keep his bride in line?

dangerously, from a jeep on the ground. Mom did not go back to Manhattanville. In December 1941, four months after their wedding, the Japanese bombed Pearl Harbor and the United States was at war. I was born in July 1942. Mom was nineteen, about to turn twenty. Late in 1943, Dad was sent to the Pacific. Sheila was born shortly after he left. When he came home two years later, there were more children - seven more, one after the other. Pregnant every second year, Mom had no time or energy for art. And when there finally was time, some thirty-odd years after leaving Manhattanville, the impetus was gone. "I never had any real talent," she used to insist. "I was only a draftsman." But if she stopped believing in her own talent, she believed in Mercy's. She wanted Mercy to develop her gift and study art.

Dad, for his part, saw art as a frill - a feminine frill. He believed that careers for women - in art or otherwise - were a poor second choice. He felt that a woman without a husband and children was missing out on true happiness. But at the same time, he believed it was important for a woman to be able support herself in the event of hard times. He had graduated from Yale in 1935, the middle of the Depression. The only job he could find was selling tractors. Although he and his family had weathered the Depression in comfort, the plight of the farmers he met on the job, as well as the fortunes lost by his father's acquaintances deeply affected him. He wanted his daughters to have "something to fall back on". In Sheila's and my case, it was typing and shorthand. He wanted us to go to secretarial school and it was only through Mom's intervention that he agreed to send us to college. Perhaps he justified the expense by thinking that at college we would find suitable husbands.

Fifteen years later, computers were looming on the horizon and, for Mercy, instead of prescribing secretarial skills, Dad was advocating data entry. College was the next best in his mind - but Mercy rejected both. In her journal, she explored her options:

Ma was talking about [me] finding something to do this fall. Oh dear. I'm doing what I wanna do. I'm [gonna be] away from the east and living in a land that seems so much more realistic than these eastern highways and suburbia. I have room to move. But my mind and talent. How can I let them go on being undeveloped. Well I figure if I need a school to develop them for me, then they're not ready to be developed. I can't see myself going to school. but what? Find a job and an apartment. but I need someone to share an apartment with. Oh where are my buddies. . . I want my prince charming to come galloping along and sweep me off my feet.

Later that night, up in her room after dinner, she added,

I feel a lack of something so I stick a chew [of tobacco] in my mouth still flavored from that sticky Benedictine. . . no still something's missing. Maybe I should draw a pretty picture. Maybe I should be with my prince under the stars that dance head to toe. No I think no matter what I could be doing at the moment I'd be kind-a-lonely and kind-a-empty. It just happens that way. I think there's always something that will be missing at sometime or other. Yes, that's the way it goes. Oh my sweet dreams."

As it happened, the job at the Teton Science School came through. Relived and excited, she wrote in her journal: "Wyoming here I come. I'm going to be at TSS on the 3rd of June. . .Oh I'm coming home WY."

At the Teton Science School's summer session, Mercy helped out with pack trips and cooking in the kitchen. She continued to resist pressure from home to enroll in college and in the fall of 1976, she moved into the nearby town of Jackson Hole, Wyoming.

In the winter of 2007, Andy and I visited both Yellowstone and Jackson. We went snowshoeing and cross-country skiing in Yellowstone and found it as magical as Mercy had - a prehistoric wonderland full of snow-covered bison and steaming fumeroles and hot pools whose turquoise blue and ochre-colored edges were rimmed with ice. We did not venture into the backcountry, however, and we did not bathe in any hot springs. There were warning signs posted at the edges of the pools and stories circulated about children who had been scalded to death.

In Jackson Hole, a picturesque Valley with stunning views of the Grand Tetons, I spent a morning in the county's new library browsing through local histories and old newspapers in an effort to get a picture of the place when Mercy lived there. I learned that at the turn of the nineteenth century, the "hole" was a hideout for horse thieves and cattle rustlers. In the 1920s, it became the first town in the nation to swear in an all-female town council - a bit of local history still proudly touted as indicative of Jackson's liberal spirit. In fact, the women were elected because none of the men would run. Once in, however, the ladies cleaned the place up. They removed garbage from the streets, installed culverts to solve the spring mud problem, and got the town out of debt. By the following decade, Jackson was a tourist destination. Then, as now, it cashed in on its Old West past. Every evening in summer in the main square, there were reenactments of cowboy shoot-outs, stagecoach rides for kids, and for the grown-ups, art galleries and high-end boutiques along town's wooden sidewalks. In winter, the area's ski resorts were a draw.

When Mercy was there in the seventies, locals decried the traffic jams, garish neon signs, and over-priced liquor. Still, the casual "live-and-let-live" attitude of the counterculture was a good fit with traditional Western respect for "rugged individualism". Jobs, although low-paying, were easy to find. Housing, however, was harder to come by and employers hired on the condition that "you have a place to live". Mercy moved into a small house rented by several of her peers. She had her own bedroom and found work first in a bakery-cum-restaurant, and then a leathercraft shop. She also babysat for a young couple she'd met at the Teton Science School. Although she found her day jobs stultifying, she relished escaping into the backcountry on her skis.

At Christmas, she was happy to stay put - perhaps to avoid clashes at home about her future. But she complied with our gift giving ritual. On the Fourth of July, Mom would put all our names - siblings and spouses - in a hat. We each would draw two names - or, if not home, delegate Mom to draw for us. By Christmas we were expected to make two presents for the names we had drawn. Store-bought was not allowed. There were always a few of us who never got around to making anything, and there were always a few whom you hoped would draw your name. Sheila, for example, once spent months knitting an exquisite wool sweater. Most of the gifts, however, fell in between: a lamp made from a craft kit, a drawing or photograph, a homemade cake. But the gifts themselves were less important than the efforts made (or lack thereof). We would open them at Sheila's after a festive Christmas Eve dinner, and it was always an occasion of much hilarity and raucous teasing.

The Christmas Mercy spent in Jackson, she sent home gifts for Andy and me. For Andy she made a cap of soft leather. She had sewn alternating triangles of mustard-colored leather and mahogany-colored leather together to form a kind elf's hat, complete with earflaps and rawhide strings that tied under the chin. When Andy put it on, he looked like one of the mischievous gremlins in her doodles. She sent me a pair of ski mittens she'd cut and sewn from the same mustard and mahogany colored leather. She had turned the leather of the palms rough side out to facilitate gripping ski poles or an icy sled rope and had used bone cuff buttons made of antler sections. She included woolen liners: one a store-bought gray rag wool mitten with ribbed cuffs; the other was softer, hand-knit from dark green wool, with a stripe of brown at the cuff.

They were as original as Andy's cap, but more practical, and in the years after her disappearance, I wore them on the rare occasions it snowed enough in Virginia to go cross-country skiing. They had a subtle power. Not that they gave my skiing any kind of boost from the Great Beyond. But each time I put them on, I felt connected to the open possibility of her.

Photo by Carol Andreae
1972. Andy and I with Tim and Morgan on our deck at Overall.

7

Mom's photo of Mercy with her niece Maria Daley on Mercy's last visit home.

Since Mercy was not coming home for Christmas, Mom mailed off a package of presents to her in Jackson. Among the gifts was a paperback copy of *The Horse's Mouth*, a novel by Joyce Cary, an Anglo-Irish contemporary of James Joyce. Cary had studied art at the University of Edinburgh and lived in Paris as a painter before deciding his talent was not large enough to warrant a career. He returned to Ireland where he studied law at Trinity College, then, after a stint in Africa with the British Colonial Service, he settled in England and began writing. *The Horse's Mouth*, which was published in 1944 as the final volume of a trilogy, celebrates the power of the creative imagination. It is a essentially a comic novel, a kind of Portrait of the Artist, not as a young man spreading his wings, but as a down-and-out old man with an enormous lust for life. Along with Virginia Woolf's Mrs. Dalloway and Elizabeth Bowen's *The Heart of the Matter,* it was one of Mom's favorite novels.

The narrator is Gulley Jimson, 68, just out of prison for assault, homeless and penniless. He has a violent temper, he lies, cheats, and steals without compunction, but he has a gift for gab and for laughter. At core, he is a passionate artist who is assaulted by the sensual beauty of the world around him and is obsessed by a desire to paint the "truth." He sacrifices all - domestic comfort, wives, son, lovers - to his creative process. When his mother dies, he can't tell whether he is suffering her loss or in agony over his "failed" impressionistic watercolors. When a young admirer declares that he wants to be an artist, Gulley replies: "Of course you do... everybody does once. But they get over it, thank God, like the measles and the chickenpox. Go home and go to bed and take some hot lemonade and put on three blankets and sweat it out." The youth stutters, "But Mr. J-Jimson, there must be artists." Whereupon Gulley retorts: "Yes, and lunatics and lepers, but why go live in an asylum before you're sent for? If you find life a bit dull at home and want to amuse yourself, put a stick of dynamite in the kitchen fire or shoot a policeman . . .you'd get twice the fun at about one-tenth the risk."

The book struck a chord with Mercy. "It's influencing me," she wrote to Mom. To some extent Mercy must have identified with Gulley Jimson. Like him she had a temper which she didn't always have under control. Like him, she refused to be bound by social conventions. Moreover, Jimson began his life as an artist by doodling. As he tells it: "I was a regular clerk. I had a bowler, a home, a nice little wife, a nice little baby, and a bank account. . .but one day when I was sitting in our London office on Backside, I dropped a blot on an envelope; and having nothing to do just then, I pushed it around with my pen to try and make it look more like a face. And the next thing I was drawing figures in red and black on the same envelope. And from that moment I was done for."

Tommy remembered that when he went to visit Mercy in Jackson over his spring break that March, she was reading *The Horse's Mouth*. She took him camping in the snow. Not for the first time, he was impressed by her stubbornness. When their stove fuel leaked into their oatmeal, she insisted on cooking it up and eating it anyway. Perhaps she inherited her stubbornness from Dad: the incident reminds me of one family sailing cruise during which Sheila and I were assigned galley duty. We had been out several days and the lamb chops in the icebox had spoiled. The stink of them turned my stomach. Over Mom's and our protests, Dad scraped off the green, soaked them in seawater, and ordered us to cook and serve them - which we did. As Dad was fond of saying, at sea the Captain's word is law and he was definitely the Captain. After faking several bites, I surreptitiously slid my chop overboard.

Tommy recalled that during his spring visit with Mercy, they sat on the snowy bank of a creek while she talked about her conflict with Dad. She confided that she thought Dad was paying her friends to influence her to go college. "Even at the time, it struck me as grandiose," he said, then added with laugh, "Not that she didn't have Dad pegged!" Trying to control his children with money was a knee-jerk strategy.

Although Mercy's fears may have been aggravated by weed, they were not entirely unfounded. In 2009, at the gathering after my mother's funeral, our cousin Jane Hoffman, with whom Mercy and Tom had bonded during their skiing trip to Aspen, told me that in fact, Dad had gotten on Mercy's case. No money was involved, but he did pressure her to write Mercy and persuade her to go to college. Dutifully, if reluctantly Jane did as he asked. "It was pretty hypocritical of me," she said ruefully. "I wasn't about to go to college myself."

"What was Mercy's reaction?" I wondered.

"She never wrote back," Jane said. "I never heard from her again."

In April, perhaps inspired by Gulley Jimson, Mercy quit her job in the leather craft shop. Although she doesn't say so in the letter she wrote to Mom about it, the "meaninglessness" of the job must have been heightened by the fact that she didn't need the money to survive. Despite Dad's disapproval of her choices, he continued monthly deposits of her allowance into her bank account. She could live, albeit in a stringent, counter-cultural mode, on money from home. So while she was relieved and happy to be free of her job, she felt pressure from within, as well as from home, to find a worthwhile path. Like Dad, Mom was pushing for college or art school - an opportunity she herself had never had. At the same time, I think she gave Mercy permission to do whatever she wanted to do.

A dozen years before, when I was just out of college, confused and in an emotional crisis, she wrote me a letter that I imagine must be similar to the advice she gave Mercy. I had declined to join the family on vacation

Adoration of the Holy Eucharist. The chapel was the center of our school life. If Mercy's high school years were relaxed, Sheila and mine were tightly laced with prayer. Daily Mass, prayers before and after each meal, prayers before and after each class, Sunday evening Benediction, processions and litanies on saints' days.

Sacred Heart Convent Gate

in Bermuda and had decided instead to hunt for a job in New York. She wrote:

> I hope you are straightening out inside and remember that job hunting isn't the
> important thing - or the job - but it is what is inside you that makes the difference
> between a success and a failure as a human being. We all know successful - or
> know of - successful writers, painters, business men etc - that are failures in the
> only thing that counts - so it is good to work for success - but be sure to keep your
> values straight about what is success - Thus ends today's sermon.

Letters from Mom were always reassuring. She wrote to us all the time - to whoever was away from home. She wrote to me regularly over a period of forty years - from the time I went away to the Convent until "that time when everyone was dying" as she refers to Patrick's and Dad's deaths in 1995 and 1996. Then she stopped letter writing altogether.

The Convent was only half a mile down the road from home, located in the old Collander mansion at the end of the Point, but behind its wrought-iron gates, we seventy-odd girls were as isolated as students on the moon. Radios and newspapers were not permitted, there were no TVs, and no access to the telephone, so our only contact with the outside world was by mail. Letters were distributed at lunchtime in the Refectory, a room with a bare wood floor, a high ceiling and a large window that allowed a view of the Sound sparkling beyond the hockey field. I remember sunlight falling in patches on the round, darkly varnished tables and glinting off the heavy silver-plated coffeepots that held chicory-flavored café-au-lait - the milk usually curdled from boiling. And I remember the pleasurable relief of getting a letter. All our mail came with the envelopes slit, as our incoming and outgoing letters were censored by the Mistress General, the nun who served as head of school, but I doubt she bothered to read Mom's or any other parental letters. However, letters from boyfriends were scrutinized, and some boys, knowing their letters were read, would make suggestive comments or write nervy notes to the censor, and the girl would be called in and reprimanded. Some girls would pray novenas to get letters from a certain boy, and there were shrieks and squeals of delight when a long-awaited letter was passed out. But I didn't have a boyfriend, so Mom's letters were the next best thing, a comfort if not a thrill. They were a reminder that beyond the Convent's wall, I had a home, a real life without demerits, without the guilt of failing to meet the nuns' perfectionist standards.

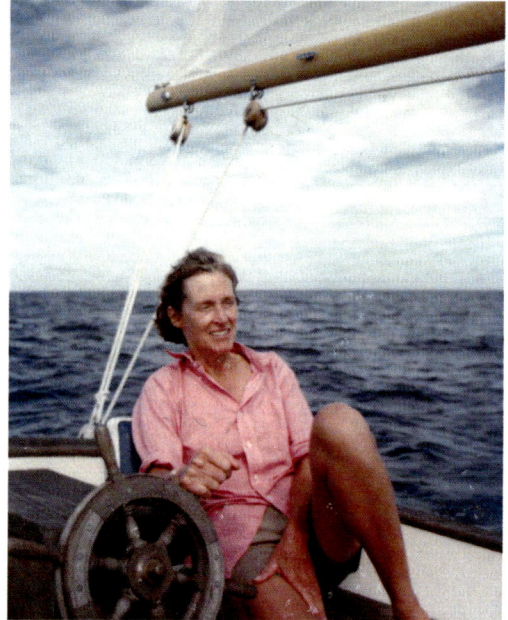

Mom at the helm of *The Houston,* the 22 foot Hereshoff they kept in Bermuda.

Mom wrote about the little ones - how Mercy and Tommy, her sun-flushed towheads, had learned to swim and how Pat was learning to crawl. She wrote about books she had read and flowers she photographed with a new lens. ("The yellow hibiscus is really spectacular… it has been so satisfactory… just like a talented child.") She wrote about the sailing trips she took with Dad and how, when they were away on one of their cruises, Mercy found our beer-drinking cleaning woman passed out on the laundry room floor and thought she was dead. As we got older, Mom wrote more confidentially, allowing herself an occasional ironic remark. She described a family wedding at which the bride and groom had mashed wedding cake into each other's faces. "Charming," she commented.

Clearly letters were an outlet for her, and although she insisted they were "boring" she found some pleasure in writing them. Letter writing was a respite in her day, a welcome duty that gave her a chance to sit down and reflect. Sheila once remarked that her letters sounded like Virginia Woolf. Certainly she wrote in a conversational, stream-of-consciousness way and her tone had a Britishy wryness. Her letters were most relaxed when she and Dad were on vacation together, either off sailing by themselves on their boat, or in Bermuda where they played golf and rode pedal bikes around the island. She liked to see her husband unwinding, leaving Wall Street behind, putting aside the weight of his role as Family Provider, and the additional weight of his own father's financial successes: Buck Ewing, Sr. had been one of the original partners in the Morgan Stanley Investment Bank. On vacation, my father and mother had fun together. It was a side of my father that I never knew, but now and then would glimpse when his eyes would light up with mischief and he would toss a firecracker at a pompous cousin at our annual family the Fourth of July picnic or, in Bermuda, rev up his motor bike and take off across a golf course to jump a sand trap, pretending he was Steve McQueen in the movie *The Great Escape*.

In one letter to me from Bermuda, Mom lists the letters she has yet to write: she had written "the little ones" as well as Marie, our nurse, and her mother Mercedes, but still had Billy and Fritz to write to in their respective boarding schools. My sister Sheila and our cousin Michael Crimmins were in Bermuda with her. Mom wrote that she was sitting on the deck overlooking the turquoise cove below their house. I imagine she was sweating in the late morning sun and probably drinking a beer after a game of golf with Dad. She noted that she wearing her favorite pair of cotton madras shorts, faded and soft and thin with age, and she worried that she wouldn't be able to find a replacement at Trimmingham's, the department store in Hamilton where she liked to shop: Shetland sweaters and tartan skirts imported from Scotland, shirts and shorts of madras imported from India. She looked at her knees which glistened with oil and were turning brown in the sun.

> I am most unsatisfied about my baggy knees & have to wear longer & longer shorts
> - & I cannot get into my last years Patchwork ones - & I go on and on drinking
> beer and planters punches & I wonder if I should just give up trying to be chic -
> which I've never been able to be - and become reconciled to middle age spread
> - consoling myself with the untrue thought that it comes from 20 years of fruitful
> child bearing - and try desperately to feel sorry for those other slim trim chic
> ladies of 40. There is a chameleon next to me with tiger stripes on his back - have
> never seen one like it before.

This was April of 1963. Mom would turn 41 in September. I was 20, a junior at Manhattanville College. I shared her worry about getting fat, but her worry about her knees surprised me. It never occurred to me that anyone would worry about baggy knees. When Mercy left Noroton in July for the Fiji Islands, Mom was filled with a gut-level dread. The whole time she was gone, her worry persisted below the day-to-day flow of ordinary pleasures and annoyances. Airmail letters between the remote islands of South Pacific and Connecticut could take more than a week to arrive. Mom wrote often, but Mercy had no fixed itinerary and sometimes Mom's letters missed her and were returned unread. For example, the first week of Mercy's trip, Mom sent her three letters in care of "Burns Philip South Sea Co. LTD in Suva, Fiji Islands." In them she wished Mercy a happy birthday and described our brother David's wedding. She confided that she was looking forward to "getting off on the *Maria*" (their forty-foot sloop) with Dad for two weeks and that she worried about leaving Tom (then seventeen) alone at home. Although she undoubtedly was more worried about Mercy, she wrote nothing of her fear, but sent her hopes that "things are going fairly smoothly for you" and "lots and lots of love".

In October, these letters were returned marked "N.O.B." - Not On Board. Mom put all three unopened into a single envelope and sent it off to General Delivery in Suva. "I don't really want to reread them," she told Mercy in a subsequent letter. It was frustrating to realize that Mercy had never gotten the letters - and the love and implicit support that went with them. Nonetheless, despite gaps and delays in communication, Mercy was writing home regularly, not only areograms to Mom, but also postcards and letters to siblings as well as our elderly cousin, Grace Jennings, who had doted on Mercy since she was small. In addition, Mercy was sending home souvenirs - boxes of shells, rolls of film to be developed, a woven mat. Mom was not entirely reassured by Mercy's letters which confided her ups and downs, both emotional and physical. Nonetheless, she took vicarious pleasure in the Mercy's great adventure. She saw the trip as a valuable life-learning experience and so gave advice sparingly and with restraint. In one letter she wrote:

> The Tongan stamps are really great - I think the 4s one shaped like a banana is marvelous - what a wonderful idea - the possibilities are endless - I was thinking - if you continue to be allergic to mosquitoes - why don't you try an antihistamine when you get bitten & it starts to blow up -

On October 17, she wrote:

> Your letter arrived this morning - I'm answering it right away - sometimes it is hard to react when I let much time pass between receiving & writing - Don't stop writing because it's a drag - it isn't really futile to explain - or try to - what's going on around you or in your head - even if I don't always understand it doesn't matter, I'm interested, and of course care a great deal and I do worry when a long time goes by without word. I keep thinking of leaking boats and typhoons & sharks etc. I thought that you would not be allowed to work in New Zealand - why do you have a problem trusting people - I wonder. Have you often been betrayed - or

do you think perhaps you expect too much - If Asia seems too much - fly over it & come home after going through the Middle East, Greece etc. Asia has been there a long time & will remain - & there is no reason you cannot go back - you don't have to do the whole bit in one gulp. I wrote last week & sent it to Suva - will they forward your mail to you?

The following week she wrote:

I now have the Atlas out and see where you are - or were. I cannot find Napuka (sp?). You really have covered the Islands in detail - where in hell is Toga - I cannot find it in my maps - you don't - you cannot possible mean TONGA - can you? In my National Geographic Atlas I have a map of the Oceans - a contour map of the land under the sea so I can see the Fiji Islands as if I was in a plane and there was no water in the ocean - it is rather spooky but interesting indeed. . .the Fiji Basin or Plateau is 1800 to 1121 deep but whether feet, fathoms, or meters - I don't know - This map of the Ocean is really fascinating - I will try & get a copy to send you - it adds a whole new perspective.

In a P.S. written on a scrap of paper, she added:

Tom called this afternoon and he is fine - got on the honor roll. . .Also talked to Jessie last night - she wondered if you have received her letter - I had not realized that you were so very homesick - though I know that if it had been me I would have been. It is a dreadful disease and I'm glad it is better. We - I - all of us miss you - often very much indeed. They had 12 in of snow in Eastern Penn yesterday with the autumn leaves still on the trees. . .

A week later, she told Mercy "I'm going to try and get a chart of the Fiji Islands." She and Dad were aboard the *Maria* anchored in "very pretty small harbour off Narragansett Bay."

It is cool but sunny - for a wonder - and blowing quite hard from the Northwest...I'm just as happy we will not be sailing today. It is really beginning to blow quite hard - I seem to worry more about sailing in bad weather than I used to - and I'm not sure if it is because I am older [Mom was 55 and Dad 65] - and so is the Maria - we had one really wild sail across the Sound from Port Jefferson to Saybrook - very clear like today - cold as all get out and blowing about 30 knots - & quite large seas - we were reefed and not too wet or uncomfortable - but I kept waiting something to give - a stay or a spreader or a sail or something - & in that case we could have been in serious trouble - with only 2 of us. & neither of us as strong as we used to be - and if one went overboard - well that would have been even more complicated.

An October 23rd letter was written in four different places: "I'm now parked behind the Church" waiting to pick up Sheila's little boys from catechism class; "Now I'm home again"; "Now I'm on a plane" flying down to Virginia; and finally "Friday morning at Christie's". On the plane she wrote:

I've just finished the newspaper - do you get a newspaper - I must say its depressing - editorials still about the latest hijacking - have you heard of it - the German air liner taken over by German terrorists that are Arabs - they ended up in Africa after shooting the pilot in the aisle. . .there is no happy news today. A man in Queens was shot on the street & killed in front of about 50 neighbors & no one will tell the Police who did it - why? - no one knows - Mafia? An Italian neighborhood. It is very foggy - & we are now in a cloud. . .

In November, Mom and Dad went down to Bermuda with their friends Houston and Gusty Huffman. Sheila, who was picking up Firwood's mail at the Post Office, knew that Mom was becoming increasing worried about Mercy so when a letter from Tonga arrived, Sheila called Bermuda and read the letter to Mom over the phone. In the letter, Mercy told Mom that she was hitching a ride on an orange catamaran and expected to be in Auckland by Thanksgiving.

From Bermuda, Mom wrote to Mercy in care of General Delivery in Auckland. As usual, it took her two pages of news - a kind of epistolary warm-up - before she got to her core concerns:

There is no point now in telling or asking you to be sensible or wise in selecting a job or ride on a yacht - when you are at sea the Captain is king & you have no recourse - & you might find yourself in a nasty mess - in an unseaworthy boat - anyway if you receive this letter you will have arrived - so there is no more to be said. Usually if a boat is clean it is well kept & apt to be sound - look at the lines - halyards - sheets - etc - are they worn thin & likely to part - anyway - I cannot remember all your letter - is being so alone beginning to get to you? that was a thought that passed through my mind as I heard [Sheila read] your letter.

Thanksgiving came and went without word from Mercy. Mom showed Mercy's slides to the family over the Thanksgiving weekend. ("They were all good & some were excellent," she wrote Mercy. " & the one of the 2 girls & the boy in the tree was terrific - what a handsome girl - It will be more interesting when you can give us a lecture on them."). Every time the phone rang, Mom's heart jumped. But there was no call. And no more letters.

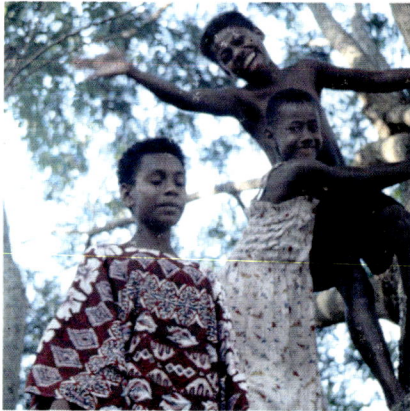

At the beginning of December, Mom's letters - all the ones quoted above - began coming back. Ones sent to Fiji came back first, then the letters in care of the steamship company, then letters to Tonga. This time, Mom opened and reread them - a kind of slow torture. She jotted down the dates of their return on the back of the envelopes: 3/12, 12/12, 21/12. On December 30, her letter advising Mercy on how to choose a seaworthy boat was returned.

Dear Mera -

~~Saturday~~
Friday -
Bermuda -

Sat morning - & she read me your letter - so I'm writing to Auckland - & if your check is there when we get home Daddy will make arrangements with the bank - or he probably will anyway & I'll write & let you know the details. There is no point now in telling ~~me~~ or asking you to be sensible or wise in selecting a job or ride on a yacht - When you are at sea the Captain is king & you have no recourse - & you might find yourself in a nasty mess - in an unseaworthy boat - anyway if you receive this letter you will have arrived - So there is no more to be said. Usually if a boat is clean it is well kept & apt to be sound - look at the lines - halyards - sheets - etc - are they worn thin & likely to part - - anyway - I cannot remember all your letter - but look forward to the map - is being so alone beginning to get to you? That was a thought that passed through my mind as I heard your letter -

We anyway - the sun came out yesterday in all its glory & we

ahead of Sheila before I mail in address for you. We the Huffmans got in today was nice & so was been put in the water go to the Airport bag - We got there & cliff to get ashore. in coral. You know makes. & we were due in for another ark we decided tell everboard arrived at our waiting on the place - there the hill having them weaker - but is interesting He is is more going out

"...there is no point now in telling you or asking you to be sensible or wise in selecting a job or a ride on a yacht..."

April 5, 1977
Jackson, Wyoming

4/5

Dear Ma,

I went into give my Boss two-week notice yesterday...And my emotion ran away with me...I ran on about how I really couldn't be happy doing that, and how the job was starting to run my life and on & on...I was surprised the way it slipped out... came out pretty good.

"You're fired!" he said. "Why are you firing me?" "No one quits from here, they're fired...you can leave now, have a good day..."

He was laughing the whole time - weird.

I wonder if he said that so I wouldn't collect unemployment... am I eligible for unemployment? I don't think so.

Well I'm out of work. I feel free... everything is dream-like and the only thing on my mind is to make a decision about traveling or staying, walking with the neighborhood dog "HOBO" and drawing...spring is in Jackson for the moment 50 - 60 during the day - full moon at nite- I'm sure this state of mind wouldn't last for long. I'll soon become tormented & desperate about my decision... But for now I'm relaxed and just working on trying to understand what's right for me to do.

Well my dear mother, your letter loosened me up...maybe too much...I don't know how much of this is coherent...and I don't wanna save it for a day and read it over later. I wanna get it off to day off to you.

Soon I'll write a letter to you & Dad very soon.

Thanx so much for your letter. It helped because it sounded so real...like you really meant it. Thank-you...I'm just working on being alive and I guess a lot of this comes from realizing how much I should have hated that job... so many people work the 40 hr week and miss out on the finer points of living... am i being unreal?

Do i need a slap in the face? to bring me back to reality? A career? A stable future? Well, it's beautiful out i'm going to mail this off. thanks again for that great letter so so so much love and admiration. Mercy

May 5, 1977
Jackson, WY

5/4

Dear Ma,

Got back from a trip to the Grand Canyon on Monday. That's when i got your letter.
Oh it was so incredible...95 degrees and up.
So hot — just what i needed to thaw out.

We hiked down to the bottom and in and out the different side canyon. We didn't see anyone the first couple of days. But after a while we got into the better traveled canyon and there were many people. You really get a feeling of how old that canyon is hiking down in it.. Down Down

Down.

It's a long way down there.
I'm thinking of going to New Zealand on June 14th or 15th. There's a freighter leaving San Francisco then and i've got a cabin on board for $850. Could you please send me my passport right away. I need it to get a visa... i have no idea of where it is.

In my room a round my desk?....or i think
it might be in the bath room on that
self below the slanting mirror or in the
cubboard to the left. Thanks a lot.

I'm not sure if i'm going or not. I'm trying to
plan it out really well. And, if i don't get
every thing together in time...i guess i won't go.
But it's looking pretty positive right now.

So, yes, i need that pass port.

I'm getting kind of scared to just go over
there by myself. I'm scared of leaving Jackson too
cuz I know i won't be able to come back and have it the
same...i feel like there's more i wanna
get out of this town...and i won't be able to
if i leave in June specially if the weather keeps up.

Its been snowing & melting every day since I got back.
We need the rain so bad but i like sunny days.

My visa can only last for 3 months and its
really hard to get it renewed, so i'll probably be
back in this area in the fall.

Well, i'll call you and let you know what's up.

Much love Mercy.

8

Until I began to sort out the notes and cables Dad had saved in his manila folder, I was convinced that Sheila and I were the ones who had nudged our parents out of disbelief into action. The way I remembered it, our drunken New Year's Eve fight was the catalyst that prompted the search. But this was, I discovered, a perfect example of Memory painting a self-portrait without warts or wens. In fact, Dad's first cable was sent at 5:31 p.m. EST on December 31st - hours before our midnight phone calls to Tonga. This, no doubt, was why Mom had looked so depleted that evening: she had finally given voice to her worst fears and convinced Dad that something had to be done. It had been two months since Mercy's last letter. It was unlike Mercy not to write or call. "People just don't change character," she insisted over and over.

She and Dad must have worked on the cable that afternoon: she with the National Geographic Atlas of the World open on the dining room table showing him place names gleaned from Mercy's last letter and helping him with a description of her (he would not have known how

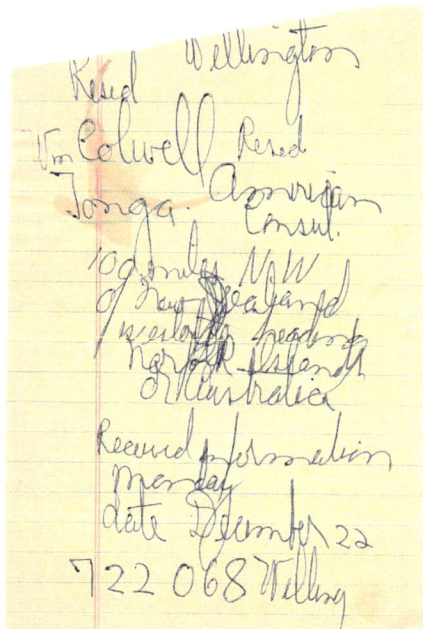

Dad's notes

92

old she was - he never knew how old any of us were); then he retreating to his study to compose the cable on two sheets from a memo pad incongruously decorated with sepia drawings of violets and roses. He wrote with a pencil in block letters. His draft read:

MERCEDES EWING OUR DAUGHTER 20 YEARS OLD,
5 FOOT 7 INCHES TALL BROWN HAIR AND EYES LAST
HEARD FROM IN LETTER WRITTEN NOV 9. WAS THEN
SAILING IN Vava'u ISLAND GROUP ON WAY BACK TO
KAPA ISLAND IN A BOAT BUILT IN NORWAY WITH A MAN
CALLED STEVE WHO HAD A TORN SAIL AND HAD IT
MENDED ON KAPA. HE HAD SAILED FROM TAHITI. HER
LAST ADDRESS WAS GENERAL DELIVERY NUKU'ALOFA
CAPITAL OF TONGA ON TONGATAPU MAIN ISLAND OF
TONGA, MEMBER OF BRITISH COMMONWEALTH. IN LAST
LETTER OF NOVEMBER 9 WAS PLANNING TO LEAVE FOR
AUKLAND NEW ZEALAND IN A COUPLE OF WEEKS ON
A 65 FOOT TWO MASTED TAHITIAN RED CATAMARAN
OWNED BY AN EX AIRLINE PILOT WITH A TAHITIAN GIRL
FRIEND AND AN AMERICAN COWBOY. DON'T KNOW IF
SHE SECURED PASSAGE ON THIS BOAT. SHE HOPED TO
BE AUKLAND, NZ, END OF NOVEMBER. TODAY RECEIVED
POSTCARD FROM CAROL A GIRL FRIEND SHE HAD MET
IN FIJI ISLAND AND HAD BEEN TRAVELING WITH. IT WAS
ADDRESSED TO HER AT HER HOME NOROTON, CONN.
ASKING WHERE SHE WAS AS THEY HAD PLANNED TO

MEET IN AUKLAND, NZ., A MONTH AGO AND CAROL HAD
NOT HEARD FROM HER.

WOULD CATHOLIC PRIEST HEAD OF CHURCH IN
NUKU'ALOFA MAKE INQUIRIES AT IMMIGRATION TO
FIND OUT IF SHE HAS LEFT TONGA. SHE WROTE THAT
SHE HAD OVERSTAYED HER 30-DAY VISA AND WAS IN
TROUBLE WITH IMMIGRATION. WOULD APPRECIATE
EFFORT BASED ON ABOVE INFORMATION TO TRY TO
LOCATE HER. DID SHE LEAVE TONGA. DID SHE LEAVE ON
65-FOOT CATAMARAN.

LAST LETTER NOV 9 MENTIONED FRIENDS ON KAPA
ISLAND WHOM SHE HAD BEEN STAYING WITH. NAMES
WERE LANTAIMI AND SALEVI. THEY MIGHT KNOW OF
HER PLANS.

ANY EXPENSE INVOLVED IN LOCATING HER WILL BE MET.
WILL WIRE MONEY. PLEASE ADVISE WORRIED PARENT AS
SHE HAD BEEN WRITING REGULARLY EVERY TWO WEEKS.

The final draft was a quarter of the length, omitting the description of Mercy and calling her "Mercy" instead of "Mercedes". Also edited out was the description of where and what Tonga was, the mention of the ex-pilot's girlfriend and the cowboy, the appeal to the Catholic priest and the postcard from Mercy's friend Carol. It was addressed to the manager of the Marine Broadcasting Commission in Nuku'alofa on Tonga Island and it provided our home address and phone number.

If the draft admitted to parental worry, the cable Dad ended up sending was military in its precision - nothing more than the immediate facts. His cables and notes have the feel of a military mission. Among names and phone numbers he scrawled on the backs of envelopes, there were runic-looking diagrams of circles intersected by lines at different angles - something an army navigator might draw to indicate the movement of the sun. A series of typed letters from a New Zealand contact have a manly-man tone, as if the correspondent were reporting to a Captain in a World War II era movie. The command post for the search was Dad's study at Firwood.

Originally the room had been part of a butler's pantry that served the dining room which was large enough to accommodate John D. Crimmin's massive oak table. (It had been made to order in Ireland and with all its leaves in, it could sit twenty adults in matching carved chairs.) When Dad and Mom bought the house from Mercedes' sister Evelyn, they divided the pantry into two small rooms - the half equipped with a zinc sink became a well-stocked bar; the other half was paneled in knotty pine and the pantry shelves were converted to bookcases and a rack for Dad's shotguns. Like the dining room, the study's ceiling was 12 feet high but its floor space was small - just large enough for a desk, a small sofa upholstered in a masculine rust-colored tweed and an end table. The sofa and the table were always piled two or three feet high with old newspapers. Sometimes they also covered the top of the radiator below the single window.

Dad's newspapers were a family joke; he was devoted to his newspapers. Every evening when he got off the train, he carried his briefcase in one hand, and with the other, hugged three papers to his chest: the New York Times, the Wall Street Journal, and the New York Post. Once his hoarded piles of newspapers almost killed him. During a Thanksgiving dinner, in order to take a Polaroid of us seated at the massive dining room table, he pulled the end table from his study into the doorway into the dining room. He climbed atop its stacks of newspapers. He ordered us to smile, and as he peered through the lens waiting for compliance, the pile of newspapers slipped out from under his polished loafers and he fell with a great, horrifying crash to the floor. There was a rush to assist him, but he ordered us back to our seats and climbed back up onto the now bare end table to take his photo. (The fact that his holiday photos were always blurred throw-aways never deterred him from trying to capture the moment.)

When Dad called you into his study for a talk, you had to move the newspapers off the sofa so you could sit in the hotseat. On these occasions, he would sit at his desk in a Windsor-type Captain's chair with the Yale crest on its back. When he wasn't there, we would sit in the chair to use the black rotary phone on his desk, careful not to disturb any of the papers on his blotter. There were only two other phones in the house: one in the kitchen and one on Mom's desk in her bedroom, so if you wanted to talk privately, away from her, away from our nurse Marie, and away from the comings and goings of the younger kids, the phone in the study was the surest choice.

The desk was furnished with a lamp whose base had been made from a knee-high riding boot of polished leather. The boot had belonged to Buck Ewing, Sr. - the "Old Man" as he and his father used to call each other. After the Old Man's death, Dad's sister Grace had his boots made into lamps and had given one to Dad. Dad thought it a fine gift and took comfort from it. He had had a deep affection as well as an unwavering respect for his father. Mom, however, didn't like the lamp. In her view, the Old Man

Jessie Vallé Ewing

was a judgmental, demanding father who withheld approval from Dad and his sisters. She found it a bit creepy that even after the Old Man's death, Dad worked under the light of his boot. Buck Ewing, Sr. inspired feelings of maternal anger in her.

She felt the same protective anger at Dad's paternal grandmother Jessie Vallé Ewing. Dad's mother Maria (pronounced Mariah) had few mothering skills - perhaps because her own mother had died when she was still a child or perhaps mothering wasn't in her personality. Dad's oldest sister Jane once remarked that their mother "wouldn't come near us when we got sick," but when

one of her horses was sick, "she'd go down the stables in her nightgown and spend the night in its stall, rubbing it with brandy." Dad was the first born and the subsequent pregnancies and births (three girls) must have swamped Maria. When Dad was four, she sent him to live with his "Grandmere" Jessie who had an apartment above the family's New York brownstone. Dad once told a story about how he had climbed out on window ledge of his grandmother's apartment and hung down over the street, hoping that his mother would see his legs and come and reclaim him. According to Dad, his grandmother Jessie Vallé promised that if he would come back inside, she would let him go see his mother - but when he was safely back inside, "she gave me a whipping!" He told the story as if it were a great joke - a boyish prank that landed him in hot water. But I remember being appalled by the story.

Another time, not long after I'd finished college, I was sitting in the hot seat in his study asking him for money so I could start seeing a psychiatrist. I expected him to say no, but to my surprise, he supported my request. He told me that his Grandmere had taken him to see a psychiatrist when he was small. His problem was driving his family to distraction: whenever he was asked a question, no matter how innocuous, he would invariably answer,

Frederick B. Ewing

"I don't know." Threats and punishments failed to produce a straight answer. Finally Jesse Vallé marched him off to a psychiatrist. If Dad was, say, eight years old, the year would have been 1920. Psychiatry was in its infancy. Jessie Vallé must have been both forward-looking and desperate to "fix" the grandson in her charge. But after several sessions with the doctor, there was no improvement and she became impatient. "Bill," she ordered, "you tell that doctor what's the matter with you! He's costing me twenty-five dollars each visit!" During the next session, he obliged her by discovering the cause of his problem. He remembered that the nuns at school had told him he

97

would go to Hell if he told a lie. So he had decided to avoid all possibility of telling a lie by saying "I don't know."

"She cured me," he told me in all seriousness.

Mom never knew Jessie Vallé first hand, but from Dad's accounts of his childhood, Mom concluded that, in addition to being "as tight as a tick" with money, she was a humorless martinet who regularly punished Dad for being "disobedient". Although giving away a four-year-old was both unimaginable and unforgivable to Mom, her anger skipped over the maternal ineptitude of Maria and landed on Jessie Vallé. "They say her husband was alcoholic and never amounted to anything," Mom once vented. "But if you ask me, she drove him to drink."

An early photograph (now lost) of Jessie Vallé, showed a proud looking woman in a pale evening gown - taken perhaps in the 1870s when she would have been in her twenties. Her carriage is aristocratic, reminiscent of a young czarina, and the gown, with its tightly corseted waist, looks expensive. She is handsome rather than pretty: a strong jaw, a wide mouth with narrow lips, and intelligent dark eyes. Above a fine brow, she wears her hair in pinched little curls. She was descended from an old St. Louis family who had made their money in the fur trade around the time of Lewis and Clark. "Coming from good stock," was an important family value, as were good looks and money.

In a family album, pictures of her husband, Frederick Berthold Ewing show a nice looking man with slightly sleepy eyes and a dark mustache drooping over soft, full lips. He ran a cattle ranch in Arizona which eventually failed. In one picture he poses in his "ranch clothes": riding boots, a white shirt blousing over a cummerbund and a wide-brimmed hat. He is standing stiffly at attention as if under orders. Judging from the photographs, Jessie was clearly the stronger personality. When life on the ranch with Frederick became intolerable to her, she took her children off to Austria. By the time Dad was born in 1912, she was a widow. In an informal family photograph, it is summer and she is seated on a porch in a loose-fitting, lace-trimmed pinafore. She is heavier, with a double chin. Escaped wisps of gray hair soften her face as she smiles with pleasure at the curly headed baby boy - my father - in her lap.

As a substitute mother for Dad, she no doubt was strict, and perhaps even harsh, but they were close to each other. When he was sent off to boarding school at age 13, she sent him care packages of oranges and crackers as well as the things he asked her to send: books of stamps, a Bible and prayer book, starched shirt collars, his sled. His letters to his parents were formal, but he began letters to her with the salutation, "Dearest old fellow Grandmere." In his first letter to her, he declared that he was "going to like it here a great deal." In the next line he confided that on his first night in the dorm, he had been sick to his stomach and had thrown up: "I couldn't find the toilet for a long time. It sure was some stomach ache and it doubled me up like a knife. Gosh! I surely did wish you were here. . ." In a subsequent letter he told her, "It is awful nice up here but I would much, much, much,

much, much, much rather be with you. I miss you very much."

He worried about her weak heart. Writing in the spring of his first year, he expresses his concern:

> I have received your two awfully nice letters. I'm sorry you feel lonesome and sad
> but don't think about me. Because I will see you this summer and we will have a
> fine time. As long as I am here there is no use feeling bad because it doesn't do any
> good. So cheer up. I am sorry I haven't written quicker but it slipt [sic] my mind. I
> am going to write to you as much as you write to me. I bet I will too. . . They asked
> me if I wanted to play golf on the links and all the Form was going to so I did.
> Please tell me what I should do about getting some golf clubs. . . But promise me
> this that you will get help or I will be sore at you forever. Because the box [of golf
> clubs will be] awfully heavy. . . "

Jessie Vallé died later that year. Her daughter recalled that "Bill was really broken-hearted (for a boy) and said to his father, "I just don't see how we can get along without Grandmere."

Despite the "lickings" she gave him, Dad remembered her with affection and gratitude. In his study, on the knotty-pine panelled wall above his desk, he hung her photograph - not as gray-haired grandmother, but as a younger woman in her czarina pose. Thus, along with The Old Man's boot, the indomitable spirit of Jessie Vallé presided over his search for Mercy.

July 2, 1977
Vancouver, BC

7/2

Dear Ma,

We're in Vancouver now, and we're leaving today at 5:00. Sailing for the Fiji's. I really have an urge to call you again, but phone calls always leave me feeling so empty...i'm really scared to go and the thought of stepping off the boat and forgetting the whole deal seems really easy. But how could I ever do that. I'd be kicking myself for the rest of my wanderings....So i guess the next you'll hear from me i'll be on Fiji. Coming down the West Coast was so nice, gave me a preview to traveling on my own and i really like it. Being on the boat is kind of driving me bezerk...Very English Blue Star Lines, and being a passenger kind of awkward, really awkward...being waited on at meals and having a steward....I'm not very good at handling it all, but am learning to just ride along with it...Carol and John, a English couple, are trying to teach me the English ways. How to drink tea, — with mint sugar of course, ugg...which fork to use and when, how to lay your napkin at your lap...how to talk to the steward etc...Ugg.. its so gross... so fake and English...can't wait till i can be primitive with the Fijians. God, i'm so antsy—we're gonna be leaving pretty soon...My camara's bust or somepart has fallen out...What do you expect...

I read this book Pan by Knut Hamsun, a Norweigian writer, i really liked it, the way he describes his interaction with people...Its so personal and accurate...its almost embarrassing...Ya know?

I started to ready the Aenid of Virgil, but it keeps putting me to sleep...so now i'm reading Even Cowgirls get the Blues by Tom Robbin. Good book to read while you're on the road.

Well, the boats about ready to pull off and i wanna mail this before i leave. Just wanted to let you know that i was thinking of you and would of liked to see you in Vancouver before i left. I'll be in touch—don't worry...please.

so so much love   Mercy.

9

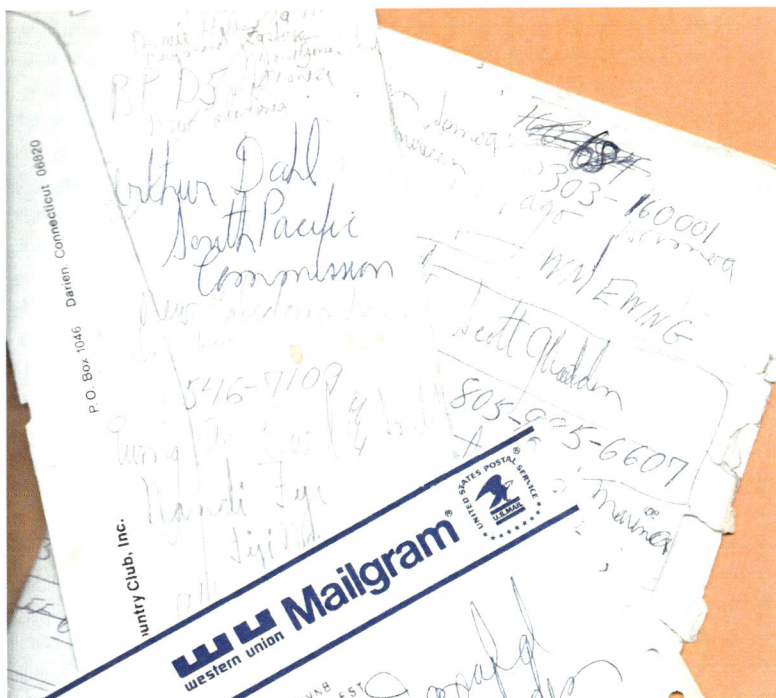

Dad's notes

While Dad and Mom waited for a reply to their cable, Dad began making the first of hundreds of telephone calls he made over the next six months. One of the people he called was his brother-in-law David Challinor, who at the time was the Assistant Secretary for Science at the Smithsonian Institution and well connected in Washington, D.C. circles.

From David Challinor's journal:

Tuesday, 3 January 1978. Buck Ewing called in the a.m. to say that they'd not heard from Mercy when she wrote to say she was going underground because her visitor's visa to Tonga had expired. They thought she was going to sail from Kapa in the Vava'u group to Auckland, NZ in a 65-foot red 2-masted catamaran owned by an ex-airline pilot, but they did not know whether she'd ever left. A friend she was supposed to meet in Auckland wrote home and wondered where she was! Buck seemed very casual about it all and said he was calling to ask for my help even though Mary did not want to "bother" me. I immediately got in touch with Jim Sherburne who gave me the name of Jim White, the Peace Corps Director in Nuku'alofa, Tonga. I sent him a long cable asking him to inquire among his volunteers. I also contacted Ray Fosberg, but he had no connections in Tonga. I purposely didn't contact our State Department because if Mercy is still underground, the State Department would have to turn her over to the Tonga government if she surfaced. If I were Buck, of course, I'd have long since gone to Tonga to start looking for Mercy myself. . .

The ellipses after "myself" are David's and indicate text he had omitted. When I asked him what he had left out, he cheerfully admitted that he had "bowdlerized" (i.e. censored) the passages in which he had vented his anger at Dad. Neither David, nor his wife Joan, liked Dad. From their firm stance as liberal Democrats and progressive intellectuals, Dad was a die-hard Republican throw-back, too involved in Wall Street to take any real interest in his offspring. Dad seemed genuinely oblivious of their disapproval, but Mom resented her brother's judgements on her marriage and her choices. Although in old age she and David finally became friends, at that point in her life, her relationship with her brother was distant and carefully polite. I probably widened the existing chasm between the families, first as a teenager and later after college, when I found a sympathetic refuge from my conflicts with Dad in the Challinor home.

David kept his anger at Dad within the confines of his journal. After Dad's phone call, he followed up with a letter written the same day telling Dad that he had asked the Peace Corps Director in Tonga to inquire among his volunteers if they knew Mercy and whether she had left Tonga on a red catamaran. He goes on to advise:

> "It will take a couple of weeks to get an answer. Telephone service is virtually non-existent in Tonga except possibly through the Embassy or Consulate. If Mercy has indeed "gone underground", should she get involved with our consular officials they would be obliged to turn her in - that is why I thought the Peace Corps route would be best. They're all about her age. Please keep me posted and I'll see what else I can think of.

My uncle David Challinor in 2007 at age 87. His daughter Mary drew this graphite portrait as a present for her mother Joan's 80th birthday.

In the Kingdom of Tonga, after word of mouth, the primary means of communication was by radio or radio telephone. Local radio stations on the main Tongan islands would broadcast news from the "outside world". In emergencies, the station manager would send and deliver messages by short wave radio.

In Connecticut, the fastest, least expensive way to communicate with someone on the other side of the world was by cable. This involved calling Western Union and reading your message to the operator over the telephone. The operator then sent it out and mailed you a copy of your message. This confirmation copy would arrive at your Post Office a day or two later.

Along with requesting help from his brother-in-law, Dad began tapping into his own network of friends on the East Coast and gradually making new contacts and new phone friends in Pacific time zones. On weekends, he was in his study on the telephone virtually round the clock. On weekdays he would commute to his office on Wall Street, then resume his calls after he got home in the evenings. Conveniently, when it was eight in the evening in Connecticut, in New Zealand, it was in the middle of the next working day, so he was able to reach his contacts at their offices. It is impossible to reconstruct the chain of these calls, to sort out whom Dad called and in what order. The telephone bills, which ran up in the thousands of dollars each month, were not saved. But there are dozens of phone numbers and names scribbled in pencil and in ballpoint on the backs of envelopes and in the margins of the undated notes he kept on pads of yellow lined paper.

The place names are exotic to me: Pago Pago, Marquesa Society Island, Tongatapu, Tomatola, Suva, Fiji, American Samoa, Navau, New Caledonia. Not surprisingly given that time, the names of his contacts are all male: William Oliver of the Samoan News; Captain Frank Hunt, "Nautical Officer, Marine Division, Ministry of Transport", New Zealand; Jack Rickleman "Asst. to the Governor or secretary to Gov." of Tonga; Stewart Indor, "Pacific Islands Monthly, Sidney, Australia"; a Lt. Carl Smith in Fiji; one Peter Coleman in "Pango Pango"; Kenneth A. Wills, "General Manager Felt and Textiles of New Zealand."

At the top of a small sheet of yellow lined paper, "Cyrus Vance" was written in ball point and underlined. No title, but the name rang a distant bell. I googled Cyrus Vance and was reminded that he had been Secretary of State during the Carter Administration. In 1978, he had played a crucial role in the Camp David Accords between Egypt and Israel. So his name had been prominent in the news the year of Mercy's disappearance. Had one of Dad's friends suggested contacting him? Like Dad, Vance was a Yalie, but several classes below Dad, so it was unlikely that they knew each other. Dad's handwriting looks tentative: Secretary Vance's name is at once is smaller and fainter than the firmly written address below it for Air Sea Rescue in Honolulu. If at one point, Vance's name gave Dad slight hope, later he scribbled it out with an impatient pencil.

At the bottom of the "Vance page", he had pencilled a fragment in tentative French: "Ma fille, Mercy Ewing sur le bateau J'laime tu - est elle" - then he stopped. This was another small jolt of discovery for me: my father knew French? The idea of Dad speaking French was utterly incongruous to me. French was the language of high culture, a mark of sophistication. In college, I had struggled through French classics Moliere to Verlaine in an attempt to master the language and join the ranks of the literati. But if I had intellectual pretensions, Dad had none. He was, at least as I knew him, throughout his life entirely focused on the business of making money. However, when I stopped to think about it, I realized that his Grandmother Jessie Vallé had probably spoken some French as well as German. In addition to whisking her children off to Austria for a year, as a widow, she and a cousin sailed across the Atlantic several times to "take the cure" in German spas. Moreover, I guessed that Dad would have studied French at St. Mark's - along with Latin and perhaps some Greek.   Today, the modern languages of choice are Spanish and Chinese, but in Dad's day as well as my own, it was French.

After my mother's death, more packets of old letters surfaced and among them I found a report card from St. Mark's for Dad's first year there. He got a "9.3" in Latin and a "7.0" in French. Along with the report card was a carbon of a typed letter from his father:

> Dear Bill,
>   I have just received your report for the month ending May 10.
>   I am very much disappointed that you did not do better.
>   I am not speaking of French, as I know that is hard for you and you have not had a good start but there is no excuse for the other subjects.
>   There are fourteen in your form, and you are tenth, which really tells the story.
>   I very much hope this last month [of school] you will make a showing. It is most important, especially at the start.
>   With much love,

Ma fille Mercy. . . Some fifty years later, Dad was resurrecting the French he had struggled with as a schoolboy. Had he been composing a cable? Preparing for a phone call?   One of the few non-Anglo-Saxon names in his notes sounds French: Andre Petre - or Pitre - of Nerimea, New Caledonia. If Dad in fact called New Caledonia, surely he would have been relieved if M. Petre spoke English.

Ma fille Mercy Ewing sur le bateau J'laime tu..." "J'laime tu" was his attempt at translating the name of catamaran, *I Love You II*. Sometime during the first weeks of his search, Dad had learned the boat's name. When I first heard it, I thought it was *Love You Too* and I groaned inwardly. A hippie name. Captain Groovy. Peace and Love and mellow sailing in the Pacific. No wonder she'd gotten on board.

On one of their train rides into New York, Dad confided to his son-in-law Tom Daley that he also had contacted William J. Casey, a spy and Washington power-lawyer who later became director of the Central Intelligence Agency. Dad and Casey were business acquaintances. Both happened to be investors in a fledgling company that had invented a new film-developing process. (Ultimately, like so many of the ventures Dad backed, the company went broke.) So Dad had no qualms asking Casey for information about the *I Love You II*. When Casey got back on the matter, he cited hush-hush sources, and said that the CIA had the catamaran "under surveillance." Whatever that meant. Casey did not have a reputation for straight dealing and his "under surveillance" could have been a brush-off, an easy way to satisfy Dad and keep him from being a pest.

Somewhat fuzzy polaroids of the *I Love You II*.

To Dad, however, "under surveillance" suggested that the *I Love You II* was still afloat and that our government had suspicions about her activities.

Later Dad obtained two photos of the boat. She was a two-masted catamaran, ketch-rigged with the shorter mast set forward of the helm. One photo shows her twin hulls up in dry dock. They are painted orange or red - it is hard to tell - with a white waterline and white frieze-like bands along the length of her rails. The bands are painted with primitive-looking glyphs: perhaps they had personal significance for the Captain; perhaps they were traditional island designs.

Allowing for the fact that the boat had been hauled out of the water for repairs, she does not look very ship-shape: her lifelines are casually draped with laundry. The same is true of the picture of her at anchor. Although the mizzen and main sails are furled along their booms, the jib lies in a loose pile on netting between the two forward decks. Nonetheless, this photo has a romantic look. The boat is anchored in a cove hemmed by rugged-looking mountains that rise as sharply as a fortress wall from the shore. Her twin prows have the sharp lines of a Polynesian canoe and her wooden masts are slightly raked, like an old clipper ship's. There is none of the aerodynamic sleekness of the aluminum-masted, fiberglass "cat boats" I'd seen on Long Island Sound. Moreover, she was bigger than any catamaran I'd ever seen. Sixty-five feet of boat is a mansion in the water. You have to study the photo carefully before you notice the tiny, naked torso emerging from a mid-ship companionway.

If Dad had hopes that Mercy had not set sail on the *I Love You II*, they plummeted when, ten days after his New Year's Eve cable, he received the following reply from Fusi Malohi, the "Broadcast Commissioner" or radio station manager in Nuku'alofa, Tonga's capitol and largest town which, at the time, had a population of approximately 47,000 souls. Mr. Malohi had done his homework. He wrote:

MERCY EWING BOARDED TAHITIAN CATAMARAN
18 NOVEMBER 1977 BOUND FOR AUKLAND STOP
CATAMARAN HAVE NOT ARRIVE DESTINATION   RESCUE
PARTY SEARCHED AREA SO FAR NO INFORMATION ON
IT WHEREABOUT POSSIBILITY CAPTAIN CHANGED
COURSE HEADING DIFFERENT DESTINATION OTHERWISE
CATAMARAN LOST AT SEA STOP POLICE STILL LOOKING
FOR INFORMATION LEADING TO WHEREABOUTS OF
CATAMARAN STOP PLEASE REMIT TWENTY DOLLARS
COVER EXPENSES

Shortly after receiving Mr. Malohi's cable, Dad sent a cable to Mr. William Colwell, the American Consul in Wellington, New Zealand:

COULD YOU ASK PORTS OF ENTRY IN NEW ZEALAND,
NORFOLK ISLAND AND AUSTRALIA TO NOTIFY YOU
WHEN 65 FOOT RED CATAMARAN NAMED LOVE ME
TWO ARRIVES AND IF MERCY EWING IS ABOARD. WIRE
OR PHONE ME COLLECT. FORWARD ANY EXPENSES AND
INFORMATION. WILLIAM EWING

His mistake of the boat's name was repeated in a second cable to Fusi Malohi:

HAVE YOU RECEIVED MONEY   LOVE ME TWO
WITH MERCY EWING ABOARD REPORTED 100

MILES NORTHWEST OF NEW ZEALAND HEADING

WESTERLY DIRECTION ON DEC 22. CAN YOU SEND

LIST OF PASSENGERS AND ADDRESSES   HAVE YOU ANY

INFORMATION ON BOAT OR PASSENGERS   IF SO CABLE OR

PHONE

W EWING

I found no record of how Dad knew about the December 22 sighting. But two days later, he cabled Mr. Malohi again asking whether it was a plane or boat that sighted the catamaran, repeating his request for the names of the passengers, and asking for Mr. Malohi's thoughts on organizing a search party. He sent the same cable and the same requests to Mr. Colwell, the American Consul in Wellington.

Mr. Malohi replied to Dad's cable on the same day it arrived. Two days later, on January 25, the Western Union operator called Noroton to deliver a three page telegram from Nuku'alofa. Dad was at work and Mom scribbled down the information as the operator dictated it to her. Mr. Malohi confirmed that Mercy had joined the crew of the *I Love You II* at Vavua, Tonga, on December 11, 1977 and had sailed for Nukualofa, Tonga, with New Zealand as the final destination, on the same day. "The vessel did not arrive Nukualofa which lies 185 miles south of Vava'u," he continued, "and has not been heard of since." He goes on to describe the vessel as "orange-coloured," 57 feet long with "fifty foot yellow masts."

Orange or red? Did it make a difference? And 57 feet long? Mercy in her last letter home had described the boat as 65 feet long, and I doubt she would have paced it off. It is fair to assume the measurement came from the Captain. Had he exaggerated the size of his boat when asked, "How big is she?" Alternatively, perhaps the boat's official length was measured at her waterline and the Captain had used the longer, topside measurement.

According to Mr. Malohi, on October 30, the catamaran had arrived in Vava'u from Pago Pago in American Samoa with a crew of five, all with American passports. Two of the crew, a journalist and his teenaged son got off the boat and returned to Pago Pago where the father worked for the local newspaper. The Captain and two others remained on the boat in Vavua until mid-November when they set sail with Mercy.

The cable went on to say that a "so far unsuccessful search" had been organized by a Captain Hunt of the Marine Division of the New Zealand Ministry of Transport. Mr. Malohi reported that Dad was not the only worried parent. The mother of another girl on the boat had also been in contact. He concludes:

> CHECKS MADE CONSTANTLY THROUGHOUT TONGAN
> ISLANDS BUT NO SIGN STOP POLICE HERE STATE NO
> KNOWLEDGE OF CLAIMED SIGHTING OF VESSEL 22.12.77
> NORTH WEST NEW ZEALAND AS REPORTED YOUR CABLE
> TODAY STOP WOULD WELCOME FULL DETAILS OF
> SOURCE AND EXACT INFORMATION SOONEST

Mom's heart must have plummeted as she wrote out the message on one of the yellow pads on Dad's desk. As impossible as it was to think of Mercy as dead, it was even more impossible to think that if she were alive and safe, she wouldn't have been in contact. Had there been a storm at sea? In one letter home, she had mentioned that November was the start of the hurricane season - the cyclone season, as they called it in that part of the world. Mom wanted to know about what kind of weather the *I Love You II* had encountered. What had the winds been like? What about the seas? How seaworthy was *I Love You II*? How well had she been provisioned? Was there a life raft aboard?

From Mr. Malohi, Dad learned that the Captain was an American, a retired airline pilot, from

Malibu, California. His name was Donald Glidden and he was born on May 4, 1927 - which made him fifty years old - five years younger than Mom. His girl friend was twenty-six year old Taire McMillan of Papeete, Tahiti. The "cowboy from Wyo" was twenty-one year old Steven Wolf from Portland, Oregon.

If Mom was struggling with a Lost-in-a-storm-at-sea scenario, Dad, encouraged by what he had heard from the CIA, latched onto the suspicion that Glidden was hiding out somewhere from the law - perhaps even forbidding his crew any contact with their families. In his notes, he instructed himself to find out "about the character of Donald Glidden, how he supports himself, what airline he worked for and if he had a good record. Also what bank he uses so a check can be made if money has been forwarded to any location and where last checks were cashed." At some point someone told Dad that Glidden had faked an inner-ear problem to qualify for early retirement. The source of this information is not in Dad's notes, but we didn't question its truth and it left a bitter taste in our mouths. True or not, the rumor served to heighten Dad's suspicions about Glidden.

Glidden's only address was a Post Office Box in Malibu. Through a dozen more phone calls, Dad learned that the box had been in use for the past six years. He also learned that a secretarial service forwarded Glidden's mail to him. From that service, he obtained an address for Glidden's son Scott. He sent Scott a cable:

> HAVE YOU HEARD ANY NEWS OF YOUR FATHER HIS BOAT
> 2 MONTHS OVERDUE AT AUKLAND, NEW ZEALAND MY
> DAUGHTER ABOARD.

A few days after Mr. Malohi's long, helpful telegram, Dad received a copy of a typewritten report from the Tongan Prime Minister's office in Nuku'alofa. It was addressed to the "Tonga

High Commissioner" in London, England, and was dated January 18, 1978. The report provided several new details. A month after the journalist William Oliver and his son left the catamaran at Vava'u, Glidden went through Customs/Immigration and was cleared for passage to Nuku'alofa and New Zealand with two passengers on board: Tiare McMillan and Steve Wolf. The report goes on to say:

> But on actual sailing out of NEIAFU harbour, Vavua on 18/11/77 a fourth person - a woman named MERCEDES EWING of Noroton, Connecticut passport F 1289754 issued on 16/6/75 in Washington - was noticed on board.
>
> The catamaran did not arrive in Nuku'alofa and nothing has been seen or heard of her since leaving Vava'u.
>
> Vava'u gossip reported radio and engine both giving trouble and intention to repair on reaching New Zealand.
>
> The weather reports for the two weeks immediately after the vessel's date of departure from Vava'u, i.e. 18/11/77 did not indicate abnormal sea conditions.

Perhaps Mom was reassured by the weather information. But both Mom and Dad, as experienced sailors themselves, must have wondered what sort of Captain would have set sail on 1500 mile passage in hurricane season without a reliable radio and engine. Then there was the bit about Mercy being "noticed" on deck as they left. Presumably, she had been worried about her expired visa and Glidden had allowed her to remain hidden below when he and his crew tied up at the main wharf in Neaifu Harbor and presented their passports and the catamaran's papers to Immigration. This doesn't say much for his honesty.

Nonetheless, the officials who later spotted Mercy on board and intercepted the boat on its way out of the harbor, were content to let her sail after taking her passport number. Had Mercy pleaded with them? Had money changed hands? More likely, in that pre-9/11 era, the local authorities were casual about formalities and had simply concluded that as long as she was leaving, there was no point making a big fuss about an expired visa.

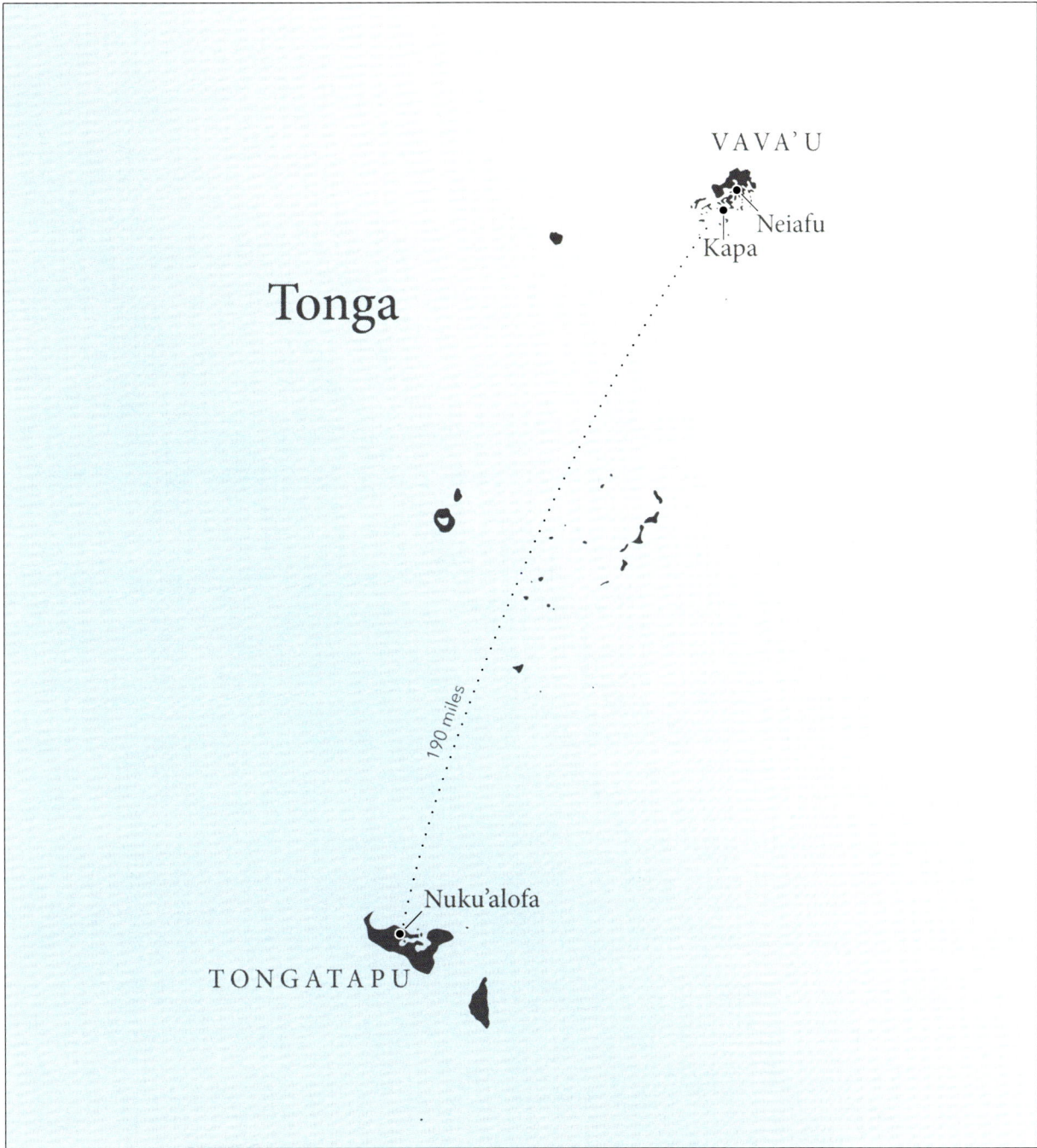

VAVA'U

Neiafu

Kapa

Tonga

190 miles

Nuku'alofa

TONGATAPU

Looking back at the incident, it is hard to brush aside the thought that if the police had detained her, she would not have been lost with the *I Love You II*. As it happened, however, off she sailed. She must have been relieved to have passed though the official hurdles, to be underway, up on deck with the wind in her hair, heading out through Vava'u's chain of little islands to open waters.

July 19, 1977
(Mercy's 21st birthday)
Suva, Fiji

7/19

Dear Ma, thanx for all your letters...it was good to hear from home...got into Suva last nite found a hotel for the nite + i guess now i'm just getting everything together. Don't really know where to start. Here i am — what now?

The [freighter] ride was nice, but I'm really glad to be off and given a chance to start seeing some country...it was so peaceful, a good feeling just floating on top of ocean 8 miles deep....5,000 and some odd miles to Fiji....seeing the sun rise and set over the unbroken horizon. Dolphin were jumping along side of us, on and off, all the way here, saw many rain bows left over from distant storms.....and had lots of time to read and read and read...i even dreamed i was reading — never done that before.

Well, i don't like being in this town Suva at all,...so i guess i'll get a bus out to the country and find a place to stay there for a while until i find a way to get over to New Zealand. The customs agent has been a real help to me, getting my visa, finding me a hotel, and he even mentioned something about getting me a job on a sail boat going to Auckland. Sounds good but he's so busy i hate to go and bother him...can't wait to get out of this town though.

Yes, the Jesus people, they were in Seattle...wow, what a bunch of fanatics. It just didn't seem healthy the way they adored him and he was every thing to them...i mean everything, they only sang Jesus songs, only listened to Jesus music, only ate Jesus food, ugg, and only did Jesus things... Jesus was in control of every thing they did..." well if the lord has chosen this road for me i'll go."

And everything was so sloppy and ugly around the house...i mean if you're gonna have a commune, a common house, then you may as well put some energy into it and have it look nice. Half of them weren't working either...so I don't know what they were up to. Jesus i suppose. It just seemed like they were using him as an escape, Well, listen to me. how can I pass judgement on them? i'm not into Jesus but the real drag of it all was that they really thought that they were going to "save" me. That's all they would talk to me about...and if you tried to change the subject....it would inevitably come right back to "Jesus wants you"

"Do you want to know Jesus? He wants to be your big

Daddy." Ugg. and on and on so i left.

Well, gotta go...

i'll write more later.

Much love Mercy...

P.S.   don't think that i'm looking badly on every thing that's happening on this trip...really good thing have been happening too. you just asked me about the Jesus people so I told you.

so long.

10

```
         HKD063(0627)(1-00096SC027)PD 01/27/78 0624
TLX SECSTATE WSH
ZCZC 1239 COLLECT SD WASHINGTONDC 1/27/78
PMS MR WILLIAM EWING
    BOX 3412
    NORTON, CT 06820
WELLINGTON 432


1.   IN VIEW OF PROVISIONS OF PRIVACY ACT, EMBASSY IS
UNABLE TO FURNISH NAMES OF CREW OF "I LOVE YOU II".,

2.   UNCONFIRMED SIGHTING OF "I LOVE YOU II" MADE BY
AUSTRALIAN ORE CARRIER "JEPRAIT" AT 0900 HOURS
DECEMBER 22, 1977.  LAST CONFIRMED CONTACT WAS IN TONGA
IN NOVEMBER 1977.
```

On January 27, three weeks after Dad's cable to the American Consul in New Zealand, the wheels of our government finally turned out a response. The telegram arrived collect from the American Embassy in Wellington. It had numbered paragraphs. The first one read:

1. IN VIEW OF PROVISIONS OF PRIVACY ACT, EMBASSY IS
UNABLE TO FURNISH NAMES OF CREW OF "I LOVE YOU II".

This struck us all as bizarrely outrageous and I remember howling with indignation when I heard. But, as confirmed by Dad's subsequent telephone calls, according to the laws of our country, any law-abiding citizen over the age of 18 is allowed to disappear. Still, as frustrating as the Privacy Act was, it was irrelevant since the Tongan government had already given Dad the passport information of everyone on the catamaran.

The following paragraphs were more forthcoming:

2. UNCONFIRMED SIGHTING OF "I LOVE YOU II" MADE
BY AUSTRALIAN ORE CARRIER "JEPRAIT" AT 0900 HOURS
DECEMBER 22, 1977. LAST CONFIRMED CONTACT WAS IN
TONGA IN NOVEMBER 1977.

3. EMBASSY LEARNED TODAY FROM NEW ZEALAND
SEARCH AND RESCUE THAT EFFORTS ARE AGAIN
IN PROGRESS TO LOCATE "I LOVE YOU II". PORT
AUTHORITIES THROUGHOUT NEW ZEALAND, AUSTRALIA
AND SOUTH PACIFIC ISLANDS HAVE BEEN ALERTED.
EMBASSY WAS ADVISED THERE IS NO REASON TO
SUSPECT CATAMARAN IN ANY DIFFICULTIES BUT EXACT
WHEREABOUTS UNKNOWN.

4. EMBASSY BELIEVES ALL POSSIBLE EFFORTS LOCATE

YACHT ARE BEING TAKEN.

The unconfirmed sighting offered some hope - or at least another lead. But paragraphs three and four carry a whiff of bureaucratic impatience: "We are doing everything we can. We have three governments on alert for your daughter's yacht. Please stop calling."

Dad was oblivious to the subtext. Or perhaps he got it and ignored it. He immediately called the Embassy in New Zealand to quiz Mr. Colwell on the sighting. He also called Captain Frank Hunt of the Marine Division of New Zealand's Ministry of Transport - the man in charge of the search. Sometimes Dad called both men two or three times in the same day. This was typical of Dad's modus operandi: he rarely accepted an answer to his questions at face value. When he asked, say, "How are you doing at college?" my proud answer "Fine, I almost made Dean's List," would not satisfy him. He would ask how many people in my class were on the Dean's List, what grade point average was necessary, what was my grade point average, and so on, until inevitably, he would reach a point of resigned disappointment. He would shake his head and urge me not to study so hard. He worried that his plump bookworm daughter would never find a suitable husband. By the time Mercy came around, however, his focus had shifted: he wasn't worried about her finding a husband; he worried about her not going to college. He would have been relieved to have her glued to books in a college library rather than traveling footloose around the world.

In his search for her, he tested and retested his questions, asking the same ones over and over, measuring one answer against another. From the American Consul Mr. Colwell and from Captain Hunt, Dad learned that the reason the ore carrier *Jeprait* had not made positive identification of the *I Love You II* was because they did not know it was missing until four or five hours after it was seen. Thus the *Jeprait* had not attempted to contact the yacht, nor had the ore carrier deviated from her course to check it out. After more questioning, Dad also learned the *Jeprait*'s deck officer had sighted the boat through binoculars "close to dawn". The yacht was under sail, and might have been a catamaran, but the color of the boat's hull had been indistinguishable, making any identification dubious.

Even more questionable than the identification was the yacht's location. It was sighted about 150 miles northwest of New Zealand heading either towards Norfolk Island or Australia. Norfolk Island was some 300 miles away from the yacht's spotted position and the coast of Australia over 1000 miles away. If this boat was the *I Love You II*, that meant that by December 22, Glidden had safely sailed all but 100 or 150 miles of the 1500 mile passage from Tonga to New Zealand, then veered away from his declared destination in a northwesterly direction towards Australia.   Of course, the other explanation is that the *I Love You II* actually made landfall sometime before December 22 in New Zealand and then had set sail for Australia.

As much as Mom would have liked to believe that the *I Love You II* and her crew had not perished, she was unshakable in her belief that if the catamaran had made landfall somewhere, be it New Zealand in December to reprovision or Australia in January on a final leg of the voyage, Mercy would have found a way to contact home. Even if she had decided to skip New Zealand and go onto Australia, she knew that "Ma" would be worrying. Why had she not mailed a letter or called home if they had made landfall?

Other families had the same question. Steven Wolff, the 21 year old crew member whom Mercy had described in her last letter as a "cowboy," was in fact a dental student taking a year off to hitchhike around the Pacific islands. Like Mercy, he had been writing regularly to his mother in Portland, Oregon. By January, his mother was distraught at not having heard from him. She contacted the Red Cross - to no avail. In desperation, she called the newspaper in American Samoa. International telephone calls were expensive, and to avoid the cost, she placed the call from her daughter's place of work in Portland. The staff at the newspaper gave her Dad's name and phone number. They told her that he was "co-ordinating" the search and had news of the *I Love You II*. She made a second long-distance call to Dad in Connecticut. So it was he who ended up having to tell her that in all probability, the catamaran had been lost with all hands. (He described her as a "poor widow" but in one of the letters in his folder, she is referred to as Mrs. Shaw, not Mrs. Wolff, so perhaps she had divorced Steve Wolff's father and had remarried a Mr. Shaw who had died.)

Dad also talked to the mother of Tiare McMillian, the Captain's 26 year old half-French, half-Polynesian girlfriend who had worked as an airline flight attendant before setting sail on the *I Love You II*. Tiare's mother, Denise Higgins, was living in Paris with her second husband. Independently of Dad, in January she had called New Zealand authorities demanding that a search be made for the catamaran. Like Dad, she had been directed to Captain Frank Hunt of New Zealand's Marine Division of its Transport Ministry.

Hunt appears to have been a kind and patient man who never brushed off Dad's repeated calls. In January, when he heard from Dad and from Mrs. Higgins, he was already involved in a multi-national search for a Tongan ship that had disappeared at the end of December. The ship was called *Tokomea* and it had been lost in a storm with more than 60 people on board. Hunt added the *I Love You II* to the search for *Tokomea* survivors. The scope of the search included the Tongan islands - two parallel chains of more than 150 islands scattered over some 300 square miles of ocean. Of the islands, only 36 are inhabited year around. Tongan Search and Rescue workers were joined by the American Coast Guard out of Samoa who checked out all the uninhabited islands by air in a large plane especially built for searches. The Royal New Zealand Air Force and all ships in the area were ordered to be on the lookout for any evidence of the lost vessels. Five hundred miles west of Tonga, where ocean currents might have carried wreckage or survivors, the Fiji Islands were searched. (Hunt personally contacted the chief of the Fijian navy as well as the prime minister and hereditary chief of the Lau group of islands and had requested that each island be searched for the *I Love You II*.) Over a thousand miles southwest of Tonga, the Australian Marine Operations Centre searched Caledonia, the New Hebrides, and even further southwest, Norfolk Island. Hunt was particularly pleased with the thoroughness of the Australians. "If the Australians say they have searched," he commented to one of Dad's contacts, "they have searched." None of the searches, however, found a trace of either the *Tokomea* or the *I Love You II*.

News of the loss of the *Tokomea* was as startling as the sudden blast of a foghorn. It cut through my own fog of hope and denial and jolted me into an awareness of the stark reality: a whole shipload of people had disappeared. Not one survivor, not one body or piece of wreckage had been found. What hope was there of finding Mercy?

Dad, however, kept on asking questions. He pestered Captain Hunt, and anyone else he contacted, about the *I Love You II*'s seaworthiness. He was told repeatedly that she was a "good vessel", a U.S. registered yacht whose papers were in order both when it cleared from Pago Pago and when it left Tonga. "In good shape," Dad wrote more than once in his notes.

Other questions swirled around the catamaran's owner and captain: On a sheet of yellow lined paper, Dad organized them in pencil. "How good a sailor is Don Glidden? Navigator? What kind of man is he? Does he smoke pot, use hard drugs? Did they ever talk about disappearing and leaving the world behind them?"

Over this last question, he wrote in dark ballpoint, "Rumored that he left." Perhaps his source for this was William Oliver, the newspaperman who had sailed from American Samoa to Tonga with Glidden in October. Oliver's name and telephone number is at the top of the list of questions. Or perhaps it was Captain Hunt - or both. Hunt was familiar with the inclination that some yachtsmen had for disappearing. As a hydrographer, he had spent time in the New Hebrides, a chain of islands which were something of a haven for fugitive sailors. They were not hiding from the law, Hunt emphasized. They were simply "dropping out" to escape from family or business entanglements. Hunt suggested contacting Stuart Inder, Editor of the Pacific Islands Monthly in Sidney, Australia, and see if Inder's sources among the yachting crowd could help locate the *I Love*

You II. In a January 29 telegram, Dad alerted Inder to the fact that his daughter and the catamaran were missing. He went on to cable:

"GLIDDEN RUMORED TO HAVE DISAPPEARED BEFORE
FOR SEVERAL MONTHS." He ended: "CAN YOU HELP."

Two days later, he received a terse response:

AUSTRALIAN MARINE KEEPING WATCH FOR CATAMARAN
I LOVE YOU TWO NO FURTHER NEWS. INDER.

Perhaps the idea that they were fugitives, either from the law or by whim, allowed him to hope that Mercy was still alive.

Frustrated by the lack of solid information, on January 31 Dad flew down to Washington, D.C. to knock on doors there. David Challinor met him cordially and escorted him around. Dad's apparent lack of urgency, his slow, methodical fact gathering was a worry to David. Afterwards, he jotted down an account of the day in his journal:

> I accompanied Buck Ewing over to the State Department to see Bill Galligher, the New Zealand desk officer. He shares a suite of offices with Ed Hurwitz, whom I met at C.S. Squires's when John Smith, the Governor of the Gilbert Islands, was here. Galligher was very nice and very cooperative. He made a number of suggestions that Buck might do in contacting people in Pago-Pago. He said he'd also call Colewell, our Consular official in Wellington to see if there was information that he could tell Galligher, but not Buck. He also reinforced my argument that Buck should go out there as soon as possible to follow up these leads before they became too cold and people forget all about the boat. Buck was stubborn and I had the feeling that all the action he was taking was primarily triggered by Mary. I took Buck to the Federal City Club for lunch. . .

The following week, on February 5, a New Zealand freighter called the *Tasman Enterprise* reported the wreckage of "the starboard hull of a catamaran some 60 feet in length with orange hull, white trim." *The Tasman Enterprise* was under way from Brisbane on the West Coast of Australia to North Cape, the northern tip of New Zealand. The wreckage was spotted at 10 am in the Tasman Sea at a latitude of 32 degrees, 4 minutes south and the longitude of 167 degrees, 2 minutes East - approximately 150 miles south of Norfolk Island and more or less in the vicinity of the unconfirmed early morning sighting from the decks of the tanker *Jeprait*.

But what had the *I Love You II* - if the wreckage did indeed belong to her - been doing in the Tasman Sea? And what about the missing hull? Dad's phone calls discovered that port hull was where they lived and slept. Had it sunk with them in it? Was it floating somewhere with survivors clinging to it? Did Donald Glidden have a life raft on board? If so, was it equipped with water? Was Mercy adrift and dying of dehydration in a rubber life raft?

If initially Dad had balked at David's suggestion that he fly out to Tonga and New Zealand, he now determined to make the trip. He reserved a seat on a TWA flight to Los Angles, arriving Friday evening, Feb. 10th. From there, on Saturday morning, he would fly Pan AM to American Samoa, arriving on Sunday, February 12 for a flight to Tonga. He refused to let Mom come with him. I remember being shocked at this fiat, and surprised that she had not put up a fight. Several of us volunteered to go with him, but he firmly rejected all offers. When my oldest brother Bill, took a day off from work at his New York bank to get a passport and announced that he was going, Dad became angry. He insisted that he "did not want to be responsible for anyone." Ironically Billy wanted to accompany him because he felt responsible for his frail-looking, 66-year-old father. As for Dad being "responsible" for Billy or Mom or any of us, it had always seemed to me that Mom was the responsible one. She was the tower of strength, the one who took care of us all, who fed and clothed us, got us to school, to the doctor and the dentist. Through the lens of a child, the fact that Dad paid the bills was too remote to count. Even as an adult child, it always seemed to me that Dad was more dependent - at least emotionally - on Mom than vice versa. His sister Grace had the same take: in a 1995 letter she told Mom, "As the poem says, you are his East, South and West, and his North star." But not on his trip to Tonga.

Almost forty years later, Mom maintained that she had no desire to accompany him. "There was no point to it," she said. "By then, I knew Mercy was dead." On the other hand, several of us remember that at the time, she had been torn, initially wounded by his rejection, then stoically resigned to being cut out of the action. I imagine that some part of her wanted to go, wanted to see the places Mercy had written to her about, wanted to connect with the Tongans Mercy had counted as friends, but at the same time, another deeper part of her felt it was an exercise in futility. More certainly, she and Dad were not getting on. Mercy's disappearance had inserted a wide wedge of anger and guilt between them. For Mom, the idea of traveling with Dad, listening to him obsessively quiz anyone and everyone about Mercy, listening to him attempt to discover who she was and what she was up to, would have been beyond bearing.

As for Dad, I think his declaration of responsibility was exactly what he felt. Like his father before him, he took his role as head of family very seriously. He believed it was his solemn duty as a father to find out what had happened to his youngest daughter and to rescue her - if she were still alive. A therapist today might describe Dad's trip as "grief work", as a way of working through the guilt and pain of Mercy's loss. But he himself saw it as a mission - a manly mission with no room for women and children. He did not want to have Mom - or any of us - questioning his moves. In happier times, when we sailed with our parents on the *Maria*, sometimes they would argue over how much sail to set or which course to take to avoid running aground. Dad's word was law - he was the Captain, as he often reminded us - and although Mom had grown up on the Sound and had more sailing experience than he did, she obeyed his orders. Nonetheless, her tight-lipped silence was a protest loud and clear. Later, when we were safely at anchor in a snug harbor, the tension between them would dissolve with jokes over a drink before supper in the cockpit. But this was cruising in Long Island Sound. Dad's trip to Tonga was no vacation. Perhaps he sensed that Mom's presence would make navigating the sea of his questions more difficult. Certainly he had not ruled out evil-doings stemming from involvement in drug running, so perhaps wanted to shield Mom, whom he knew was especially close to Mercy, from whatever hard realities he might uncover. So in the end, he took off for the South Pacific alone.

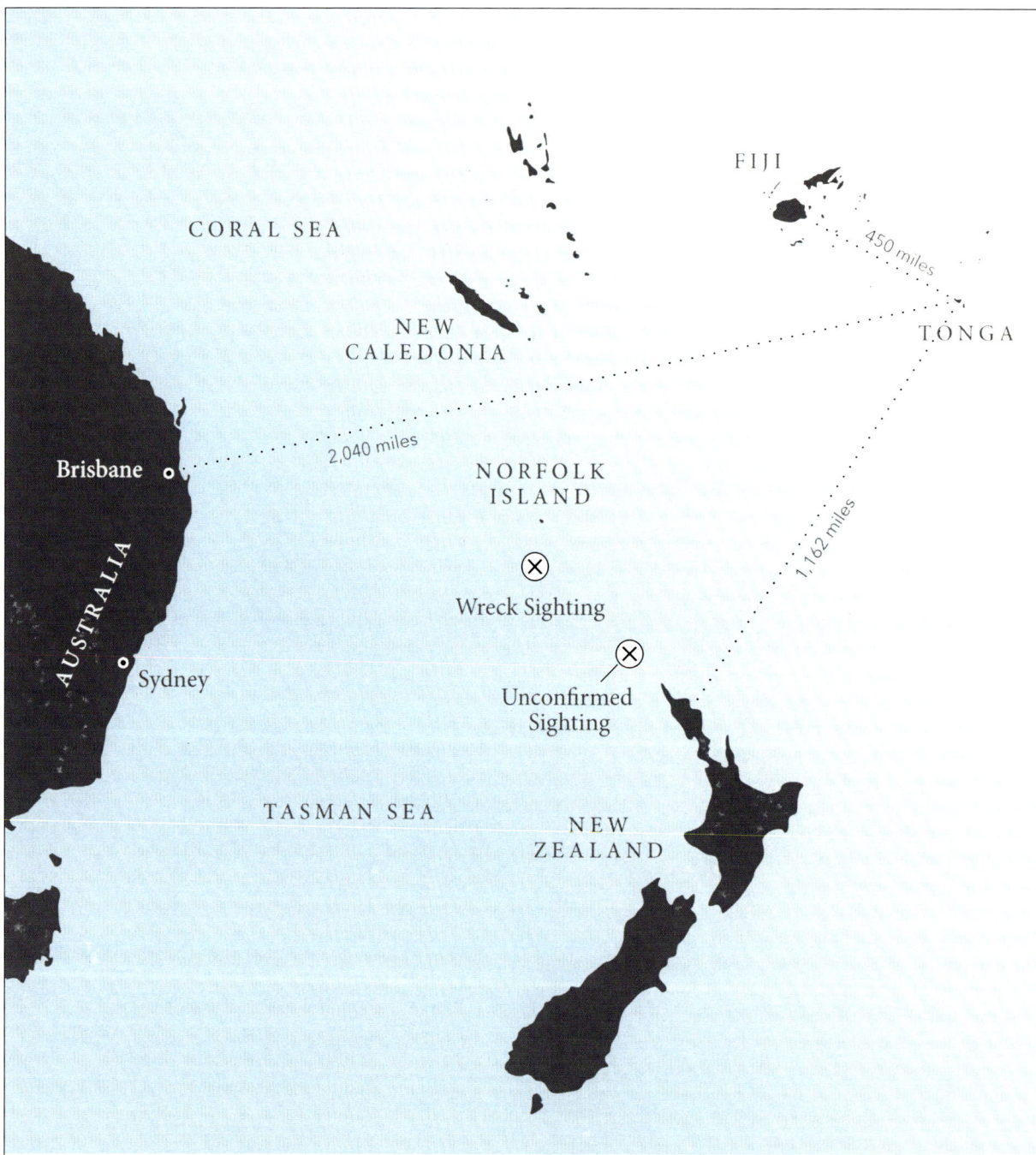

FIJI

CORAL SEA

450 miles

NEW
CALEDONIA

TONGA

2,040 miles

NORFOLK
ISLAND

1,162 miles

Brisbane

⊗
Wreck Sighting

AUSTRALIA

Sydney

⊗
Unconfirmed
Sighting

TASMAN SEA

NEW
ZEALAND

July 28, 1977
Suva Fiji
South Pacific

7/28

Bula, [Hello]

     still alive and living in that bura i was talking about.

     Its so nice out here...there's a rain bow in the water fall every after noon and the fijians always drop in to look at it. I've met a couple of families...they're so friendly and interested, even though they get a fair amount of tourists staying here. They always want to take me home and feed me and show me their homes...Most speak English pretty well, so communicating is no problem....

     Most are very poor in money, but live very well off the land..so much food grows in these wet jungles. Dalo [taro plant] and hassava are both like potatoes...really starchy & the main source of food along with coconata. This is the rainy season here. Just before i came they had 14 days of straight pouring rain and now i guess it's slacking off a bit.. lucky...

     These islands have really captured my curiosity

     Along with everything else on the outer islands around fiji.. (the Lau group). Tourists hardly ever make it out there. That's where i want to go. People tell me its not too hard to get out there...just hang around the docks and find a supply boat that going out...The natives are still living their old life style and have that fijian hospitality. I've heard so many stories...of people going out there and being invited into families and they all have a feast and celebrate. And you really get to see how the natives live..untouched by western society.

I've paid rent here until Aug 1st and after that i guess I'll go back to Sava and try and find a ride out. I also want to look around the main island more (Viti Levu.)

Well, here i am in another Fijian village. Cora. It's really nice, long beach Bananas, Dalo, pineapple, coconut, paw paw, bread fruit. Today's Sunday, church day, and i'm getting dressed up in a sulu [wrapped cloth skirt] and going to meeting with the family. Then there's a feast after church, then bathing...the rest...ahh the famous fijian rest... rest before you do anything "first we take rest" in the middle of doing anything. "Ahh i think it time for another rest' and after its all done "Now we done, we get to rest."

Tomorrow i'm going out on the reef with the woman and going fishing, & looking for shells to sell to the tourists.

I feel pretty comfortable here, nothing much to worry about. I'm with a family and they take care of you, protect you. Rape is very common on all the islands...that just how they treat strange women – Before white man came, there was no such thing as rape, that just how things went. But with a family, they take care of you...I guess they feel responsible... But they really do look after you. Tell you where to go and where not to go swimming and who to go with and who not to go with.

There's just one thing that's bothering me... the old man keeps saying i'm going to marry him when i come back to Fiji. Hmmm. I keep saying he's crazy. I tell him I'm not going to marry him and then i make up a story that i'm engaged to a man in New Zealand. But he still keeps talking about the business we're going to have in future times. Maybe he's just kidding...that's how i'm treating it.

Well, every things well. I like living in this village...the good-life. I guess I'll stay here until the end of the week and then try and get out to some of the outer islands. Fiji paradise...not really. You can see Westernization setting in pretty fast...soon there will be no place felt where people aren't striving for T.V. sets, radios, hair dryers and cars. It's so sad. Their lifestyle is so simple. And there's so much love... family unit tight and all. When people start striving and striving...they loose it. You can see it happening already here. They think with a T.V. they'll really be happy...and then a radio and on and on...And there's no way to stop it... The world is doomed.... I'm lucky to be able to see the last of the old world...Times seems to go so fast, but then i realize the I've only been in Fiji for a little over a week. Every thing happens so fast and i'm learning so many different things to do.

Its not hard at all to get on a sail boat as a crew member and get a ride to New Zealand or the New Heberdies. I already looked into it and had a chance to get on one boat but it was leaving too soon...Maybe I'll get another chance, maybe not. I can always fly...but it would be nice to sail...Well every things just hunky-doory. Write more later when some more plans fall in to place. Mauvay.

Oh and if you write...write to General Delivery...Suva, Fiji. South Pacific. I don't want to keep in touch with any one...I don't want tooo...see? Its just easier this way. General Delivery.

Much love Mercy.

Mom and Dad always hosted Fourth of July
celebrations at Firwood where generations
of cousins and neighbors gathered for a
morning parade, afternoon baseball on the
lawn and evening picnic at the seawall.
There was a bonfire at dark and fireworks
gleefully exploded by Dad.

11

Mercy's ink sketch for my book *Seances and Spiritualists.*

Sometime after the February 5th wreckage report and before he left for Tonga on February 10th, Dad contacted an old army friend, highly placed in the Carter administration, and managed to get the American ice cutter Burton Island to search the area in which the wreckage had been found. The ice cutter was based in Antarctica, but at the time the wreckage was reported, she happened to be in Wellington on a passage to Fiji. Thanks to Dad's string pulling, the Burton Island took a detour through the Tasman Sea.

While the Burton Island was on its new course, he followed up another long shot and went to visit a psychic. When I heard about it, I was shocked. I wondered if he'd gone off the deep end. It seemed pathetic. At the same time, I was curious. I thought, well, why not? The more I thought about it, the more it seemed in character. It was not only a matter of leaving no stone unturned. Dad was as curious about the occult as I was. Two years before, in 1975, Lippincott had published my first book, a young adult book on 19th century teenaged mediums and their alleged paranormal powers. Mercy had done some drawings for it. It was the only one of my books that Dad ever showed an interest in. "So do you think there's anything to it?" he quizzed me more than once.

"I don't know, Dad," I would tell him. And in fact, I didn't. Researching the book, I had spent a lot of time reading texts from the Library of Congress's Harry Houdini collection and I had found it impossible to either dismiss or credit the old eyewitness reports. I decided to present the facts and let the young reader make up his or her own mind. I liked my solution. I thought it had a certain pedagogical virtue. But the one and only review I got complained that the author had copped out and never revealed where she stood.

When Dad pressed me, I told him, "Well, it's pretty clear something out of the ordinary was going on, but whatever it was, it's hard to say." There was (and still is) a part of me that believes with Hamlet that indeed there are more things in heaven and earth than we mortals dream of. But there is also a skeptical part of me that questions the literal reality of paranormal phenomena. So I am most comfortable sitting on the fence between belief and disbelief.

The psychic Dad visited was famous for finding bodies. "The police use her," he told me, as if to justify the move. "She lives in New Jersey," he said. Presumably one of his contacts had suggested her. He didn't confide in Mom about his visit: she was skeptical and dismissive.

He never told me the psychic's name, but when I googled "New Jersey psychics" I found her. Her name was Dorothy Allison. She was an Italian-American woman, the wife of a contractor and mother of three teenaged children and she lived in the blue-collar suburb of Nutley, New Jersey. When Dad visited her, she was in her fifties. According to her autobiography which she published in 1980, two years after his visit to her, Allison had been having visions since she was fourteen years old when she "saw" a sign of her father's unexpected death. The vision was intense and insistent: several times over a period of two days she saw white lilies, her father's drawn face, white funeral crepe on the front door of her house. At the time, her father was sick in the hospital, so it is reasonable enough to interpret the vision as a surfacing of unconscious fears rather than as a paranormal glimpse of the future. In any case, she was frightened by her vision and confided in her mother who, as it happened, took some pride in her own visionary talent, and reassured her daughter by telling her that she had a special gift - "a gift with sting," she warned.

Allison, however, came to relish her gift, along with the special status accorded her because of it. In 1968, she achieved some measure of fame after approaching the local police to offer help in a missing child case. When the boy's body was found, some of the details she had "seen", fit the facts of the case. She had "seen," for example, that the boy's shoes were on the wrong feet and this proved to be the case. There were, however, misses along with her hits: she predicted the boy would be found in a drainage pipe and police manpower was wasted digging up a pipe she indicated. But when the boy's body was found floating in a pond, she claimed it as a "hit" because she had "seen" water as a clue.

Although she was championed by the chief of police in Nutley as a finder of missing children, he admitted that her predictions were "very difficult to verify when initially given." He went on to note that her "accuracy usually could not be verified until after the investigation had come to a conclusion." Skeptics call this "retrofitting" and believe it is the secret behind most psychic successes. Allison herself did not claim to understand or sort out her visions at the time she had them. She would study a photo of a missing child, or hold something the child was attached to - a toy, an article of clothing, a piece of jewelry - and receive "strong impressions" from the objects. Sometimes she saw numbers or colors; sometimes she saw places or faces. Then she would tell what she saw to the police or the families of missing children. The color silver, for example, might indicate silvery hair, a silver spoon, or the name "Silverman." It was up to her clients to make sense of her visions. "I know I get my cases confused a lot of the time," she declared unapologetically. "It just happens that I pick up things that may have something to do with a case I'm working on or in the future. Imagine how confusing it is for me."

In 1974, her increasing fame prompted Randolph Hearst, the newspaper magnate, to consult her on the case of his teenaged daughter Patty who had been kidnapped by the radical group Symbionese Liberation Army. Hearst was desperate and when he offered to pay for her services, she retorted with her usual snappy comeback, that there was no price for a child. Nonetheless, Hearst paid to fly her and her "team" out to San Francisco. Her team was composed of a Nutley detective and a psychologist/hypnotist with whom she had worked on previous cases. Hearst put the three of them up in a first class hotel, but after two days of "searching" for Patty Hearst in a hypnotic trance, the only thing she "picked up" was that Patty was alive, frightened, and in a small, dark place. Again, not an unreasonable supposition for a kidnapping case.

By the time Dad visited her in February 1978, Dorothy Allison had become a celebrity in police circles. From police departments across the country, she had received a collection of honorary badges for services rendered and these she proudly displayed on velvet in an oak case in her home. She enjoyed working with detectives on missing child cases and they enjoyed working with her. Sometimes she became involved in as many as twenty cases at once and visitors were surprised to find her home looking like a squad room: her bookshelves and dining room table piled high with stacks of newspapers and police files. Photographs from that time show a short, stocky woman with a large bubble of jet-black hair, thin arching eyebrows, and classical looking features. She had a buoyant wisecracking personality, but was warm and earth-motherly towards frantic parents - in some cases, feeding them meals with her family and staying in contact till the child or its body was found. She believed that finding a body and holding a funeral were great comforts to parents, but according to her autobiography, she made it a cardinal rule never to tell a missing child's parents that she knew the child was dead. Perhaps she worried that she might be wrong.

Dad never said much about his session with her. Perhaps, despite Nutley's police chief endorsement of her, he was embarrassed to have gone to her. I'm guessing that he brought photographs of Mercy to her, and maybe some of her letters as well. She probably encouraged him to lay out all the facts of the case, from the unfruitful multi-government search for the catamaran, to the report of the wreckage floating in the Tasman Sea. No doubt he offered her money and no doubt she came back with her standard line that St. Anthony, "did not like to charge for finding kids." (As a Catholic, Allison had a special devotion to Saint Anthony of Padua, the patron for people who had lost precious things. Our nurse Marie Burns also relied on St Anthony and when we were children, she encouraged us to pray to St. Anthony to find things we had lost. The more valuable the object, the more money we promised him to find it. I don't remember St. Anthony ever failing, and on Sunday, we would insert coins saved from our allowance, or folded dollar bills in extreme cases, into the slot in the wooden "poor box" at the back of the church.)

With Dad, however, Dorothy Allison broke her cardinal rule and told him that she believed Mercy was dead.

I remember asking him: "Is that all she said?"

"She said she saw a fire."

"A fire?"

"She thought there had been an explosion on board." He grimaced and gave his head a sad, little shake - whether for the uselessness of Allison's visions or for the idea of Mercy's death I couldn't tell. Maybe it was for both.

"What was she like?" I pressed.

He shrugged. "She was just a housewife."

In Mercy's case, Dorothy Allison was pretty safe. Given all the circumstances, the chances were extremely slim that Mercy was alive. And the chances of anyone ever verifying a fire on board the *I Love You II* were even slimmer. Moreover, Allison's vision of "fire" and "an explosion" was vague enough to be made to fit any number of situations: a passionate argument, a burst of lightening in a storm, a gun shot. Still, regardless of whether or not she had genuine psychic ability, she clearly had talent as a sympathetic listener. Estranged as he was from Mom, perhaps he found some comfort in telling his story to Dorothy Allison. And perhaps her suggestion that Mercy was dead helped banish false hope and aimed him toward acceptance of her loss.

August 7, 1977
Suva Fiji
South Pacific

August 7th

    i got on a boat as cook August 1 that was sailing over to the other side of the main island. They've been sailing around the Solomon's, New Guinea, Australia. Thought I'd try it out. 65 ft. motor sailor owned by a rich American Hippi. Heard rumors around the Yacht Club that he was a big time thief.....?

    Well, he had every thing on board, motor cycle, wall to wall carpet, 2 t.v. set, whirlpool bath radar range.... and Jesus the navigation equipment and radars...I've never seen so many. at the bus stand and an old man came over and asked me where i was going...I guess I looked kind of lost and young... The American Dream Boat. Kinda of disgusting....but it was nice sailing and i knew it wasn't going to last long. We anchored at a couple of small islands on the way around the Big Island. Beautiful... Well i got off the boat yesterday and was waiting for a bus to Singatoka, There were some small beach cottages there i was going to stay at..I was sitting I told him and he asked me to come and stay at his village with his sister-in-law. Village on the beach, away from the road...sounded nice...so i

went with him. You think it dumb that I trusted him?
I'll write more later. Much love, Mercy

My sister Jessie took this photo of Mercy on their
trip to Scotland. It was one of Mom's favorites.

143

12

Dad arrived in the Kingdom of Tonga on a Sunday afternoon in February 1978. When he climbed out of the small plane onto the tarmac, the humid scents on the warm Pacific air must have reminded him of the war. He had spent most of World War II in the Pacific Theater as a

David Challinor and Mercedes
Crimmins at Orly during WWI.

forward observer. This meant he would drive in a jeep to the front lines and radio positions for bombers. "It was dangerous work," Mom told me. "If the enemy didn't get you, your own bombs might. He had some close calls." He also flew as an observer - partly to rack up airtime that counted toward furloughs and partly to combat boredom. (This was family history repeating itself: Mom's father, David Challinor, Sr., had flown biplanes during World War I in France. He had been stationed at Orly airport outside Paris. There he met and fell in love with Mercedes who was there with the Red Cross. One of her most difficult duties, she told me, was notifying the kin of pilots who, out of boredom, had been flying stunts in their biplanes and had crashed and died.)

Dad never talked about his war experience - partly, I suppose, because he was reluctant to revisit whatever suffering he had witnessed, and partly because he saw nothing special about his service. He had done his duty like everyone else and that was all there was to it. It was not a subject for an adventure story. The only recollection I ever heard from him concerned the destruction of Tokyo. He had been there with the occupying forces after the surrender and the sight of the entire city flattened by our incendiary bombs and the firestorms they caused had deeply shocked him. "It was terrible," he recalled somberly. "There was nothing standing for miles."

When he landed at Nuku'alofa, the capitol of the Tongatapu group of islands, he had been flying for three days. Perhaps he had taken the time to shave along the way, but the habitual dark circles under his eyes would have bagged like bruises. At sixty-six, he wore his silver hair cropped close to his scalp and he kept himself fit swimming laps. The people whom he met would have seen an unassuming older man with exhausted but determined brown eyes, wearing a rumpled business suit and carrying an armful of American newspapers that he had read on his flights and didn't want to discard. Like all businessmen of his generation, he always traveled in a coat and tie, but he was not a sharp dresser. He had a sentimental attachment to his old suits, a few of which were relics from his college days, and though they belonged in the wardrobe of a school drama department, he wore them with pride, glowing with the pleasure of being able to still fit into them. He was also attached to a tweed overcoat his mother had given him in the 'thirties during the depression to keep him warm. When he wore the coat on Wall Street, its moth-eaten fur collar and sagging lining gave him the forlorn look of a man who had lost his fortune. Nonetheless, despite his sartorial shabbiness, to the native families of Tonga, he was obviously a very rich man. He had flown all the way from America, his daughter had been sailing on a pleasure yacht, a gold signet gleamed on his right ring finger and he was armed with a wallet full of more dollars than they would ever accumulate in a lifetime.

As with his war experiences, he told us little about his trip in search of Mercy. I imagine that while in Nuku'alofa he visited with Fusi Malohi, the broadcast manager at the radio station who had answered his first telegram. Perhaps he also visited the family Mercy had stayed with before she moved onto a sloop owned by Steve Abney, a fellow American and kindred free-spirit whom she had mentioned in her last letter home. Dad then flew to Vava'u and went to the island of Kapa where Mercy and Steve had found locals to mend his sail. Mercy's stay on Kapa was one of her happier times. She formed a bond with a family named Nasilai who put her up in their home. While there, she and Steve Abney joined the locals in a wild Tongan-style benefit: a night of feasting and dancing to raise money for a fence to prevent the island's overpopulation of pigs from destroying crops. A few days after the feast, she and Steve returned to help build the fence.

Three months later, Siliva and Lautaimi Nasilai received Dad warmly and he was touched by their sympathy and openness. "They killed a pig for me," he said. "They held a feast in honor of Mercy." Although Tongans are known as party lovers and reputedly will hold a feast at the slightest excuse, he was moved by what he saw as a great sacrifice of their meager resources. In gratitude, he gave them a transistor radio. As it happened, Mercy's loss turned out to be their good fortune. For years afterwards, they stayed in touch by letter and sent photos. Their first letter was written by Siliva, the wife, in halting English on pages torn from a small notebook. She wrote two letters on four sheets, one to "Dear Buck Ewing" and the other to "Dear Mary Ewing". In both she spoke of her love of Mercy ("I told Mercy you are my sister") and how she kept Mercy "in my home in 2 or 3 weeks, sleep & eat and stay not cost." She ended both letters stating "I am very poor" and asking Dad to sponsor her husband so he could come and work for them in the States.

Dad might well have been willing to import Lautaimi: he had no hesitation trusting strangers met by chance. He once hired, sight unseen, the sister of a Polish cab driver he had talked to on the way to LaGuardia. She came to work for us as a cook and made kettle after kettle of paprika-red goulash despite the fact that no one in the house wanted to eat it. It was a short-lived employment. Mom discovered that her monthly food bill had doubled and that most of the food the woman cooked - from goulash to puddings - was being hoarded in bowls under her bed. At the time, it seemed inexplicably strange to me, but now I wonder what kind of deprivations the woman had suffered as a child during the war.

Mom was dead set against the idea of importing a Tongan man to work in the house. Her youngest children were finally away at boarding school, she had managed to get our nurse Marie back to Scotland, and she did not want to have to cope with the needs of a foreign stranger as she grieved for Mercy. She never came out and said so. Instead she declared, "He would be miserable here." Just as she had declared Marie would have been miserable staying at Firwood.

Photographs the couple sent to Dad show Siliva as a pretty young woman with smooth brown skin and long black hair pulled back behind her head. In one shot, taken at night indoors, she and her husband sit cross-legged on a floor mat in front of a kerosene lantern. A bare foot pokes out from her madras sarong. On top she wears a blue and white checked shirt. There is a red flower tucked behind her ear - a heilala blossom perhaps, the Tongan national flower. She is smiling, her face aglow in the lantern light. Her husband looks more dour - maybe ten years older, and his skin is darker than his wife's. He has bushy black eyebrows and he glances at the camera with a slightly worried expression.

Another photo, probably taken some years earlier, shows the couple posing outdoors with four young children wearing only short white pants that, to my eye, look like underpants, as if the kids had been pulled into the picture half dressed. But surely this was wrong; the parents are dressed up. Siliva is wearing a long green calico dress and Lautaime a white shirt with his tupenu - a knee-length wrap-around for men. In this picture, he has a beard - a sign of mourning for a relative. Although obesity is a health concern in Tonga as it is here, the children and Lautaime are slim, and while Siliva is matronly looking, she is not overweight. Behind them in the background, at the edge of a forest, is a two-room clapboard cabin on stilts, its whitewash wearing off.

A third photo, black and white, crinkled with wear shows three of the children. They pose in traditional ta'ovalas, soft white mats woven from ocean-bleached fibers of the pandanus plant and worn wrapped around the waist. The small girl, flanked by an older brother and a younger brother, displays a trophy plaque, and from the pleased expressions on their faces, I imagine they won it at a Tongan dance contest.

Siliva's second letter to Dad, written in October 1978, eight months after his visit, again thanked him for his gift of the radio:

> We are now using the radio to hear news, music from our studio A3Z. My children are very happy to listing to the radio. I have five children two boys 3 girls. Now Lautaimi sick and can't go out fishing again. Flu is now acquired a lot in the Vava'u group.

She also thanked him for his "big present one hundred pa'anga Tonga" - about fifty US dollars - and enclosed a snap shot of a new fishing dingy they had built. It sits on a sandy beach, just above the tide line. *Mercy* is painted on the bow in red letters and beside it stands a small girl in a red dress. "Buck," Siliva wrote, "you know my small daughter change her name [to] Mercy because [your] Mercy is my sister. My small daughter have 5 years old." She signed off sending love "and wishing you happy time."

Four years later, after their house was destroyed by a hurricane, he sent them enough money to rebuild and received a joyous thank you written by Siliva. It was dated 9 October 1982:

> Dear Buck.
> Hello! What a wonderful and marvelous surprise we have received from you. We can not believe that we should have been so lucky, and we thank you very much. . .
> Our house will have a cement tank for water. Two rooms, a cooking house, lavatory, bathroom and a fence all around. It will be the best house in Falevai. After we have finished the house we will make a boat and buy a new motor.
> The chief and the people of our village are very happy because it is the first time anyone in our village has received such a large present from a palangi.
> . . .I prayed to God and thanked him for our present. We cannot tell you how grateful and happy we feel.

She encloses a photo of their daughter Mercy, now nine, in a flowered print dress. Her jet-black hair has been partially tamed into two long ponytails tied with red ribbons. She has inherited her father's heavy eyebrows, straight as hyphens, and they make her look older than nine. Her mouth is wide and her almost-smile is calm and as secretive as a small Buddha's. Her mother proudly reports that she has been first in her class at the Falevai primary school, "every term and every year - never second," and expresses the hope that she will "be lucky and go to High School in Nuku'alofa".

The final letter in the file is from Lautaimi, the husband. It was written in April 1983, five years after Dad's visit. Lautaimi dictated it to a visitor from California, so it is written in standard English, and addressed to Dad's Wall Street office. I think that Dad, having sent the money for a new house, must have asked for a progress report because Lautaimi's letter has the tone of "accountability" that I recognize from many of Dad's letters to me. Lautaimi writes:
I was not able to send the photograph you requested because I did not have camera. However

people from California are here with a Polaroid camera.

> We have the basic house finished; the floors, walls and tin roof with louvered windows. We also have built a cistern of concrete blocks to catch the rainwater. There are two rooms in the house, but we do not yet have a kitchen. Your picture hangs on our living room wall. . .
>
> Myself, my wife and family all express our love for you.

The Polaroids show the new house. It is maybe 20 feet by 12 feet and sits on posts, a couple feet off the ground, a small, raw plywood cabin with white curtains in the louvered windows. Siliva and Lautaimi pose in front of it with their three girls. Mercy, the youngest, is holding a framed photograph of Dad. I suppose that at some point, Siliva or Lautaimi must have asked him for

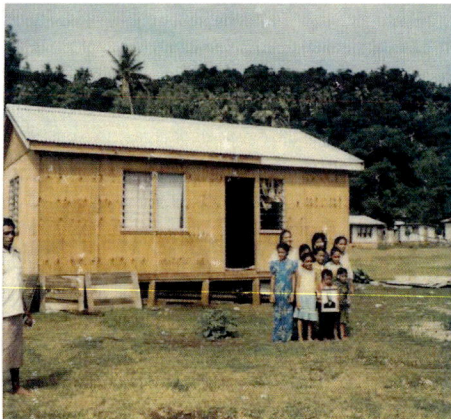

his picture. What he sent them was a studio portrait, the kind of black-and-white headshot found in annual reports or on board room walls. But in this Polaroid, the Nasilais are no less formal: the girls and Siliva wear bright Sunday cottons, and they all wear pleasant, dignified smiles. Only if you study the picture for a while, do you catch a glimpse of the life behind their formal Thank You: in the background, a small face peeks out from the doorway of the house; and Lautaimi, again in his best white shirt and tupenu, holds a cigarette down at his side, as if to keep it out of the camera's eye. Dad, a former smoker himself, never hesitated to tell people they should stop smoking.

The image of little dark-skinned Mercy holding Dad's business portrait is an odd role reversal:

the benefactor held by the donees - supported by them, as it were - and it makes me think that in a very real way, the family supported him as much as he supported them. He was moved by their poverty and no doubt helping out the family was a satisfying sort of payback for the generosity and kindness they had shown his lost daughter. I'm sure it occurred to him that they were exploiting the connection, but he would have shrugged it off with a half-embarrassed roll of his eyes. He knew their need was genuine and he was always sympathetic to those less fortunate than he was and willing to help them out - especially if they took his advice. But more importantly, I think, his continuing relationship with the family was a way of connecting with his grief, of refusing to let it be buried under the more immediate concerns of his everyday life. The money he sent to Siliva and Lautaimi was a way of staying in touch, however remotely, with his own Mercy.

Nasilai family holding Dad's portrait.

There is no statute of limitations on loss. Fast forward twenty-six years to 2015. In the last week of October 2015, the same time of year Mercy was lost, a phone call in the middle of the night woke Andy and me. In the dark, I felt a stab of alarm. Had someone died? Andy handed me the phone. It was my sister Jessie Ewing. She was calling from Fiji and, due to her dyslexia, had miscalculated the time changes. She was traveling without her spouse Carol Anshaw who was busy teaching in Chicago. Ever since Mercy had been lost, Jessie had wanted to see what Mercy had seen, to walk where she had walked. Now she was in Nadi, the main town on Fiji's main island Viti Levu. She was about to embark on a Lindblad/National Geographic cruise and was calling me in the woods of Virginia for information about the Nasilai family. Jessie wanted to see if she could connect with the Tongan girl who had been renamed Mercy.

The next morning I dug up Dad's folder in my studio in our barn and found the family's letters. I emailed Jessie their names and the address on the backs of the blue airmail envelopes and she went to the tour leaders and told them the story.

"I cried talking about it," she said. "They told me they would make locating the family their mission. I didn't want to talk about it to any of the other passengers on the boat. I had an overwhelming sense of psychic anticipation. I kept feeling I was going to meet Mercy. At the same time, I knew that in reality I couldn't connect with her. But I could connect with the real place she had been."

As it happened, the tour leaders located a first cousin of the Tongan Mercy. Her name was Neeta. Her father was a brother of Lautami Nasilai. Neeta said that Lautami had died and her cousin Mercy was living in the States with her two sons and her mother Silivia. Neeta thought they had settled in Oakland, California. The rest of the family had either immigrated to New Zealand or was dead.

Neeta was born in 1979, two years after our Mercy was lost. She was 38 when Jessie met her but she looked considerably older than Jessie who was 65. She reminded Jessie of our nurse,

Marie Burns. "A kindly faced version," she emailed. She attached photo taken by a tour leader. In it, Neeta stands a head shorter than Jessie whose eyes are hidden behind dark sunglasses. She looks as if she is trying not to cry.

"It was a very emotional meeting," she told me in a long phone call after she got home. "Ten minutes before we docked in Nuku'alofa, the tour leaders called me and said they had found her. She had traveled by ferry to meet me. I walked down the gangplank and saw this short, stocky woman. We hugged and we both cried. It was almost like Mercy had come back."

It was Halloween, the Day of the Dead. Neeta spoke little English. "It was mostly non-verbal," Jessie said. They walked along Nukualo'fa's waterfront holding hands. In a lighter moment, Jessie plonked her Panama hat on Neeta's head and snapped her photograph. With the Lindblad passengers, they visited Botanical Gardens, watched native dancers perform to the music of a garage-type band.

"It was so cathartic," Jessie said. "I also met Neeta's sister who had more English. I got that our Mercy was perceived by Tongans as friendly and genuine. We walked past a bar and Neeta said that her adopted daughter's father had been killed there."

Jessie remembered going out to visit Mercy in Jackson, Wyoming, in 1976. "We walked in the foothills and argued about Mom."

"What about Mom?"

"Who she loved most!" Jessie laughed.

They also visited Jackson's public library. "Mercy showed me all these books about Tonga and Fiji. She wanted to go there. She saw it as a way out of the bubble of our society. She felt the bubble was becoming anachronistic."

"Being where she had been," Jessie reflected, "I came out to the other side of grief. The trip made me feel proud of Mercy. She rejected the part of society that excludes people who are different. Things have changed since the time she was lost. Our family's consciousness has expanded and Mercy's death was part of that expansion."

Jessie in Tonga with Neeta Nasilai

August 1977
Fiji

8/12

Moved out of that village, Cora. i was getting sick staff infection on my leg, pussy boils just waiting to explode...3 of them. Feels like the puss is flowing through every vain, just circulating making me sicker and sicker...i'm staying in a bunk house in Korotogo...waiting for recovery. it's pretty nice, right on the beach..and at the low tide you can walk out on the reef. That's usually early morning when I'm felling pretty good. When you go out to the very edge of the reef where the surf is breaking. there's so much life, Coral, fish, snakes, eals...Well the reef is like sponge and has all these holes that are real deep. You're walking on the sponge reef and a wave comes breaking against it and you can hear it gurgling underneath you and then little fountains of salt water spurt out of all the pores in the reef. It was so cool...gurgling underneath you and then the rock bust out into fountains...Made my boils feel better...see? It's a pretty nice here good people and nice beach...i go to the hospital every afternoon & get a penicillin injection and have all the dressings changed...should be all cleared up by the beginning of next week or around then...i guess I'll go over to Lautoka on the western side of the island and try and find a boat out to the Yasawa group...maybe find another village to stay at... and be able to really explore the Fijian life style.

Living at Cora, was an experience. The old guy that brought me there just had it in his mind to marry a European woman and move out of Fiji. i guess i was one of his many brides-to-be. It left me with a bad feeling about Fijians in general that i've gotta get rid of ...

i stayed there in all about 4 days..and learned a lot of customs and was able to sit on a ceremony-feast they were having for a dead brother. Every 5 days they mix a huge bowl of Kava (that local Fijian drink) [mildly narcotic drink prepared from Polynesian pepper shrub – Piper Methysticum] and say a bunch of blessings over it...then pass a coconut shell around to every one...clapping 3 time before you drink & then 3 times after you gulp it down.

Then the feast –eels & kava...they gave me a fish boiled in coconut milk instead of the eels, but i did taste the eel, not bad just the feeling of swallowing it.

Just thought i'd let you know what's going on. Right now mostly reading & relaxing & recovering, and thinking & planning of how to get out to the Yasawas.

Time is so weird..going so slowly..time to absorb everything but still everything is happening so fast...can't explain.

i'll let you know when i head out to the Yasawa, I won't be able to write from there, no mail boats, or anything.

Much love Mercy

13

"I never should have let her go."

–Buck Ewing

From Tonga, Dad flew to Wellington, New Zealand's capitol and most populated city. Originally inhabited by Maori people, the harbor was discovered and settled by Polynesian explorers in the 10th Century, then rediscovered and colonized by the British in the 18th Century. Today it is long strip of city sandwiched between a bay and high mountains. In aerial photographs on the net, Wellington looks beautiful, clean and white, curving around an expanse of blue sea, and I wonder if Dad, as his plane came in for a landing, found the sight reassuring: here was civilization, here was solid ground and the competence of Captain Hunt, the man in charge of the New Zealand search effort, here was the hope of some answers. By this time I don't think he held out much hope for finding Mercy alive, but he had not yet accepted the idea of her death, and the likelihood of it must have been a constant underlying nag. At the same time, I'm sure, his head was buzzing with questions and just trying to keep track of them was a distraction from any inchoate pain of loss.

Certainly one of the big questions in his mind was whether or not the wreckage seen in the Tasman sea belonged to the *I Love You II*. The strings he had pulled in Washington had yielded no clue: the American ice cutter Burton Island, which had been diverted for exercises in the area of the wreckage, had found no sign of the orange hull, so perhaps by the time she reached the reported coordinates, the hull had drifted away or sunk—along with any certainty of its identity. That left the report from the *Tasman Enterprise*, the freighter that had spotted the wreckage on February 5. The report was addressed to the Branch Manager of the Union Steam Ship Company which owned the freighter. It is a single typewritten sheet with Hunt's notes in a small, legible script at the bottom. I imagine that Captain Hunt went over it with Dad in his Wellington office. "Dear Sir," it began and went on to say on February 5, the *Tasman Enterprise* spotted the "starboard hull of a catamaran some 60 feet in length with orange hull and white trim." The freighter circled the hull twice, "passing close each time," a maneuver that took 15 minutes. The report continued:

> [The hull] was upside down, heavily encrusted with marine growth, the fibreglass bow sprung open and from the appearance of its thwartship members it indicated the hulls had parted with some force. There was no sign of human life, mast, rigging, or port hull of the catamaran.
>
> From message issued by Auckland Radio 0500 GMT 17 December 1977 we conclude the wreckage is that of the American ketch rigged catamaran "I Love You 2" which left North Tonga for Bay of Islands.
>
> The hull could be troublesome to navigation. Radio Auckland were informed of our find and at 05/0015Z proceeded on our passage.
>
> Weather conditions at the time of sighting were:
>
> ESE at 12 knots. Slight ESE sea. Low E Swell. Excellent visibility. Part cloudy, fine and clear."

One clue in the report was the "heavily encrusted" marine growth seen on the "upside down" hull. Hunt's investigation found that the *I Love You II* had been dry docked in Pago Pago in August, before Gliddon set sail for the Fijis. At that time, her bottom had been scraped and painted with red anti-fouling paint. Was it possible in the space of six months for a hull treated with anti-fouling paint to become "heavily encrusted" with barnacles and seaweed? Hunt called the paint manufacturer who said no, the paint would have prevented a heavy build-up of marine growth. So did this mean that the wreckage was not the *I Love You II*? Had the wrecked hull belonged to some other orange catamaran? How many orange catamarans could there be sailing around the Pacific?

Hunt then interviewed the *Tasman Enterprise's* master who revised his estimate and admitted that the words "heavily encrusted" had been used loosely: when pressed, he told Hunt that the wreckage had had less barnacles than his own ship. This revision casts a doubt on the accuracy of the whole report. What did "upside down" mean? If it was entirely upside down, how had the witnesses on the deck of the freighter seen the white trim? But suppose the hull had been floundering on its side—or the wake of the circling freighter had exposed the orange side and both its white waterline and the band of white trim below her rails. The side of the hull might well have been "heavily encrusted" since only the portion of the hull below the waterline had been treated with anti-fouling paint. Which would mean that the hull could have belonged to the *I Love You II* after all.

Who or what to believe? At the time, we were told that the *Tasman Enterprise* had been unable to retrieve the wreckage because of high seas. But the freighter reported a "slight SES sea" with a "Low E swell." I suppose that having made certain that there was "no sign of human life," the master decided it wasn't worth the major amount of time and effort, as well as risk to the crew, that it would have taken to secure the hull and raise it onto the freighter's deck.

Hunt also told Dad that there was a fleet of Japanese fishing boats in New Zealand waters. He speculated that perhaps the *I Love You II* had been run down by one of them. It was not uncommon for large commercial vessels to be on automatic pilot and have no one on the bridge. A fishing "factory ship" which processed catches on board could weigh thousands of tons. Some were over 400 feet long. A 63-foot catamaran might weigh about 8 tons. So the *I Love You II* could have been hit by a fishing behemoth and sucked under without causing a blip on the screen or a shudder below decks. Moreover, as Mom told us later, if the reports were true that the catamaran had left Tonga with a malfunctioning generator, she would not have had running lights. Thus, Mom reasoned, even with a lookout on deck of the trawler, the *I Love You II* would have been invisible at night. The catamaran would not have been the first pleasure yacht to be victim of commercial shipping but this possibility only confirmed their view of Glidden as a sloppy captain. They had to wonder about his navigational skills: what was he doing in shipping lanes? Had he sailed into them by mistake?

Another question that plagued both Mom and Dad was the issue of the *I Love You II's* seaworthiness. During their sailing years, they owned two boats, both designed and built in Norway during the 1950s, both wooden sloops with traditional lines and heavy lead keels. The first, 32 feet long, was christened the *Njord* after a Norse wind god. I had found the name in a book of Norse mythology and, at age 10 or 11, had been pleased and proud that my parents adopted it. The *Njord's* replacement was an expanded version by the same designer, 40 feet long and more comfortable for taking five or six kids on weeklong family cruises on Long Island Sound. This one was built with money that Dad had inherited after his mother's death in 1956 and he named his new boat the Maria in her honor. Despite the lovely, sleek lines of both boats, neither was particularly fast, especially when compared with the new fiberglass sloops that were beginning to be popular. Fiberglass boats, with their aluminum masts, tended to be roomier below, and required less maintenance, but Mom and Dad—especially Mom—were traditionalists: they liked the look and feel of a wooden boat, liked the slap of stays against a varnished wooden mast, took pride in the teak decks and brass winches. Swabbing the decks and polishing the brass was a daily chore for us kids when we cruised with Dad and Mom. They took pride in having the boat look ship-shape whenever we entered a harbor.

Both sloops handled well in heavy weather. I remember one scary incident on the *Njord*: a storm warning had been posted—I think a hurricane was sweeping up the coast—and we were racing across the Sound, trying to beat high force winds and rain back to the Connecticut shore. It was rough going and Dad ordered all the younger children to put on life jackets and to stay below deck. Sheila stayed below with them, but I was allowed to remain in the cockpit, either because I was the oldest and biggest and might be useful, or more probably because I was seasick and being below deck made it worse. Dad was at the tiller and Mom was working the sheets, and despite a reef in the mainsail, we took a knockdown. The boat heeled over so far that the mainsail touched the waves. Grey seawater started pouring over the leeward rail and into the cockpit. I was clinging to the windward rail, ready to abandon ship, and saw the keel rising to the surface like a giant red fin. Mom, thinking we were about to sink, yelled to get the kids up on deck, but before we could slide back the cabin's hatch and pull out the first kid, the wind spilled out of the sails, and thanks to the lead weight in her keel, the *Njord* righted herself. She bounced back like an inflatable toy weighted at its base, and the kids in their orange life jackets were flung around the cabin like so many padded dolls.

Mary sailing *The Maria* close to the wind. Buck took the photo from the dingy.

A catamaran, however, would not have bounced back: it has no lead keel. If a catamaran happened to take a knockdown in high wind, there would be no counterweight to right it and instead of bouncing back like the *Njord*, it would be likely to turn turtle. To prevent this, at least

Mercy and Tom on a family cruise on the Maria. Mom's photo albums were also logs in which she recorded sea conditions, winds, and anchorages.

one multi-hull designer of that era installed a Styrofoam disk at the top of its mast—a safety feature that added to the boat's peculiar appearance. If the boat was blown over, the disk was supposed to keep the catamaran lying on its side and thus give its crew a chance to escape.

If this sounded like an ominous safety measure, catamarans had some intriguing pros. They could sail twice as fast as a conventional yacht. Moreover, catamarans promised a smoother ride in rough weather. Twin-hull fans cited a tale of the skipper of an ocean-going catamaran weathering high seas: when he came on deck for his watch, he left a glass of wine on the salon table. Four hours later at the end of his watch, he went below and found not a drop of the wine had spilled.

When I was sailing with my parents, you didn't see many catamarans on Long Island Sound, and those you did see tended to be small, day-sailers like the Hobie Cats. The sight of a large catamaran was rare enough to bring everyone up deck for look. In a catamaran the same size as the *Maria*, we kids might have shared staterooms instead of being packed into close communal quarters with pullout bunks that converted the cabin into one large bed.

But to Mom and Dad, catamarans were suspect. It wasn't simply a matter of salty snobbery.

It was also a matter of seaworthiness—the ability of a boat to handle safely in all sea conditions. As they saw it, choosing a catamaran was taking a risk. It was choosing speed and creature comforts over safety. It was as if Donald Glidden had chosen a new-fangled bus equipped with a racing car's engine instead of a standard station wagon: the bus might go 150 miles per hour, and it might carry twenty people and all their luggage in luxury, but could it take a corner at speed without turning over?

The glossy magazines *Yachting and Rudder* reported some spectacular wrecks. Some twin-hulled boats were broken into two pieces when a wave hit the bridge between the hulls. Others were victims of their own speed: they would plough into a wave and keep on diving, turning a fatal stern-over-bow somersault. Given the stories circulating at the time, Mom feared the *I Love You II* was more vulnerable to weather conditions than conventional boats. The fact that Donald Glidden had left Tonga at the start of the cyclone season only added to her fears of the worst.

But, but, but: According to Captain Hunt and the drift experts he consulted on the case, if the *I Love You II* had been lost on its way to New Zealand, the ocean currents would have carried the wreckage toward the Fijis. The orange hull found in the Tasman Sea was thousands of miles southwest of where it should have been—if the catamaran had kept to her planned voyage.

Together with the report of the ore carrier *Jesprait's* sighting west of New Zealand in December, the wreckage in the Tasman Sea raised the suspicions of the New Zealand police. If the boat in both these positions had been the *I Love You II*, Glidden had either by-passed New Zealand despite his declared destination or he had entered the country without notifying port authorities—in other words, illegally. The police began working on the theory that Glidden and his crew were running drugs from Tonga to Australia.

Mom dismissed this hypothesis with a derisive snort. The rest of us were not quite as certain as she was, but it seemed unlikely. The *I Love You II* may have held a bunch of potheads, but unless Mercy had gotten way in over her head, it was a stretch to imagine Glidden as a criminal in the drug business. He was living his dream. He had his airline pension, his custom-built boat, his girlfriend as first mate, a sweet life in the South Seas. Why put it all at risk? What more could he want? And if he were innocent of criminal activity, why would he have avoided landfall in New Zealand? Putting aside the report that he planned to have his engine and radio repaired in Auckland, and ignoring the fact that Mercy planned to get off the catamaran in New Zealand to meet her friend Carol, surely after a long, rough sea passage he would have wanted to reprovision with fresh fruits and vegetables, and to fill his water tanks before heading for Australia.

From Wellington, Dad flew to Auckland, New Zealand. There he rented a car, bought a book of road maps, and drove some 230 kilometers north to the Bay of Islands, an area comprised of 144 islands and coves, where the New Zealand police speculated that the *I Love You II* might have made landfall. It was high summer in a place known for the wild, unspoiled beauty of its secluded beaches and clear blue-green waters, but I doubt Dad took

Dad's shell map shows Bay of Islands and Russell, the northernmost port of the legal entry. There were rumors that north of Russell at Mangonui, the *I Love You II* had made an illegal landfall.

much note of the scenery. In New Zealand, as in England and Bermuda, cars drive on the left side of the road, and while he had had practice riding his motorbike on the left in Bermuda, in the best of times he was an absent-minded driver, so between the challenges of adapting to left-lane

Photo by Joan Challinor

Dad in happier times on the Fourth of July.

driving, navigating unknown highways and his preoccupation with his mission, it's lucky he arrived safely in Kawakawa—the town underlined on his map.

There he had consulted another psychic—a man this time, a dowser with a reputation for finding bodies. "He held a little pendulum over a nautical chart," Dad told me. "It was on a red cord. He moved it back and forth across the chart and when it started to circle over an area, he said this was where she had gone down." When he told us this, weeks later, he was skeptical about the psychic's talent, but also sheepish—like a boy who had caught in a foolish escapade. Perhaps the psychic had requested "a donation" for his services. If so, Dad would have forked over without question. His next step, and the next outlay of cash, was to hire a small plane and a pilot. For five hours they flew over an area indicated by the dowser's little pendulum. "We didn't see anything except water," he said. He shook his head. "I knew how vast the Pacific was. I'd flown over it during the war." Then he added bitterly, "I never should have let her go."

14

While Dad was searching in Tonga and New Zealand, my sister Jessie flew home to Firwood to be with Mom. Jessie lived in Illinois, where she worked as a photographer for the Springfield Times. She had a close connection with Mercy. They had attended the same grammar school and in the summer of 1975, two years before Mercy's Fiji trip, they had traveled together in Scotland. Mercy had just graduated from high school, and Jessie, despite the handicap of severe dyslexia, had just finished college. Our nurse Marie Burns had come over from Glasgow for a summer visit and Jessie and Mercy had accompanied her back home, then gone on to tour the highlands and the Shetland Islands. Their styles and tastes were often in conflict. Jessie wanted to stay in nice hotels; Mercy wanted to camp out. At times, Jessie, who was eight years older, unexpectedly found herself cast in the role of disapproving older sister. She recalled Mercy going off to party with drunken strangers one night. She had met them in a pub, and she did not return till daylight, leaving Jessie alone and frantic in their room.

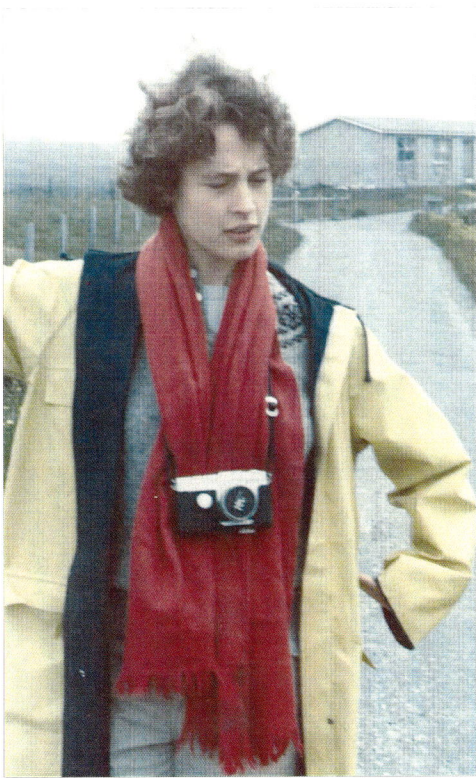

Jessie's photo of Mercy in Scotland.

"We had a lot of fights," Jessie remembered. "Then I'd buy her a candy bar—a kind of peace offering. She'd gobble it up and then get mad at me for making her fat!" She laughed. "We had a fight on the boat over to the Shetlands. The walls of our cabin were paper thin, and when we stopped for breath, we heard the people next door fighting. We started to laugh and couldn't stop!" Thanks to a common sense of the ridiculous, their friendship survived the trip. At Mercy's invitation, Jessie visited her in Jackson before she left for Fiji. Mercy also wrote to Jessie from Tonga and confided feelings of homesickness.

During Jessie's visit to Firwood, Mom, without the distracting irritant of Dad's endless overseas phone calls, was able to give some space to what she knew in her heart as well her mind: that Mercy was never coming home. While Dad was off on his fact-finding mission, Mom's own mission was to get the rest of us to accept the fact that Mercy was dead. So she and Jessie flew down to Virginia for the weekend to visit me. I made bread for them—a version of baguettes I had adapted from Julia Child's Mastering the *Art of French Cooking*. There were no artisan loaves in our supermarket then—only packaged "air bread"—and I was proud to pull out my own bread from the oven for them. I remember admiring the warm loaves through a blur of tears.
After their visit I wrote Mom a letter and thanked her for "coming down and sharing so much" of what she was going through. " I hope it wasn't too much a drain," I worried as I pecked away at my Smith Corona. It was a quiet February morning, the boys were in school, and I sat at my desk at the top of our hand-built redwood tower in a closet-sized room that had once been "the baby room" and was now my study. My desk was a sheet of plywood over a pair of file cabinets and that's where I labored away at short stories (on spec for "little" magazines) and at feature articles (on assignment for a regional glossy called *Virginia Country*). As a kind of warm-up exercise—a way of easing into work—I often wrote letters to friends, but most often to my mother. I wrote to her about what I was reading and what I wanted write, and now, after her visit with Jessie, I was

writing in an attempt make sense of what was happening to our family:

I know I have a tendency to ask too many questions, which is really just a habit of thinking out loud, I think. I find myself thinking of Mercy all the time—something I never did before and also something I never felt before which is the experience of family as an entity independent of its members, as if the family had its own soul or body and that what happens to one effects the other in a real way—as if a limb were cut off and I, another limb, feel the absence, though not as much pain as the head—which would be you and Daddy, if you can forgive the corny metaphor. I know granny [Mercedes] felt this, and I think I never really understood it before. The concept of the reality of the group as larger than its members is something we seem to have lost today with all the emphasis on self-fulfillment and I think (though I haven't really worked it all out) that it must be the key to good mothering which should be seen not as self-immolation, but as creation (participation in something larger than one's self?) and I think you are a very good example for us and the whole thing with Mercy is a testimony to it—whatever guilt haunts you. It is not just luck that Mercy grew up free and strong and able to follow her own way—and if she is not able to come full circle, to move from family to creating an individual to creating a family (not literally, but in the sense of giving to others), then in some way, what has happened may be a catalyst for us (off-spring) to grow less self-centered. I know and it is really the only thing I'm positive of, that the self is an illusion. I think I told you that two years ago I had the experience, a kind of gift, of letting the Self go and that I didn't want to come back—and even at the time I was struck by the irony of it all, that I had for so long (all those years on the [psychiatrist's] couch, etc.) trying to "find" my self....

Could this letter have brought any comfort at all to my mother? She saved it, but she saved every letter she received from her children, be it a misspelled, homesick note from a son at boarding school, or one of my typed, four and five page epistles. After her death in 2009, we found all of them neatly bundled in her desk. Now re-reading my letter to her makes me wince: it seems analytical and unfeeling. I went on to write about how a friend and neighbor had coped with the death of her teenaged son who had been killed in a car accident, but I did not address my mother's own pain. For someone concerned with "letting go of Self", my letter seems pretty self-absorbed. In a penciled PS, I had second thoughts: "I know some things are best left unsaid & I hope this isn't one of them—sorry if I've blundered." I had no doubt that if I had blundered she would forgive me. And she did. In her next letter to me she made no comment on my speculations but reported on latest developments of Dad's search. She signed it as usual: "with love to you my dearest".

In addition to keeping her children informed, she also kept her brother David Challinor in the loop. From his journal entry for February 24, 1978, it is clear that despite her grief, she allowed him no false hope:

> Mary Ewing called this a.m. to say that Buck was back from the South Pacific and that there was absolutely no news. Three months later was obviously too long a delay. Mary could barely talk on the phone and I can't blame her. The uncertainty must be overwhelming. It certainly would be for me. I do not know how long she has to be missing before she can be declared legally dead, but now for the first time I'm beginning to accept the idea of her death. It's going to be hard for me to be civil to Buck this summer. . .

After his visit with the psychic in the Bay of Islands, Dad returned to Auckland and met with a ham radio operator named Noel Curtis who, two months before, had just taken over the job of managing the Pacific Maritime Net. This was a volunteer organization that handled radio communications between sailing and motor yachts. Today the network exists as the Pacific Seafarer's Net, but instead of radio, it relies on communication satellites, mobile phones, and Internet postings on its website. Back in the 1970's, vessels in transit would call in their positions and weather bulletins to the net's controller who then would broadcast the information to other vessels, relay messages to cruising friends and families on shore, and in emergencies, call in Search and Rescue. Since New Zealand was a favorite place for yachts to sit out the hurricane season between November and April, daily check-ins with the net could total more than 60 yachts at peak times. Thus Curtis had a firm finger on the pulse of the yachting community. Not only did he monitor around-the-clock for SOS calls; he kept track of all the gossip—who went where when. He was a logical resource.

Curtis lived with his wife Marney in Titirangi, a mountainous coastal area about 20 minutes from Auckland. Artists and hippies, attracted by the scenic views and lush growth of native trees and shrubs, had begun to move there into the modest working-class houses. The Curtises welcomed Dad warmly and with great sympathy. Noel Curtis had collected a thick file of rumors on the missing catamaran. He and Dad spent an afternoon reviewing known facts and sorting out rumors. One bit of yachtie gossip had Mercy in a French jail in Noumea, the capitol city of New Caledonia. A call to the Noumean police eliminated that scenario. The following day, February 23, Dad left for home with Noel Curtis's promise to keep him informed. He reached Connecticut two days later, exhausted and unsatisfied.

The weekend after his return, my sister Jessie again flew out to Connecticut. Of all the girls in the family, she was the closest to Dad and she wanted to hear in person what he had to say about his search. As was Mom's habit when one of us came home for a visit, she invited her other children who lived within driving distance over for dinner. These invitations were not exactly "command performances" but not take-it-or-leave-it, either. And this time, she had an agenda beyond maintaining family ties. So along with Jessie, there would have been my sister Sheila and her husband Tom Daley, my brothers Bill, Fritz, David and their wives, and our youngest brother Tommy who was a senior at boarding school and home for spring break. The only absentees were Andy and I down in

Overall, Virginia and my handicapped brother Pat, who remained at The Woods School in Pennsylvania.

In a letter to me dated March 7, she took up the first page and a half relating how she and Sheila had attended a lecture on the modern novel at Manhattanville, the college I had attended in Purchase, New York, about a half-hour's drive from Firwood in Noroton. Mom listed the books she was planning to read: Toni Morrison's *Song of Solomon*, John Fowles' *Daniel Martin*, Margaret Drabble's *Ice Age*, "and that new book about Alaska [by John McPhee] and a book called *Staying On* by Paul Scott who just died."

Then, having primed the pump as it were, she described Saturday night's gathering—which turned out to be a kind of wake for Mercy:

> We all got drunk and talked and talked and wept and wept until two o'clock in the morning—except Fritz who smoked one of Daddy's cigars and didn't feel so good and Daddy folded after his second brandy. Anyway I guess it was good. I think it sort of cleared the air, and every one had seen everyone weep and come through more or less intact except for some really rather spectacularly monumental hangovers on Sunday. I can not help but think that Mercy would have approved. I guess that you have been in touch with Sheila. You know that we managed to get the Coast Guard vessel [the ice cutter Burton Island] to search for the wreck and try to make a positive identification. There doesn't seem to be much hope that they will be able to locate it again...but they will if any one can as they have a helicopter. As of last night they had no news. I don't really know what our next step will be if they don't get anything. There are two more places to search, two uninhabited islands way to the north of New Zealand which Daddy has already arranged to search or at least started to arrange-everything takes so long and the other place is the Kermadec Islands which have already been searched but they thought perhaps they could be searched again. No one seems to feel that either place is in the least likely, it is simply a question of looking in every spot that there is to look.
>
> Has Sheila told you that she talked to Michael? [Michael Crimmins, our cousin who had been ordained as a priest in the diocese of New York.] I think that we will go ahead and have a Mass for Mercy on Easter Monday if you could stay

over. At first the feeling was to have it just for ourselves. However I think perhaps we had better have it for the whole family and anyone else that wants to come. I don't know why it all seems more final having a Mass. I mean, when the whole thing is pretty final anyway...and any way it is I guess better to have it final, and have it final for everyone...so well meaning people won't keep telling you that everything is going to be all right...What an odd expression, of course everything is all right, Mercy is all right if she is dead and the rest of us will be all right in a matter of time, the only thing that wouldn't be all right at all would be if she were still alive and struggling in the sea...and that is the horror of it. Now I've said the unmentionable, but it must be in everyone's mind and I guess the only way to deal with it is to try and put it out of ones head as if it were a nightmare, or to pray.

She ends the letter: "I'm going to start my begonia tubers this afternoon in hopes that someday summer will come."

Postmark:Suva Fiji
September 5, 1977

9/5

Hello, i left for the Yasawa Island on the morning of Aug. 23. That deal with the nun fell through, just as well, i met a fellow solo American girl traveler, and together we sailed out to Nauiti on a small Fijian fishing boat. Great ride! We had to hide below deck

with all the chickens and provitions untill we passed the customs island, cuz we were traveling illegally on an unlicensed boat, and with out special visas...beautiful day good wind, just heading out towards the Yasawas, Carol & i, we had Kava, rice & tea for lunch...On the way over we were planing to camp on the beach, but were invited to stay with a Reverend & his family. So now every thing was set, we had a place to stay, knew where we were going and knew we'd be safe.

it was quite an amazing week to sum-up. Most people spoke some English, but still, it is such a trial to communicate and so much was misunderstood. Their customs and manner are so intricate and irrelevant to me it was impossible to tell whose toes you were stepping on and nothing

174

could be explained because of politeness and language. Until we met a Peace Corps volunteer working in one of the next villages and ahhh sudden enlightment. For example: Fijian houses have 2 doors, side one and front one. The side one is used for honored guests & the chief to enter the house and the front one is the everyday door.

There's a constant game that's played of honoring and trying to play humble...they insist that you go in the side door, but it's considered rude if you don't refuse at least a couple of time and put up and fuss.. Tons of little customs like that. And not knowing or not having the foggiest idea of them tends to confuse situations all the more.

One thing i still don't understand and probably never will is the role that European tourists assume. I guess it always different...sometimes i feel that the Fijians are truly kind and generous but they're also looking for a ticket off of Fiji. A trip to America...Maybe we'll take them home and send them to school and give them a T.V.

My Emotions bounced around so much. On one hand, i was frustrated, tired, and sick of never being left alone, always being brought to a neighboring village, shaking hands, children swarming and trying out the only English phrases they knew. "Whats you name?" How old are you? Are your parents still alive? (that always seemed to be a big concern...?) and "love you baby." And on the other hand, when i could look from the outside at what i was doing. i got rushes of sweet satisfaction and wholeness came. Walking down the beach at dawn...sitting at the food line, swimming, eating lunch at a neighboring village.

During the day we were under the wing of a girl, Nunia, who spoke alright English, but understood excellently...she took us visiting around the island to her parents coconut plantation, where we ate lunch, made baskets, collected clams, swam and rested, one of my best days. i took a lot of pictures.

We went to visit the hospital on another island cuz my boil blew-up again.. not as bad...

On one walk down the beach Carol & i came across a woman covered in only sand, beating the hell out of an octopus-tenderizer. On the rocks next to her were 3 gigantic, huge, enormous,

wet women holding slimy pink octopii... These enormous women dive for octopus. Hard to believe [margin drawing of woman with spear and octopus] but they're good at it. i wish i could have snapped a picture, they all had goggles and spears like Neptune's.

Well, something kind of interesting and sad.. the missionaries are real successful here. The village we're staying at, No-ago, belongs to the Church of the Assembly of God....

sounded familiar, but it wasn't until I attended their service that I realized where I heard of them before. In Seattle, the Jesus Comune. That Assembly of God Village is just as intense & fanatical as the ones in Seattle. It's always a relief when we get out of there for a day. So sad, the missionares have totally wiped out the Fijian religion. Everyone's either Methodist or Assembly of God and all the Indians are Hindu. No native religion left.

Well, village living became a little too much...And when i heard of a yacht anchored over on the other side of the island I ran over an asked for a ride to the main land. i guess they felt sorry for me and said i could come along, but they were gonna do some cruising around the other islands first. So i got to do some nice sailing, too. Carol stayed on Nauiti. And we're going to meet in Korotogo, remember?, and do a hike together across the island. it's so so nice to have company, brings me back to reality and i can absorb much more cuz we can talk thing out and with 2 it's not so much of a fight to stay on top. Every thing's wonderful and it really does get better and better and time goes on and i learn how to travel...so long. Thanks again for your letter...still write to Suva...i'll have them forward it if i go on but keep Hatty's letter and any other personal mail until i know definitely where i'll be. Much love

15

Mom's impromptu wake for Mercy did not stop, or even slow down, Dad's search. Within a day or so after his return from Tonga and New Zealand, he was back on the phone. In a letter dated February 27, Captain Hunt's assistant, Edgar Boyack, forwarded a copy of the wreckage report to Mr. Caldwell, the American consul in Wellington, and asked that Mr. Caldwell send it on to Mr. Ewing. (Obviously, it would have been easier to mail the report directly to Connecticut, but Mr. Boyack was politely following the international protocol of the search.) He goes on:

> This morning Captain Hunt received two telephone calls from Mr. Ewing who has now returned home. Mr. Ewing reported on the results of his tour and the various conversations he had with interested parties at the places he visited. What he told [Hunt] adds nothing to the information we already have.
>
> This yacht is still officially unaccounted for. Should any fresh information come to light you will be informed.

Dad wondered if Steve Abney, the sailor on whose boat Mercy had stayed in Vava'u, could add any "fresh information," so along with calls to Captain Hunt, Dad called Noel Curtis and asked him to find and interview Abney. Curtis threw himself whole-heartedly into the mission. He refused Dad's offer of "remuneration" for his services, but promised to give "a summary of my actual out of pocket expenses—no more." He was as hooked as Dad was on finding answers. Moreover, his role as Dad Ewing's lieutenant gave him a sense of importance and satisfied his flair

Mom's letters to Mercy were returned unread.

for drama. He wasn't simply doing a favor for an American father in distress: he had embarked on a quest for a lost damsel.

As it happened, Steve Abney had been filling in the hurricane season doing maintenance repairs on a yacht named *Pegasus*. Curtis tracked him down and asked him to come to Titirangi to meet with him and his wife Marney. Abney accepted the invitation and the three of them spent hours discussing the *I Love You II*. Steve Abney had refused to take Mercy with him to New Zealand on his own boat, a 38-foot (11.5-meter) sloop built in Finland that had reminded Mercy of the Maria. He told the Curtises that he had not wanted the responsibility of a hitchhiking passenger on a long, potentially risky passage. On long hauls, he said, his only companion was a cat named Turkey.

He left Vava'u on a full moon tide on November 17, a day before the *I Love You II*. Both boats planned to stop off at Kapa (the island home of Siliva and Laitaimi) to pick up fresh vegetables and then sail on to Nuku'alofa to pick up New Zealand visas. However, after Abney picked up his vegetables, the weather turned. Undeterred he sailed for Nuku'alofa in the teeth of a storm. For two days, he sailed only under his jib, with waves breaking over the sloop's cabin. After a week of running with the wind, he sighted land and realized that he had been blown clear to the southern tip of the Fiji Islands. He was so far to the west that he decided to skip Nuku'alofa and head directly for New Zealand. He reached the Bay of Islands and cleared customs in Russell on December 2. He was surprised that the bigger, faster catamaran had not beaten him there. A few days later he reported the *I Love You II* missing.

According to Curtis, he expressed "a real feeling of remorse in that he did not break his solo voyaging habit and agree to Mercedes accompanying him to NZ." Of course Abney was hardly stranding Mercy in Tonga; she didn't have to sail on the *I Love You II*. She had an air ticket to New Zealand. She could have flown but she wanted to cash it in as she was running low on funds.

Abney told the Curtises that he thought the *I Love You II*'s anti-fouling paint had been blue vinyl—not the red paint on the drifting starboard hull reported by the Tasman Enterprise. Abney also maintained that the catamaran's living quarters—along with food and water—were located in the port hull. Thus, if the starboard hull found in the Tasman Sea belonged to the *I Love You II*, it had contained only fuel and equipment. He took some hope from this: he believed that it was possible that the four *I Love You II* crew could have survived by clinging to the "living" port hull. He cited the case of a catamaran that had been run down by a freighter in the Atlantic: the crew had cut their way into the "living hull", used it for shelter and food, and had drifted in relative comfort for two weeks until they were rescued. Steve suggested that if the *I Love You II's* crew had survived in a similar fashion, it was possible that they had drifted to one of the small islands that dotted the Pacific ocean and might have been able to survive off even an inhospitable landform. In which case, he speculated, they might not be found until the hurricane season ended in April and the yachting crowd resumed cruising.

Dad's response to this information was to ask Curtis to hire Steve to look for Mercy. Curtis agreed. In a four page, single-spaced, typed "report" dictated to his wife Marney and dated March 16, 1978, Curtis relates in detail his adventure of hunting down Steve:

> I had to clear the matter of re-starting inquiries for the ILU2 on my radio Maritime Mobile network. You may recall that during your visit. I told you of the police "request" that I make no further calls for ILU2 over the network. This request I honored. I had no success in my attempts to speak to the police officer concerned so decided to speak to Capt. Hunt in Wellington. . .his attitude appeared that he not only had no objections to my inquiries [sic] by radio but, in fact, would be pleased [to help].

Perhaps the most important point which arose during this talk was his comment on the drugs aspect. His words were that as far as his Department was concerned this aspect was a "dormant issue" and that it always had been with him and his staff. So this has to mean, Dad, that it was the [New Zealand] police who jumped on it and made it an important issue. We parted company on the phone, I think, in quite a friendly manner.

It is not clear why the police asked Curtis to stop broadcasting for news of the *I Love You II*. Perhaps they felt his inquiries were interfering with their own investigation of what they were treating as a drug case. In any case, Curtis' letter goes on to describe how his "assistant" (as he refers to his wife Marney) had located *Pegasus*, the yacht on which Abney was working, moored in an Auckland harbor. Marney called Curtis from a waterfront phone and a few hours later he arrived at the harbor and boarded *Pegasus*. The yacht impressed him. He told Dad that she was "immaculate, properly equipped, completely manned," and about to set sail for Tonga on a scientific research mission sponsored by "leading American interests." Curtis met the boat's co-owners, Karl Keesling and Tony Chase, as well their fellow crew member named Bill Martens whom Curtis described as a "shipwright".

Steve Abney, however, was not on board the *Pegasus*. He was aboard the *Incognito*, his own sloop at anchor 100 yards away, making preparation to leave New Zealand. Turning this setback to his advantage, Curtis quizzed the *Pegasus* crew about Steve's character:

> Their opinions were unanimous. That as a conscientious worker, unquestionably in the craftsman class, Abney is an exceptionally keen and capable man. I contributed my bit by saying that he had been very attentive, intelligent and willing during the long session of interviews and questioning at my home. . .We all had to agree that as to his past, prior to his solo voyaging, his life was pretty well a closed book to us.
>
> At this stage, Buck, I had little option but to make a decision without delay. . .I did however make one final point. . .I asked Tony's opinion of Abney's attitude towards money. Tony said he thought that Abney was not at all interested in money as money. As long as he had enough to meet his light living and sailing expenses that was about it. Karl confirmed this. I then asked that Abney be fetched. He arrived in a few minutes."

Naturally enough, the conversation centered about the disappearance of the *I Love You II*. Abney added some new clues into the mix. He told the men that Donald Glidden had had two German Shepherds on board who slept, regardless of the weather, on the main platform of the catamaran's deck. The dogs, Abney maintained, were keen watchdogs that raised an alarm whenever someone came near the *I Love You II*. He believed that even if, by some unusual circumstance, the entire crew had been asleep, the dogs' barking would have woken them if a ship were approaching.

Curtis goes on to report:

> At this point Tony Chase of [the] Pegasus interjected, "What if the weather had been rough? Would the crew have heard the dogs?
>
> Steve replied, "The self-steering gear of ILU2 would only work in reasonably good weather conditions. In rough weather the self-steering device was useless and ILU2 had then to be steered manually.
>
> She was so difficult to steer in heavy weather that a wooden strut was used to mechanically connect the two tillers together. This rig required two persons to keep the vessel on course and it was strenuous work, which could be endured by the pair for short periods only. In heavier weather conditions the effort of three persons was needed.

Curtis concludes that "under anything more than moderate seas there would have been at least two of the crew working hard to hold steerage way."

Steve Abney planned to set sail for Tonga no later than March 25—nine days hence. This would give him the safety advantage of sailing during full moon: at night he would be able to steer clear of New Zealand's irregular coastline and to avoid other vessels. He planned to clear customs from Whangarei—the city port north of Auckland—where he had friends who would help refit his sloop for the voyage. When Curtis told him of Dad's offer of $500 to look for Mercy, he accepted it. "Sure, fine, thank you," he said casually. "I would like to do that. I'm going to look at some places anyway."

Curtis was somewhat disconcerted by his off-hand manner, but he concluded:

Buck, you must place yourself in Steve Abney's hands. Of all the people I have met or heard of in this ILU2 affair he has given it the most study from the sailor's viewpoint. He is competent, intelligent and (I am certain) is dedicated to do what he can. His yacht is well-founded and an excellent seaboat.

Dad, I'm sure, found emotional support in having a companion in arms "only a phone call away," as Curtis assured him. But Curtis' letter must have kept his head spinning. Were the New Zealand police wrong in assuming that drugs played a part in the catamaran's disappearance? Did Captain Hunt's dismissal of drugs as "dormant issue" mean he didn't believe drugs were involved? Or did he mean that the matter of illegal drugs was irrelevant to his search? How reliable was Steve Abney's memory? Was the blue vinyl paint that he remembered simply wishful thinking— the surfacing of an unconscious hope that the floating hull was not Mercy's boat? Scott Glidden, Donald Glidden's son, was certain the *I Love You II's* anti-fouling paint had been red: he had helped paint the hull when the *I Love You II* was in dry-dock in Pago Pago. Not till a month later did Dad obtain snap shots of the catamaran that proved Scott Glidden correct: her hull was red, not blue.

September, 197]
Savusavu, Fiji

Hello, there. Back from the heart of Fiji. It
was the best adventure so far...hiking through the
mountains sleeping in villages, offering hava and tobaco
for the ceramony of protection.
The best part of Fiji lies in the interior...
Carol and i floated out of the bush down the tropical
river to the road on a bili-bili (bamboo raft). Next
I'm going over to Vanva Levu...See what's
over there. Could you please forward my mail to
Suva. i'll be here long enough to receive it... and i'm
dying to read my letters thanks Mercy.

185

16

On March 26, ten days after Noel Curtis tracked down and met with Steve Abney, Curtis wrote Dad another letter—nine single-spaced typed pages, again dictated to his wife Marney. He made corrections in blue ballpoint and meticulously initialed each correction on the upper right-hand corner of the page. Mid-dictation, Dad called him for a briefing ("interrupted at this stage by your phone call"). After their phone conversation, Curtis completed his missive. Perhaps a written report made the job more real, gave it a professional accountability. Or perhaps putting it all down on paper was a way of sorting out the information he'd collected. Nonetheless, despite his organized headings—the names of people interviewed, the locations, dates, and exact times of these contacts—his narrative is garrulous rather than precise. He goes back and forth between interviews, veering off course and circling around islets of gossip and speculation. So for clarity's sake, I've put the events of March 20 to March 26 into chronological order.

Tuesday, March 20: Steve Abney calls Noel Curtis

By this time, Dad had been home in Connecticut for almost a month. Steve Abney had sailed his sloop north to Wrangarei, New Zealand, and was five days away from his departure date of March 25, when he phoned Curtis to pass on a rumor he had heard. According to the yachtie grapevine, in early January, the *I Love You II* had made landfall at Mangonui, the northernmost port in New Zealand and some 40 miles north of the Bay of Islands, where they had planned to arrive before Thanksgiving.

If this was true, then the catamaran had survived the passage from Tonga and had made an illegal landfall: all yachts were required to go through New Zealand immigration and customs and there was no record of the *I Love You II* at Russell in the Bay of Islands, New Zealand's northernmost port of entry, or at any other official port of entry. The rumor of an undocumented entry added fuel to Curtis' growing suspicion that the *I Love You II* was running drugs.

There was, of course, a less sinister reason for avoiding authorities: Glidden's two German Shepherds. To enter New Zealand legally, the dogs would have had to be quarantined for six months. If Glidden was ultimately headed for Australia, as his son Scott maintained, this would have caused a long delay—a delay he might have tried to circumvent. But if the catamaran rumored to have been seen at Mangonui was Glidden's, what had they been doing between late November when they left Tonga, and early January when they supposedly appeared in Mangonui? Even if they had been blown off course in a storm (as Steve Abney had), the passage should not have taken that long. Moreover, this story raises the same old question: if for some unknown reason Gliddon had entered New Zealand illegally before sailing onto Australia, why had Mercy not called home, or mailed a letter, when they landed? If an expired visa had not prevented her from staying in Tonga, it's hard to imagine why an illegal landfall would have deterred her from contacting Mom either by phone or by one of her usual letters.

Wednesday, March 22: Interview with Captain Hunt

Noel Curtis and his wife Marney flew to the North Island to visit with Captain Hunt in Wellington. Once again, Hunt and his colleague Captain Collins reviewed the case, this time for Curtis as Buck Ewing's representative. The meeting was cordial and lasted two and a half hours. "I was treated very well," he reported to Dad. "They were only too willing to show me the file of information; to tell me of the wide ranging, expert searches which had been made. . . .There was

Abney's Search

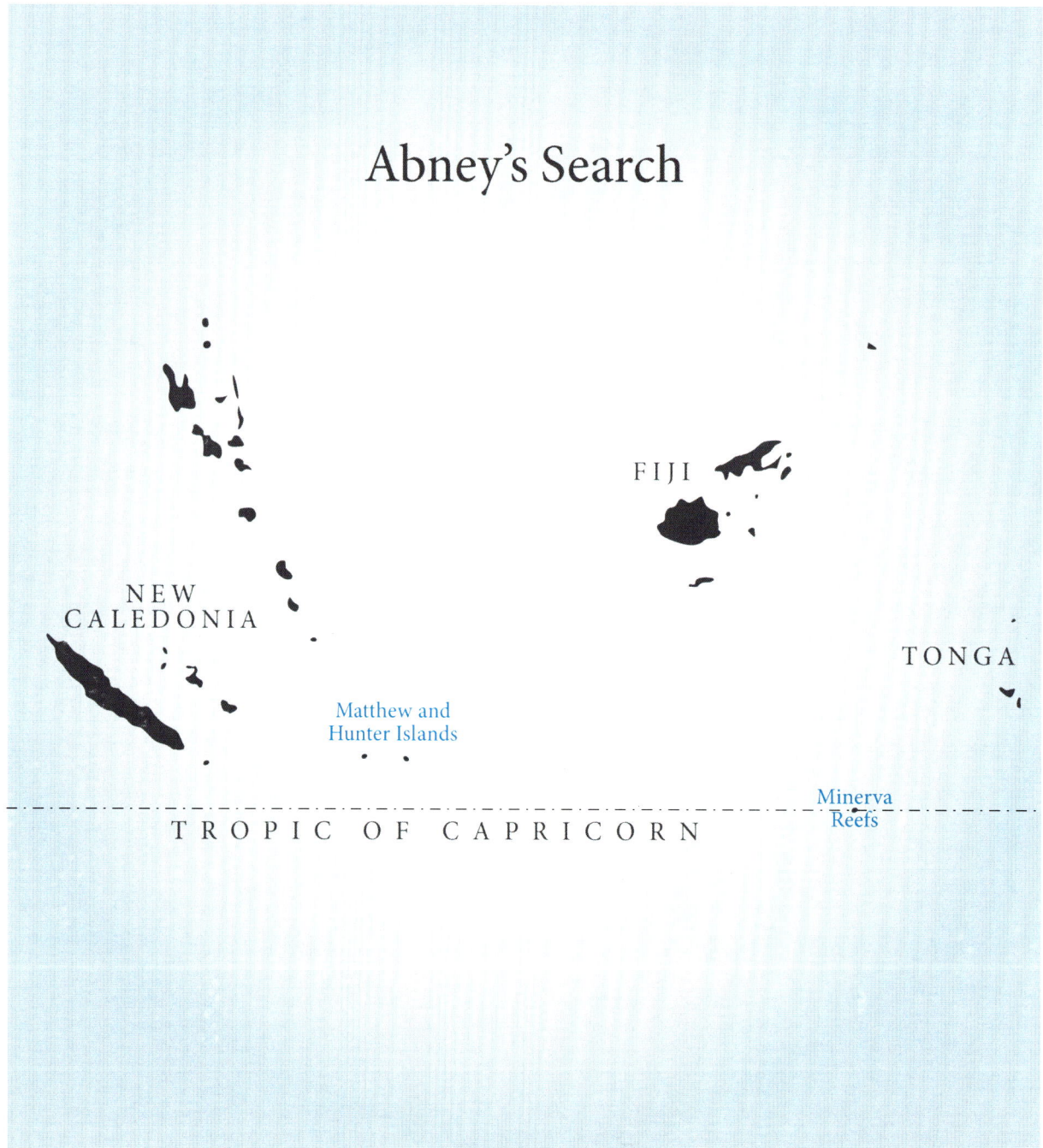

NEW
CALEDONIA

FIJI

TONGA

Matthew and
Hunter Islands

Minerva
Reefs

TROPIC OF CAPRICORN

an atmosphere of full co-operation and helpfulness." The men discussed in depth the various possibilities of what might have befallen the *I Love You II*. Captain Collins seemed to be leaning towards the "drop out" scenario with Glidden and crew hiding out somewhere—perhaps to avoid the law. He observed that if he himself wanted a "hideout", he would head for the Chesterfield Islets, a group of tiny islands to the NW of New Caledonia.

Hunt favored an "accident theory": Glidden hit by a boom and lost overboard and the inexperienced crew unable to navigate on their own. Donald Glidden had taken a navigational training course in Tahiti, but none of the crew had navigational skills and if their skipper had been lost overboard, or had succumbed, say, to a heart attack, the three crew in addition to being traumatized, would have been left without a radio to call for help. It had not been working when the *I Love You II* left Tonga. Mercy and Steve Wolff were inexperienced when it came to ocean sailing—they were simply hitchhikers. Twenty-six year old Tiara McMillan was listed as Glidden's mate in the boat's papers, but would she have been able to handle the boat without him? Hunt's best guess was that somewhere north of New Zealand, *I Love You II* had drifted into shipping lanes and had been run down by a freighter or commercial fishing ship. At the time of the year, he observed, there had been 300 Japanese fishing vessels in New Zealand waters, as well as numerous ships of other nationalities. (In Curtis' report, there's an emphatic underline beneath the word Japanese—as if the nationality were particularly significant. Enmity left over from World War II perhaps?)

Working on the assumption that an accident had befallen the *I Love You II* off the northern tip of New Zealand, Captain Hunt plotted several possible paths along which the catamaran might have been carried by ocean currents. Allowing for various sea and wind conditions, Hunt calculated that these drift paths would have taken the catamaran either to Hawke Bay (on the east coast of New Zealand's North Island), or the Coromandel Peninsula (due east of Auckland), or even Drake's Passage (between Cape Horn on the tip of South America and Antarctica).

Although both Captain Hunt and Captain Collins believed that Steve Abney's search was a forlorn hope, they suggested two areas where currents conceivably might have carried wreckage: one possibility was the uninhabited Hunter and Mathew Islands to the east of New Calendonia and just north of the Tropic of Capricorn. As an even longer shot, he suggested the Minerva Reef further to the east and right on the Tropic of Capricorn. Sixteen years earlier in 1962, a shipwrecked Tongan captain and eleven crew managed to survive for three months on the Minerva Reef, by living on fish and their own wits. Although the reef had been searched by air in December and January, there was the slight chance that wreckage might have drifted to it since the fly-overs.

As for the rumor of an orange catamaran calling at Mangonui in early January, Hunt did not dismiss it. He told Curtis that "the first preliminary report by the Police states that there is some likelihood of it having been ILU2."

As the meeting came to a close, Curtis pressed the men as to whether they thought the wrecked hull in the Tasman Sea could have belonged to the *I Love You II* but neither official would take a firm stand. The nearest Curtis could get to a statement was Collin's feeling that if the *I Love You II* had been hit near the northern tip of New Zealand, the wreckage was "too far to the west." Collins, an expert on drift, told the story of a steamer in pre-radio days at the turn of the last century. A sizeable vessel of some 4,000 to 5,000 tons, she was incapacitated by an engine breakdown. As recounted by Curtis:

> The ship was between Bluff [the southernmost port in New Zealand] and a southern Australia port. She was powerless for some six weeks. The engines were eventually repaired. When the engines were restarted and the voyage was resumed she was to the north of NZ's northernmost tip. In about 6 weeks she had moved by drifting more than NZ's north-to-south length.

Collins' point was that if Glidden's catamaran had been run down by a ship off the northern tip of New Zealand, the currents would have carried the wreckage southward for a time, but then it would have swung back north, ending up in the New Hebrides—not in the Tasman Sea. Hunt backed Collins by telling of wreckage sighted twelve days earlier on March 13, at the northern tip of New Zealand. It was a capsized black hull, thought to be steel and estimated at 14 meters long. There were traces of reddish brown antifouling paint on it. Awash, it was drifting in an east-southeast direction. Curtis comments:

> I mention this to show the odd things which are adrift in this part of the world. It, obviously could not be part of ILU2, but one cannot help wondering what it is and where it came from and who were the unfortunate persons aboard when disaster overtook that vessel!!

After their visit with Captains Hunt and Collins, Noel and Marney Curtis flew home to Wellington.

Thursday, March 23: Curtis sees Abney off

After his round trip by air to Wellington on Wednesday, the next day the Curtises rose before dawn. At "4.50 am," he notes as if clocking in, they left Titirangi by car and drove north to Whangeri to brief Steve Abney on Hunt's suggestions. It was Holy Thursday—in the Catholic Easter liturgy, the day of Jesus' Last Supper. Abney was scheduled to depart for Tonga the following day, on Good Friday. At 7:30 am, Curtis found Abney on his sloop the *Incognito* which was berthed "on the town side of the river." Together they went over Abney's charts. Abney agreed to check out the islands that Hunt had suggested. He also told Curtis that when he got to Tonga, the first thing he wanted to do was visit with Lautaimi and Siliva Nasilai—the couple on Vava'u with whom Mercy had stayed in November, and who had provisioned both Abney and the crew of the *I Love You II* with fresh vegetables before the boats sailed from Tonga. Abney wanted "to question the Nasilais as to whether there had been any signs of argument or squabbles among the members of the ILU2 crew before the yacht's departure." When Curtis asked Abney "for his reasons for such questioning he became rather casual about it, or even evasive, so I did not pursue the matter."

Curtis left Abney with addresses, phone numbers and radio call signs that "should be useful to him. I also told him that at the first port where it was possible to do so he must telephone you, Buck. He said that he would do this." Curtis also extracted a promise that Abney would telephone him "immediately prior to his actual departure from NZ at any time of day or night. I took this precaution in case something or other turned up which could be important for him to know."

> We wished him good luck from you and ourselves and said bon voyage. He had in his hand his passport documents and left us to go to the Customs office and finalize his clearance from NZ. This was at 9 am and some half an hour later, while I was talking to Humphrey and Claire Jones in Orem's boatyard, we saw Abney moving down river on his way.

The Jones were the sailors who had told Abney the rumor of the *I Love You II*'s illegal entry at Mangoni in January. They had seen the catamaran in dry dock at Pago Pago the previous season, but not since. They referred Curtis to another sailor by the name of Jim Dragonavich who owned a Canadian registered yacht named *Halcyon* that was also anchored in the Whangarei harbor. So Curtis then hailed the *Halcyon* from a small jetty within shouting distance of the boat. Dragonavich happened to be working on the foredeck and at Curtis' request for an interview, he hopped in a dinghy and paddled over to the jetty for a talk. Dragonavich and his wife had been in Pago Pago with the Jones when the *I Love You II* had been hauled. They had heard about the Mangonui sighting third-hand, from a local couple with whom they'd become friendly during a stay in the Bay of Islands. This third couple, the Neville Wiltshires, had heard the story from a retired boat builder called "old Bill" Endine who also lived in Bay of Islands. It is not clear if "old Bill" himself had seen the orange catamaran in Mangonui, or had heard about it from other visiting yachties.

Curtis quizzed Dragonavich on the matter of drugs:

Jim did not know about ILU2 having been searched for drugs at Nuku Hiva in French Polynesia. But he did know of this being done at Rarotonga. He said the search had been a very thorough one, but nothing had been found. . . When I pressed Jim for his feeling as to whether drugs were involved he was certain that there was nothing but rumor in that story.

Friday, March 24, The rumor mill. Curtis, back at home, again was up early:

> At 0605 GMT on March 24th 1978 I made the following announcement over my Maritime Mobile Pacific network: "Information is requested on the missing ketch rigged ILU2---57ft Catamaran with orange painted hulls and yellow masts---she was due at B.O.I New Zealand about Dec. 1st from Tonga---Expert and major searches have been made by the search authorities: USCG Australia, MOC Fiji Tonga, NZ Division of Ministry of Transport--- Radio reports should be made to New Zealand---Other reports to nearest Port Captain---We request information on any sighting of the vessel or component parts---Any reports to this net or the Pacific Inter Island or the 15 metre Nets will be given priority attention. . .
>
> I mentioned, too, that the sighting of a hull on Feb. 5th [by Tasman Enterprise] is not confirmed as being part of ILU2.
>
> Within 10 minutes, Buck, I had received comments on the above statement from California, French Polynesia, Marshall Islands. The information given to me in those reports were, of course, on things already known to us (you and me).

One of the Americans who responded to the call told Curtis that he and "other cruising men in his area" had been discussing the disappearance of the catamaran and that they had raised the "possibility of hi-jacking or piracy in the ILU2 affair." This is the first time (at least in the existing correspondence) that the idea of piracy came into play. At that time, American yacht owners were concerned about piracy in the Caribbean. Stories circulated about drug runners boarding yachts, murdering the crew and throwing the bodies overboard, then using the boat for a delivery, and scuttling it afterwards. Curtis admits the notion is only speculation. Nonetheless the idea was like a dark seed that gradually took hold in the minds of both Dad and Noel Curtis.

March 26, Easter Sunday. Another long distance call.

Curtis is composing his nine-page report when he is interrupted by Dad's phone call. In Connecticut, we had all gathered at Noroton for Mercy's Mass, which was to be held the next day on Easter Monday. Mom went to early Easter Sunday Mass, but I stayed home with Andy and the boys. (By that time, Mom had given up on getting any of her children to Mass. When I went home to visit, she politely ignored my non-attendance.) Later in the morning, there was an Easter egg hunt for all the cousins. For the adults, it was Bloody Marys and jellybeans culled from the kids' baskets. About one p.m., we sat down to Sunday dinner. There would have been at least fourteen of us—Mom and Dad, eight surviving children, and four spouses. But the older grandchildren would have been seated with us, and perhaps Mom, as was often the case, had included Aunt Margaret Challinor, our great aunt, and her partner Alice Whitehouse Hodges who lived nearby. So there might have been twenty at the table. Mom didn't like Easter hams, so we probably ate roast turkey with Pepperidge Farm stuffing, canned Ocean Spray cranberry sauce, Betty Crocker instant mashed potatoes, canned Lesueur baby peas, with half a case of a good Beaujolais and vanilla ice cream for dessert. After dinner, Dad excused himself from coffee and brandy in the living room and called Noel Curtis in New Zealand. Perhaps he was hoping without really hoping for some last minute news, some hopeful piece of information that would warrant canceling tomorrow's funeral Mass—a live rabbit that magico presto he could pull out of a black hat for Mom, for all of us. But, as it happened, Curtis' extensive effort had turned up nothing new. During the phone call, Dad must have expressed his doubts regarding Abney's one-man search, because Curtis, in his letter, assures Dad that the trip is worthwhile for "these reasons":

> [Abney] is the one person with first hand knowledge of the events up to November 17 last. He has a real feeling of remorse in that he did not break his solo voyaging habit and agree to Mercedes accompanying him to NZ.
>
> Finally comes the hunch of which I have said nothing so far. It is this. Through the long sessions of talks with Abney and by subsequent contacts with him I have a gut feeling that he knows or senses something or other he has not divulged. I can say no more

because I know no more. It is impossible to describe.

It is still my firm opinion that if anything can come from a one-man effort, then Abney is that man.

So Dad attended Mercy's Mass on Easter Monday wondering where his investment in Steve Abney would lead. Compared to the thousands of dollars of oversees charges on his monthly phone bill, to say nothing of the money spent on his trip to Tonga and New Zealand, the $500 stipend was a small expense. But Dad, in his business ventures, was always hopeful of investing in the dark horse that would ultimately win the race. In this case, I don't think he dared hope that Abney, as his dark horse, would find Mercy alive on some island. But perhaps he hoped for a concrete evidence of a wreck. Or at least, an "undivulged" clue that Curtis felt Abney was hiding. Perhaps Abney, given his head, might lead them to the truth of Mercy's fate. As it was, the only solid fact of the whole situation was that Mercy and the *I Love You II* had been missing for four months.

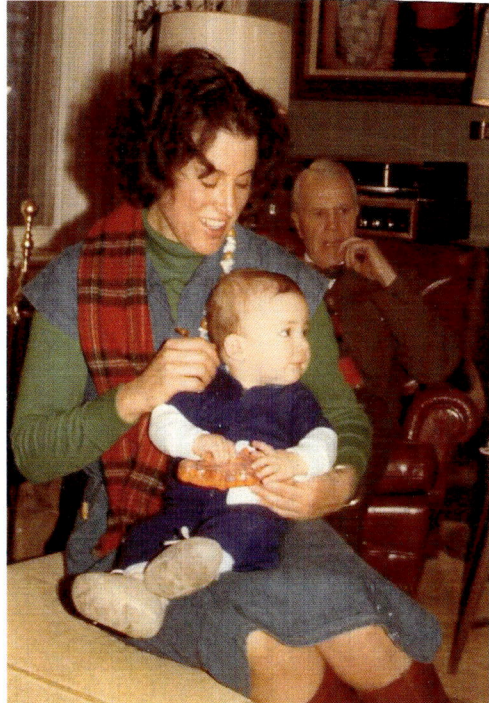

Easter Sunday 1978: My photo of Jessie with our nephew Will Ewing on her lap. Behind her, Buck in his customary chair.

[Postmark September 20, 1977
Natuvu, Fiji
aerogramme]

9/16

Dear Ma, sitting in a hotel waiting for my ride to Vapuka on the eastern point of Vanua Levu. Unexpectidly got on a copra boat last nite and arrived at Sava Sava

During the last minute rush i think i lost my hiking boots...haven't used them so far but I know i'm gonna want them when i'm in New Zealand. Oh well, maybe i'll find them.

Finished off a hike with Carol on the 14th. It was the best adventure i've had so far. The first one that I was really able to truly enjoy...It was fun...not so draining. We hiked during the day usually stopped at a stream and eat lunch and took a bath and started hiking again around 2 or 3...get into the village around 3 or 4...have a drink a couple bowls of Kava rest untill dinner, eat dinner, take a bath, drink some more Kava, and then go to sleep.. the patern was the same at each village but each village was so different.. the way we were treated, the situation on the village, the size...each nite was a totally new experience...you just knew what to expect more and how to act.

I feel like we really gotta good taste now of what the old life use to be like. its so hard to write about now. I've already started on the next leg of my journey and that hike is slowing slipping into a half remembered dream.

I think i was so good because during the day our time was our own we could hike, pick fruit, swim, rest, whatever and then when we were at the village we could enjoy it more... every thing was done for us, dinner, breakfast, cleaning-up..and all we had to do was smile with them and give a few presents out before we left people. I can't really tell what it was...just a feeling, very suttle...maybe they just seem more sincear or maybe I'm just getting used to the fijian people. its so hard to say. I relly noticed the difference when we got to the River... River people nwere so great. Just such a real friendlyness but not smothering... Rewasaw was a the head of the Suca River...And they really were straight forward about helping you out... not so many around the bush answeres... We wanted to get a bili-bili and float down the rest of the river, till we hit the road. They gave as a bili-bili and taught us how to use it. (long bamboo poles to push yourself along) and how to steer it through the rapids..(the river was very low so there was nothing that exciting thank-god)

Every thing turned out so perfectly. Good weather, no boils, every thing just nice and easy.

Now I'm over on Vanva Levu. Got on a local cargo boat last nite. Slept on the deck. Nice ride, not to rough & lots of stars...I met t[w]o girls while in Sigatoka that are working for the New Zealand Equivalant of Peace Corps. They're running a school...and said I could come in with them any time I was up for it so I'm going. This island is much nicer....much greener and not so many people. It really looks like a tropic paradice island. If you ever come to fiji for a cruise or just a rest...you should stay at Vanua Levu Savusavu is the place.

i'm siting in a resort hotel waiting for the afternoon bus.. and getting lectured by this old man. I'm getting tired of lectures from old men...They literally put me to sleep...I guess I could do something about it .... Like tryand spark it off into an intellectuall conversation, but the always seemto want to lecture so bad I can't stop them. Make sence? [drawing of map of Viti-Levu]

Heres a map of where we hiked. We covered a good pan of the island ...Hikefrom wet side to dry side...I guess I'll be leaving fiji for toga in a couple of weeks...please forward my letters, I'll be here long enough to receive them.

Much love M

Aerograms were lightweight sheets of blue paper on which you wrote a letter, then folded into a pre-stamped envelope. They were cheaper than sending airmail letters in separate envelopes. Many countries offered them, but by 2000, the US stopped producing them.

17

For Mercy's mass on Easter Monday, Mom invited the family at large—enough aunts, uncles and cousins to half fill the church. She also invited some of Mercy's friends, kids who had called wondering where she was. The mass was held at St. John's, a squat, gray stone immigrant-built church in the village of Noroton and only a mile and half away from Firwood. More than ten years before, Sheila and I, each in our turn, had been married at the church's wedding-cake altar. In 1958, Mercy had been christened there. In a family album, there is snapshot of my grandmother

Mary's Latin/English missal. By the time of Mercy's memorial, thanks to Vatican, all masses were said in English and missals were no longer used. The card I found in it is in memory of her art teacher and friend Nina Wheeler. The prayer is traditionally said as the coffin is carried out of the church to be buried.

Mercedes holding her infant namesake. It was taken after the christening outside the church and she was wearing a pale pink Liberty cotton summer dress. The obligatory black lace mantilla was draped around her shoulders—at that point, women were still required to cover their heads in church. Granny was looking at the baby in her arms and smiling. The snapshot makes me miss her. Her funeral mass was said in the church in 1966 and my brothers helped carry her coffin, which was draped with a Red Cross flag. The weight of it took them by surprise.

There was, of course, no coffin for Mercy. The day of her Mass was cold and gray—an overcast March day. Inside the church, it was appropriately gloomy thanks to the darkly varnished beaded wood ceiling and wainscoting. Today, the ceiling has been painted white, the confection of an altar has been replaced by a liturgically-correct table, and the garish plaster statues have been removed from the sanctuary to a whitewashed side wall where they are mounted like a cluster of museum pieces: St Theresa Little Flower (pressing pink roses to her breast and rolling her teenage eyes heavenward), the Virgin Mary (barefoot and stepping on a snake), and the less interesting figures of St Joseph and St Francis in monkish brown and black. But the three Tiffany-style glass windows set high in the apse are still the same. They were donated by John D. Crimmins in memory of his daughter Lily Irene who died of typhoid fever in 1895. She had been eighteen—just two years younger than Mercy.

The windows are narrow, arching to a gothic point and rendered in a Pre-Raphaelite style in hues of indigo, rose, and russet. The center one is a crucifixion scene. Christ's body hangs languidly on a cross set in a rock pile. The drape of his body is artistic, but his skin is a realistic, frighteningly gray. Mary stands to one side wearing a halo and a stark white headwrap. The two side windows show female angels with luxuriant, cascading hair and huge, ornithologically correct wings. They kneel on small rock piles of their own and adore the dead Christ. One of the angels carries a large spray of virginal lilies. This was John D's "Lily" and the thought of her as an angel in heaven was a comfort to him.

We had ample time to contemplate the windows (though I don't remember doing so) because my priestly cousin Michael Crimmins, who was driving up from his New York City parish to say the Mass, was late. My brothers Billy and Tommy, the oldest and youngest sons, were in the sanctuary waiting for him; they would serve the Mass. The rest of us took up two front pews. We came into the church through a side door at the front of the church. This would have been Mom's choice. She had an aversion to any sort of display and though no doubt we were on display as we randomly clomped into the pews, in my mother's mind, it was preferable to an organized procession of the bereaved up the aisle. I wore a tweedy maroon knit dress. I don't think any of us wore black. It was not only the ambiguity of the occasion: the sheer number of us in black would have been overly dramatic for Mom's taste.

Dad, on the other hand, had always delighted in showing off his brood. On family outings when we were little, to our great embarrassment, he used to line us up on the street in order of age and make us march after him, with Mom bringing up the rear. When he caught us out of order, straggling along in clumps, he would get genuinely angry and yell at us. "God damn it, now do what I say!" And everyone on the street would stop and stare—as if they hadn't been staring already at the sight of a handsome, black-haired man with flashing black eyes leading a line of six or seven children with a tall blond woman who could have passed for Lauren Bacall bringing up the rear.

So perhaps Dad was disappointed when, without ceremony, we appeared in the front of the church and trooped into the pews. On the other hand, given the heavy fog of his grief, perhaps our entrance barely registered. He stood at the back of the church positioned like a father waiting for a daughter to arrive in bridal finery. Father Jude, the parish priest, waited with him. I can still hear the excruciating conversation between them. Dad was slightly deaf, so as he talked to Father Jude, his voice was overloud and we in our front pews could hear every word.

"We aren't a hundred percent sure she's dead, Father," he boomed.

We stiffened in our pews, strained to hear the priest's reply, but Father Jude was responding in a discreet murmur.

"Ninety percent sure," Dad estimated. "Maybe ninety-five. But not a hundred percent."

While the occasion felt unreal to me to begin with, my father's one-sided conversation zoomed it into the surreal. I felt as if my scalp were lifting—then a grounding stab of anger at my missing sister. Anger at her stupidity, at the pain she was causing my parents. If she were sitting somewhere under a palm tree, I would happily kill her when she showed up.

Another long pause. Then Dad's voice again, loud and clear. "Well, I guess this won't hurt any." But there was a question in his voice. "I guess it can't hurt, even if she's alive," he concluded dubiously.

"Jesus!" Mom hissed up front. An explosive noise, like steam escaping from a tight valve. Her own anger was directed at Dad, at my cousin Michael, at anyone and anything but her lost daughter. Sometimes her grief would dissolve her, soften the fierce lines of her stoicism. "It's not the same as having her away, even if she never came home again," she confided later and her pale blue eyes brimmed with tears. Sheila, who visited her almost every day during the search, remembers that she cried every day. But on the morning of Mercy's funeral, there were no tears. Mom sat in the pew with her back ramrod straight, her lips compressed.

Several times, turning to see who was coming in behind us, I felt a start as one or another of Mercy's friends found a seat. Frizzy-haired, pale, androgynously dressed in baggy overcoats, any one of them could have been her. Afterwards my brother Fritz commented that it would have been just like Mercy to sneak into the choir loft to observe her own funeral, à la Huck Finn. Once she showed up unexpectedly for Thanksgiving dinner at Firwood. Everyone but Mercy had come home for it, and as we gathered in the living room for drinks before dinner, much to everyone's surprise, in she strode, wearing a short Scottish kilt and tights with her hiking boots. She had walked the five miles from the railroad station—rather than call to have someone come and pick her up. Mom was thrilled. "About as ecstatic as I have ever heard her", Sheila recalls. As for Dad, he and Mercy had been at odds, and he took her appearance as an olive branch. When he said grace at the table, and thanked God for "bringing us altogether under one roof", he became teary with emotion. Mercy clearly enjoyed the drama she had created. I was bemused—I had no idea what was going on. But Sheila was irritated by Mercy's smugness. She felt sorry for Dad.

In our front pew, Mom leaned over to Sheila and me and whispered, "Where is Michael? Why can't he be on time!"

"Maybe he's caught in traffic," we whispered back lamely.

At the back of the church, Dad was still at it, caught in his obsessive loop, loudly reviewing the details of his search for the priest's new set of ears. I sensed that the rest of the congregation was listening with fascination. Not many of my relatives knew the entire story, but we in the front pews had heard it too many times before. Still, I listened too, as if I might find something new in the recitation—some new piece of information, a new clue surfacing in the wreckage.

Mom said: "We can't keep people waiting any longer. Tell Father Jude to go ahead and start." We hesitated, looking at each other. Then, mercifully, there was motion at the side door, a blast of cold air, and Michael appeared, glowing with health in a sea-foam green Shetland sweater, his spring tan set off by the white priestly collar above the crew neck. Where had he been vacationing? Had he been to California to visit his mother? I felt happy to see him. We had grown up together, were the same age. He strode over to our pew: "Mary, I'm sorry," he apologized.

"Let's get on with it," she said stiffly.

A few moments later, the lights over the altar were switched on, the candles lit, and Michael, now vested in white and gold-embroidered robes, walked into the sanctuary attended by Father Jude and followed by my brothers Billy and Tom as altar boys.

"I will go unto the altar of God," Michael intoned.

"Unto God who gives joy to my youth," my brothers responded.

Billy wore polished penny-loafers under his cassock. But Tommy's sneakers poked out from under his, and my eyes teared up at the sight. He and Mercy were only two years apart. At the same time, I felt a measure of pride in my family, pride in my mother's strength, pride in our straight backs and straight teeth, pride that together we could provide the "manpower" to enact this ancient ritual for my sister. Like Mercy, I had spent many years chafing against the bonds of my family. Now, at her funeral, I found solace in being part of it.

Of course, it was not actually a funeral Mass—a requiem Mass. Since there was no evidence of her death, no body, no coffin in the aisle beside us, the best our parish priest could offer was a Mass for the intention of her soul. It was celebrated in English not Latin, but otherwise the prayers were the same prayers that had been intoned or sung for centuries. There were no folk guitars (a post-Vatican II innovation) and no eulogy (rare at Catholic funerals in those days). Mom would have objected strenuously had the priest proposed either. It was also a low mass: no singing or chant, no incense. Mom believed that all funeral masses should be as plain and short as dignity allowed. Twenty minutes max, was her preference. We were permitted, however, by both Mom and the Church to choose the readings and thereby infuse an unobtrusive personal note into the liturgy.

So Sheila and Jessie and I had paged through the Old Testament searching for a meaningful passage. We used the New Jerusalem Bible, a 1966 translation undertaken by an ecumenical group of scholars who had been rigorously faithful to the original Greek, Hebrew, and Aramaic. But the passages that caught our attention evoked either sarcastic snorts or dark laughter:

Proverbs 22:15: "Innate in the heart of a child is folly,
judicious beatings will rid him of it."

Wisdom 1:12, "Do not court death by the errors of your ways,
nor invite destruction through your own actions."

Ecclesiasticus 25:24-36: "Sin began with a woman
and thanks to her we all must die.
Do not let water find a leak, do not allow a spiteful woman free rein for her tongue.
If she will not do as you tell her get rid of her."

But it was in Ecclesiasticus, by chance or by grace, we finally found the right words. Ecclesiasticus (as opposed to Ecclesiastices) is not included in the King James or Douay bibles and the fact that it was outside the traditional canon, seemed to fit Mercy. Moreover, Chapter 43 is a hymn of praise for the wonders of creation, and that too seemed to fit:

> See the rainbow and praise its maker,
>   so superbly beautiful in its splendor.
> Across the sky it forms a glorious arc
>   drawn by the hand of the Most High.
>
> . . .By his own resourcefulness he has tamed the abyss
>   and planted it with islands.
> Those who sail the sea tell of its dangers
>   their accounts fill our ears with amazement:
> For there too are strange and wonderful works,
>   animals of every kind and huge sea creatures.
> Thanks to him all ends well,
>   and all things hold together by means of his word.

Even now, reading this makes me teary. But back then, when I left the front pew to read it aloud from the pulpit to the gathering of family and friends, I was too intent on delivering clearly to feel much of anything except nervousness. Still, afterwards at the reception Sheila gave at her house, a number of people said my reading had moved them and that was for me both a satisfaction and a relief.

John D. Crimmins built The Garden House next door to Firwood as a party house.
After WWI, Mercedes inherited it and used it as a summer residence. This photo is from
the 1950s when she kept a flower border at the edge of the lawn. By the time Mercy was lost,
my sister Sheila and her family were living there year round.

September 24, 1977
Suva, Fiji
aerogramme

9/24

Dear Ma,

i've been carrying around these slides and have decided i'm going to lose them if i don't send them home.

i sent off another package of junk about 2 weeks ago, with 2 roles of film to be developed. The Ektachrome has API scratched on it. I took the whole film at the ASA of the Kodachrome (whatever that is)

i was thinking maybe if you told them i screwed up the ASA they could try and fix it right while developing it. Oh and i sent the package by surface mail so it will take a couple of months to reach you. Alas.

i was looking through some of the slides and i liked the way some of them turned out. Don't lose them cuz i'd like to look at them again some day.

Just got back from trip to Vanva Levu. Went over on a freight, small copra freighter, we left at 9:00 at nite and sailed all nite. it was kind of fun. i slept on deck with all the fijians (as opposed to "shake-down" with all the indians.) Some fijian women let me sleep with them on their mat and we huddled together for warmth and listened to the deckhands sing and drink. Oh they sing so beautifully...so loud, just letting it out, but soft and high with all the harmonizing...sounded like i was in the south seas.

i left Carol back in Suva. She got on a boat & is heading for the New Hebredies...so i'm traveling on my own again, it's nice... i was almost looking forward to it... but i miss having company too. We plan to meet in New Zealand.

The freighter pulled into Savusavu on Friday morning. i missed the morning bus, so i had to wait until 3:00 for the after noon bus..went to a hotel lounge to write letters and was hassled by a lecturing Australian Alcoholic...left and walked on the road for the bus. 3:30 & the bus still hadn't come.

i was starting to get in a tizzy... asking people if i had missed it or if it was late. Nobody knew & nobody cared. Typical Fiji for "when it comes, it comes"...hmmmm...couldn't get an answer out of any one... Almost started crying & cursing up & down the main street...but the bus came in time, only a few tears escaped...gotta learn how to control my self better..Well got on the bus.

Dusty & long ride to Napolia..(where i was going to meet some girls who were working at the mission there). The busses here are made of wood and have no windows.

The roads are dirt & wind up and down the coast. The drivers are the personification of Mr. Toad on his wild ride. They're really a gas—but i need some goggles for the dust.

Jessie would go crazy.

My stay at Napolia was really nice...stayed 3 or 4 days did a lot of fishing and laying in the sun, which i haven't had very much chance to do... good swimming & diving.

Then i caught a ferry over to a smaller island called Tavevni and stayed there not very long. It was beautiful but raining the whole time... i got sick of sitting in the guest house reading & drinking beer and being pschyo-analysed by an american intellectual who was even more bored than i was...so i left when the next freighter came and came back to Suva.

Here in Suva, still raining. i'm thinking of doing another longer trip on a bamboo raft down the

Siatoha river. Don't know if i'll be able to find anyone to go with me, so i might do it alone...

Am also thinking of heading on to Tonga in the next week or so whether i find a boat or not... But i'm gonna wait here until you send the mail i had at home... After that, i'll be on my way.

And my new address will be M. Ewing C/O General Delivery, Nuku'Alofa Tonga...until mid Oct maybe.

Oh yes and there a question i have about money. i'm fine

now. Got money coming out my ears but its going to go much faster in New Zealand and Australia....i've got a blank check with me for my bank account in Conn. If i made it out to you... And sent it to you... could you withdraw all the money that's left in there and send it to me wherever i may be when i need it... just wire it to me? It sounds really easy, but i don't know if it would work or not. Well write and tell me what you think.

Lets see.... is that all? Oh and i hope you're using my stereo, if it's no trouble, cuz it's really better for it to be used. If it's too much trouble O.K., but wouldn't you like to listen to records over a good stereo?

There's something else i keep forgetting to tell you.....can't remember.

Well hope all is well. Signing Off.

Oh yea. Fiji is duty free so if you want any kind of camara of lens i can get it real cheap. i shoulda told you sooner so you could have more time to work something out, but i kept forgetting.

Oh well, let me know if there's any thing. i hope David dog* is all better by now.

Thank Dad for the nice post card.

*Mom's black lab named by our brother Tommy after his brother David.

211

18

I have learned, over the years, that grief is like a fog. We wander around in it for an indefinite amount of time, bump into dead-ends, walk in circles, and often become separated from the people to whom we are closest. This was true in Dad and Mom's case. Not only did they lose Mercy. They lost each other in a fog that was denser than most. For despite Mom's attempt to "make it final" with a Mass, Mercy's disappearance was a presumed death. Without her body, a terrible ambiguity remained.

Still, even with Mercy laid out in a coffin, I'm sure Dad still would have obsessed on finding out what happened, still would have pursued what Mom called his "guilt trip". Mom's own trip, her passage through the perilous shoals of uncertainty was more direct and swifter than Dad's. Ever since November, Mom had been worrying about "leaking boats and typhoons & sharks, etc." She had read Dougal Robertson's 1974 *Survive the Savage Sea*, a grim account of how Robertson, his wife, their nine-year old twin sons and a twenty-two year old hitchhiking Welch student had been shipwrecked on a passage from Panama to New Zealand. Their 19 ton, 43 foot schooner had been rammed by killer whales and sunk in minutes. For 38 days they had drifted in a rubber life raft, suffering extremely and slowly deteriorating from dehydration and starvation, boils and bouts of despair, until by chance (as Robertson saw it) or divine intervention (as his wife saw it) they were rescued by a 300 ton Japanese tuna fishing vessel. So Mom had graphic pictures in her mind of the ordeal castaways would have to endure to survive: images of drinking turtle blood, of improvised salt-water enemas, of ever-present shark fins cruising along side the raft. Both she and Dad must have wondered if Donald Glidden would have been as resourceful and shown the same moral fiber as Dougal Robertson. At the end of his book, Robertson gives an analysis of his survival, complete with advice on emergency equipment—everything from the type of inflatable rafts to bird charts for identifying land birds and their ranges to waterproof navigational equipment (Robertson had had none when his boat sank). "There can be no more bitter betrayal than the discovery of insufficient life-sustaining equipment after an escape from instant death," he cautions. Had Glidden read the book? Had he, like sailors then and now, benefited from Robertson's ordeal and equipped his catamaran accordingly?

In addition to Robertson, that October Mom had read Alfred Lansing's *Endurance*, the riveting story of British explorer Ernest Shackleton's famous 1917 boat journey in Antarctica. This too, was a survival story, an amazing one, and Shackleton was one of Mom's heroes. She gave several of us children copies of the book for Christmas. But in Shackleton's case, the sea was frozen. It was ice, not killer whales that had broken up his ship. And images of ice drifted into her worries about Mercy. When she learned that Captain Hunt's drift experts projected that ocean currents could have carried the wreckage from the *I Love You II* toward Antarctica, she poured over her nautical charts and worried that Mercy would be cold. She had nightmares of Mercy floating further and further south into icebergs.

At the same time, she knew that in fact, it would have been impossible for her to stay alive long enough to reach iceberg territory. The rational side of her brain told her that Mercy was dead. This was a logical deduction derived from the fact that Mercy, along with the entire crew of the *I Love You II*, had been missing for over three months. And while this inescapable fact was lodged firmly in her mind—an iron stake sinking in more deeply each day—there was also an intuitive or instinctive aspect to her growing conviction: something sensed rather than reasoned. Deep down, she felt connection between them had been broken.

As she became more and more certain that Mercy was never coming back home, Dad's search seemed less and less relevant. The circumstances of how the catamaran was lost—the whys and wherefores of Mercy's disappearance—were of minor importance to her. What mattered most was her growing conviction that Mercy was gone. She began to see all the time and energy and money Dad was spending on looking for her as futile. Moreover, it made him inaccessible. She would manage to get through the day looking forward to the evenings when he would come home from work and they could sit down and have a drink together before she cooked dinner. She was ready for distraction from her grief, for the evening news with Walter Cronkite or Dad's take on the state of the stockmarket or any conversation at all that was not about Mercy. But, as it happened, Dad had put Mercy's disappearance on hold all day at work. So when he got home, he plunged back into his search, leaving Mom alone while he closeted himself in his study and talked to Tonga, to New Zealand, to Washington, D.C., to anyone who would listen.

Mom's loneliness was compounded by her anger. Not anger at the hand she'd been dealt. "People say, why me?" she told me once. "But why not me?" She wasn't angry at fate, or at God. She was angry at Dad. If initially she had been grateful that he was mounting an international search, before long she was discomfited that he was so unavailable, so incapable of providing comfort. Moreover, she felt resentful that Dad was raising such a great fuss looking for Mercy when he had never truly known her, not as she herself—Mary—had known her. As she saw it, Dad had never been able to accept who Mercy was as an individual; he had tried to fit her into his mold of Daughter and she had refused to oblige. In fact, she had fought him tooth and nail.

Mom didn't blame Dad for alienating Mercy. I don't think she believed that Dad had driven Mercy away from home. Mom saw all our conflicts with him as a normal, if unpleasant, part of growing up. She herself as a teenager had had conflicts with her mother. Mercedes Challinor had an agenda. Her father John D. Crimmins, the son of an Irish immigrant, had made a fortune speculating in New York City real estate during the 1890s and, at a time when prejudice against Irish newcomers was still prevalent, he had striven to climb the ladder of New York society.

Waldorf Astoria, New York, New York, 1940, Mary dancing at her debut.

Reception line, left to right: Mr. and Mrs. White, Alida, Mary, Mercedes and David Challinor. I love the look of pride on my grandfather's face.

Mercedes felt it her solemn duty to maintain the foothold he had won. She arranged to have Mom "come out" as a debutante along with her Convent school friend, Alida White, granddaughter of the architect Stanford White. Mom balked at the plan, but rather than fight her mother, who was definitely a force to be reckoned with, she took the path of least resistance and submitted. For Mom, parental conflict was simply something to endure, to weather like a storm. Thus she framed Mercy's adventure not as an escape from Dad, but as an impulse towards growth, a forward movement towards new horizons, both within and without. Certainly Mercy presented it to her this way: in her letters to Mom from Jackson, Wyoming, she expressed her fear of stagnating. She was not afraid of Dad's disapproval. In Jackson, she had already removed herself from him. He was less of an adversary than a nuisance—a roadblock she had to maneuver around.

As I learned after Dad's death in 1996, if blame was cast when Mercy disappeared, it was he who cast it: "Your father blamed me for Mercy's death," Mom said bitterly more than once and usually with a vodka-on-ice in hand. "He told me that it was my fault—that I encouraged her to go. He said if I'd been a good wife, I would have sided with him and told her not to go and she'd still be alive." At this point she would break off and take a deep breath. Then let it out and with it, a burst of pent-up passion. "But there was nothing wrong with her going off!" she would exclaim. "She made an unwise choice getting on that boat, but there was nothing morally wrong with her wanting to see the world. It was an accident," she argued. "She could have been killed crossing the street at home!"

When Mom said this she was arguing with herself as well as with Dad's ghost. She didn't address the notion that her intervention could have kept Mercy at home. Maybe she could have stopped Mercy from leaving—but most likely not. Certainly if she had sided with Dad, the conflict would have been worse, perhaps cut her off from any communication with Mercy, and she was not about to sacrifice her relationship with a child on the altar of marital duty. Her role as a mother was primary in her life, and as a mother, she looked at her children's choices with a moral compass: was the course chosen right or wrong? If she believed it was right—or at least, if she found nothing wrong, if she saw no sin—she supported the choice.

Dad, however, wasn't focused on moral right or wrong. He was entirely pragmatic. He was asking Mom to protect Mercy (as he believed was the duty of them both) from the risks involved in a South Seas adventure. Implicit in the accusation that Mom was not a good wife, was the even crueler accusation that she was not a good mother—that she had not protected Mercy as she should have.

When Mom had married Dad in 1941, she had promised to "honor and obey" him. Dad was twenty-eight. She was eighteen and eager to begin her own life. For her, as for her mother Mercedes before her, a wartime romance provided an exciting exit from the parental domain. If the word "obey" in her marriage vows gave pause, it was easy enough to dismiss it as traditional formula. But it is likely that Mom accepted the concept of wifely obedience as a given. She was very much in love with Dad. He not only had the authority of being ten years older, he was a

Captain in the Army, a leader of men. Deferring to him (a soft version of obedience) would have been natural. Moreover, at the Convent, both in her day, as well as in Sheila's and mine, it was drummed into us that obedience, be it marital or monastic, was a virtue, an ideal to strive for.

Good Girls bowed to authority with humility and grace, just as the Virgin Mary had bowed to the will of God when an angel announced that He had chosen her to be the mother of the Christ. "Behold the handmaid of the Lord, be it done unto me according to Thy will."

Thirty-six years and nine children later, traditional roles were being questioned. In 1977, thanks to the feminist movement, the idea of a "good wife" was under attack as a patriarchal stereotype. The Good Wife, the obedient helpmate of the family breadwinner, had lost credibility, especially in the novels of Margaret Drabble and Doris Lessing whom Mom read and admired. What shimmered in the air, along with

Mary Challinor as bride, 1941

the notion of equal pay in the workplace, was the idea of self-realization for both partners in a marriage. By the nineteen seventies, the word "obey" had vanished from a wife's marriage vows. In 1967 when Andy and I were married, along with the "for richer and poorer, in sickness and health", we promised to "cherish" each other "as long as we both shall live."

When I asked her about Dad's accusation, Mom didn't—or wouldn't—remember if he was repetitive with it. Did he harp on it? "It's all your fault?" I imagine not. I imagine it was something that came out of him once in a burst of anger—a kind of bitter "if only". But whether once or many times, Dad's blame wounded her irreparably.

In 2008, I asked her how she managed to get through that time. "I walked," she said. "I walked and I walked and I walked. I would have gone out of my mind if I hadn't. It's true what they say about exercise being an important way to relieve stress." Every morning that winter, she would get up at six, bundle up in coat, scarf and gloves, and walk four miles down and back our road. It was dark and cold, but peaceful. There was no traffic that early, but there were other walkers and they would exchange pleasantries as they passed each other. "It was very friendly," she remembered. "People would say hello, talk about the ducks that had just had babies."

On the first mile of her walk, old maple trees arched over the road and on clear mornings, she would have seen the stars fading between their bare branches. The road sloped down to a picturesque stone bridge and a river-fed pond where ducks, herons and egrets nest in its marshy banks. Past the bridge, the road curved through residential woods to a rough stone boulder that bore a bronze plaque commemorating the fact that George Washington "had passed this spot on his way to Boston" in February 1756, June 1775, and October 1789. This was her halfway mark: here she would turn around and start back home.

The exercise itself, as well as the quiet beauty of the landscape, would be a balm for anyone, but for Mom, the route was a walk back into her past. She remembered when the road from Firwood to the bridge was dirt. It had not been paved until after World War II. She remembered when there were fields on either side of the maple allée instead of expensive new houses. And on the far side of the Pond, when she walked past the mossy stone gateposts of an older subdivision, she remembered when it had been her Uncle Cyril's Glenbreeken Farm.

Cyril was Mercedes' older brother. Their father bought the farm in 1897, a year after he bought Firwood. In his diary he noted that "the improvements on the farm have cost me quite a lot" but justified the expense with the hope that it would not only provide food for his table, but a healthy diversion for his eleven children. As a boy Cyril, one of the younger Crimmins children, took the most interest in the farm and, along with a hired poultryman, raised a great variety of chickens, ducks and geese and won ribbons for them at the Danbury State Fair. In August of 1913, John D. noted proudly that Glenbreeken was supplying Firwood with 30 dozen eggs a week, rabbits, pigs, milk from five Jersey cows, "pears and plums and figs all in abundance." Cyril inherited the farm and made improvements of his own: he converted the farmhouse to a manor house with an atrium, a "tea room" and a formal garden. After World War I, he married a Boston showgirl, a dancer in a chorus line, named Katherine Daly, and they had two sons. Although Cyril's sisters, especially Constance and Mercedes, snobbishly disapproved of Katherine, Mom often visited her Uncle Cyril's farm. She remembered that he kept carrier pigeons, a pet Irish donkey, and reindeer. He also had a white showboat parked on the banks of their pond—a party house. "Aunt Katherine was wonderful with us kids," Mom recalled. "She was so kind to us. She used to take us out for ice cream in her Pierce Arrow. She would sing to us as she drove and tell us stories about circuses and clowns. "It was a lovely car," she added wistfully. "Dark green."

These memories, prompted and intensified by the actual place, were a distraction from fantasies of Mercy blue-lipped and shivering in an ice-coated life raft. Or sun-blistered and shriveled. Or drowning in the dark—if, as Captain Hunt posited, the *I Love You II* had been run down at night by a freighter. "I had to have something to occupy my mind," Mom told me. So she turned to the past, to her grandfather's diary.

John D. Crimmins had kept detailed records of his life: notes in daily pocket diaries as well as longer accounts in ledgers, one on his desk in New York, another at Firwood. After his death in 1917, several of his daughters edited these into a privately printed tome. Most of the 700 pages are accounts of his business transactions—his real estate deals—as well as his political appointments (among offices held, he served as the first Commissioner of Central Park), many charitable works (such as organizing a relief committee after the San Francisco earthquake and fire) and his social contacts, of whom most are today obscure. (Sir Thomas Lipton, W.B. Yeats, Sir Ernest Shackleton are among the few names I recognize.) Mom had the idea of making a shorter, more accessible, edition of the diary for us kids. So she began teaching herself to touch type, and practiced on excerpts from the diary. The passages she chose for her edition were about John D.'s family life at Firwood. She found solace in reading about the life of the house a hundred years before. The project offered a sense of continuity—the reassurance that despite sorrow and loss, the family, with its many branches and offshoots, had multiplied and flourished. "I knew the house," she told me. "I knew all its sounds and smells. I knew the views of the water from every window."

She also found it interesting to get to know the man who had raised her mother and her aunts and uncles. On the surface of it, John D. Crimmins was a kindred spirit: he loved Firwood, as she loved it. He loved its gardens and grounds, took the same pride in his plantings that Mom took in hers. Never mind the fact that he had a staff of six gardeners while she did all the mowing and digging and hauling by herself. (She had a gasoline-powered mower, six feet across, and walking behind it in madras shorts and a sleeveless blouse, she would mow the three-acre lawn that sloped down to the sea wall.) John D., like Mom, had filled the house full of children. He was not a hands-on father—after the death of his wife, a maiden aunt and a nurse raised the children—but he enjoyed watching them grow into individuals, just as he enjoyed monitoring the trees he planted. In a September 1898 entry during the Spanish-American war, he describes how his son Martin [22] had enlisted as one of Teddy Roosevelt's Rough Riders, then goes on to take stock of the rest of his brood:

> John [25] is very attentive to business and takes no vacation. Tom [18] is ambitious
> to graduate from Harvard in 1900. He is required to work at his studies and I
> am satisfied that he will in after life better apply his work to his occupation than
> more brilliant boys. Mary Christine [20] assumes more of the responsibility of the

position that she occupies as the eldest of her sisters, in their care, and in that of the house. Her timidity will pass as her responsibilities increase. Constance [15] has been in better health than she has been in for years. Her sweet disposition and many charms make her most popular. Mercedes [13] is robust and enters into all healthful exercises with spirit. She promises to be a beautiful Woman. Evelyn [12] is always thoughtful and with a disposition that wins favor. Cyril [14] is a most excellent prudent boy, never requires to be spoken to for omissions for he does not appear to have any. Clarence [10] is full of energy, rides and swims well and is absorbed in his pets—a good boy, not so rigid looking as I would have wished, but never ill. Cyril and he assumed partnership in the care of their pets. I must attribute to Cyril their happy cooperation for I believe that Clarence is more aggressive and if not managed with tact, would assert himself.

Like Mom, John D. saw his children through illness and accidents, He grieved when his oldest son John lost his right eye at age 16 in a shooting accident but was proud at the "manly" way John faced the subsequent ordeal of surgery—an operation attended by a priest and performed in their New York townhouse. When Martin, at age 20, was thrown from his horse during a steeplechase and "received a serious shock to his head, producing contusion of the brain and [temporary] paralysis," John D. was both angry and anxious:

> I was greatly disturbed by this. Martin has met with several accidents, which I must attribute to his indifference to my advice. He is at school at the University of Virginia and traveled to Richmond to ride without having any experience with the horse on the course he rode over. His life was spared thank God and I have hopes that he will guide his life under reasonable conditions at least.

These selections from the diary present a benign Victorian gentleman who enjoyed his wealth, kept careful account of his investments and expenses, took pleasure in overseeing his gardens and orchard, and was devoted to his wife and family. But reading between the lines of the original tome, Mom had a rather different take on him. "I wondered why he went away to Florida to fish all winter

John D. Crimmins and his family at Firwood, about 1890, two or three years after his wife Lily died after the birth of Clarence (cross legged on the floor) in 1888. My grandmother, Mercedes, sits on her sister Susie's lap. Lily Irene, far right, took on the role of "little mother" to her siblings, until she died at age 18.

when his wife was having baby after baby, year after year. The poor woman—I'd have killed him! He was very willful. He wouldn't let Mother go overseas with the Red Cross during World War I—she had to wait till he died. And he wouldn't let Aunt Connie remarry after her husband died." (Mercedes' sister Constance became a widow when she was pregnant with her son Freddy Childs and remained a widow the rest of her life.) The girls in the family submitted to their father's will—or got around it—and he indulged them:

> The girls have their numerous occupations and engagements. . .and expect me to keep them going and never have a thought what it costs me or how I labor. Well, that is women's ways. I don't expect them to reason more than women will. I find no fault.

Mercedes told me that when World War I broke out, her father drew the line at paying for the upkeep of her beagle pack. To John D., it was an unseemly luxury. "We all have to make sacrifices," he told her. But she was not about to give up her hounds. "I sold all my jewelry for puppy feed," she used to say—with pride rather than regret.

John D. paid his sons' bills as well, but his expectations for the boys were higher than those for the girls. "I think he was very domineering," Mom decided. "The boys all hit the bottle—all except Uncle Tom." Mercedes told me how she had accompanied her brother Tom down to the Bowery, then a dockside slum at the bottom of Manhattan, to search for a drunken brother—probably John or Clarence.

Mercedes with a puppy treat in her front pocket.

John D. described his own drinking as "temperate—that is, I will take a hot whiskey and sometimes a glass of wine," and he went on to deplore "quarrels and exhibitions of temper and language" created by excess drinking. "The man who never tasted liquor is best off," he remarked. I imagine there must have been as many alcohol-fueled battles of will in John D's day as there were in ours. Near the end of his life, John D. expressed disappointment that his sons were not more "responsible" and, on account of their "indifference" to "family requirements", he deeded his beloved Firwood to the girls.

As for the boys, Cyril was a "good son" and was Tom was "the responsible one"; Tom became an engineer, took over the family construction business, and settled across the road from Firwood. John, the oldest who had lost his eye, succumbed to alcoholism. Martin, the avid horseman, escaped into the Army, and afterward to California. Clarence, the youngest, also died of drink. After serving in France in World War I, he stayed in Paris and became an expat barfly who lived at the Ritz. He died in 1931 with the Ritz bartender in attendance. He never came home. "He was probably gay," Mom speculated. "There are pictures of him on the beach dressed up in women's bathing dresses." She did not include the pictures in her edition of the diary and I have not been able to find them.

Families in the nineteenth century were more acquainted with death than families today. John D. and Lily Lalor had two babies who died before their second birthday. Lily herself died in 1888 after the birth of Clarence, the thirteenth child. After her death, her namesake, Lily Irene at age ten became the chief comforter of her father and took on the role of substitute mother for the younger children. When she died in 1897 at age eighteen, John. D. declared himself "twice-widowed". Here is his account of her death:

> For more than seven years, when events have occurred which I have considered important enough to write down, they have been of character pleasing and joyful. Today I am full of sadness and grief. On Monday morning, November the fourth at one o'clock an angel left her temporary abode here on earth to enter Heaven where her Mother will meet her. My heart, my beautiful good child, Lily Irene died of typhoid fever after an illness of just twenty-one days. She had been visiting Boston, Newport, and Stockbridge, Massachusetts where she in all probability took the germ into her system that developed into the fatal disease. My dear child had graduated from the Convent of the Sacred Heart, Manhattanville, at the same Convent where her mother had graduated some thirty-one years before. On the occasion she wore the silver and gold medal worn by her mother on her graduation… Lily was born on a bright morning the first day of June 1877. I was

present at her birth. Her mother was particularly well, and her labors were but for a moment. She came into this world in gentleness, and she left it as she had lived, gentle and loving to everyone. . .

In so many ways she was so like her dear Mother that hundreds of times I was reminded of her Mother's presence and in her features the resemblance was striking. She was somewhat taller but erect and most dignified in appearance. I had never seen either of my Lily's in ungraceful attitudes. . .

God knowest best and while my heart is overflowing with sorrow, it is loneliness, for I miss her in every place. For the three weeks of her illness I was near her every night and she was anxious for me to be near her. . .

Mercedes, who was ten when her sister Lily died, told me that on their way to her funeral, driving down Fifth Avenue to St. Patrick's cathedral, their cortege passed the wedding procession of Consuelo Vanderbilt who was to marry the Duke of Marlborough at St. Thomas's Episcopal Church. She was 18, the same age as Lily, and she had captured the public imagination with her beauty and the widely reported drama of her marriage. Although she was in love with, and secretly engaged to, a man named Winthrop Rutherford, her parents were determined to marry her off—or more accurately, to sell her off—to the Duke of Marlborough. Mrs. Vanderbilt was determined to make her daughter a Duchess. She locked Consuelo in her room to prevent her from eloping with Rutherford, threatened to murder the man, then faked illness and on her "death bed" forced a promise from Consuelo that she would marry the Duke. At the ceremony, immediately after the couple was pronounced man and wife, Consuelo's father William Vanderbilt handed the groom a check for 2.4 million dollars.

The ten-year-old Mercedes must have craned her neck in the funeral carriage for a glimpse of the bride. According to Harper's Weekly, she wore a silk gown by Worth with a high collar encrusted with pearls and diamonds, huge leg-o-mutton sleeves, and a tiny waist. But what impressed Mercedes even more than Consuelo's wedding finery was her father's severe comment: "Our Lily is far better off where she is now than that poor girl."

John D. himself had married up. Lily Lalor was, as Mom put it, "well-born." He started out as a laborer for his father, Thomas Crimmins, who worked as the head gardener on a large estate on the east side of Manhattan Island (now midtown New York). The estate belonged to fellow Irishman Thomas Addis Emmet. After Emmet's death, Thomas Crimmins and his two sons were given the business of subdividing the land, building streets and selling off lots. John D. never went to college. But unlike the Duke of Marlborough, he had married for love. The Christmas after his wife Lily's death, he reflected:

Lily Lalor Crimmins

> A part of a whole we were part of each other, fond trusting and loving. . .Twenty-two years ago I called on her. Twenty-one years ago I loved her and to me she was betrothed. My heart and her heart were glad and young. Twenty years ago she was my bride from the 15th of April. Every Christmas since, my first greeting was to the love of my heart. We never had sorrow all those years, for the consolation we found in each other, grief was soon forgotten as we forgot everything but each other.

It was not only the prospect of a loveless marriage that drew John D.'s pity for the unhappy Consuelo. His faith in an afterlife was both unshakable and literal. In the same Christmas Day entry quoted above, he professed his belief that Lily was "looking down on me and our dear children with the eyes of that beautiful soul, so worthy of a place in the exalted mansion of the good Lord. I believe in the Communion of Saints which our Church teaches, and [I believe that] death is not a separation, not a cessation of sympathy, nor is it the breaking of the ties of affection, for they who are dead in Christ are with us and they are nearer to us than they were in the days of their mortal life."

Mom too was a devout Catholic. But although she attended daily Mass during the year Mercy was lost, and found comfort in the early-morning quiet of the Church and the familiar ritual of the liturgy, she did not feel that Mercy was "nearer" to her. She doubted that Jesus' promise of "life everlasting" meant personal survival after death, and even if that proved to be the case, she found it hard to believe, as her grandfather believed, that her daughter would be "better off" looking down on her from heaven than alive and kicking on this earth. When I asked her what she prayed for, she said: "I just said 'God help me get through this'. And I said, 'Protect her'.

undated postcard
Nuku'alofa, Tonga

Hello, here in the kingdom of Tonga nice place, this little island.

People so friendly and united (religion-wise).

Staying in a guest house with other Americans and New Zealanders.

Moving out today to live with a family i met here...feel very well, thank-you. And y'all?....hope every thing brings a good and productive winter....

thinking of getting to New Zealand in Nov. till then c/o Gen Del. Nuku'alota Tonga.

THE
TONGA ROYAL FAMILY
Their Majesties and the Future
of Tonga

Prince 'Alaivahamama'o, Princess Pilolevu
Prince Tupouto'a (Crown Prince); Prince 'Ahe'eitu
His Majesty: THE KING TAUFA'AHAU TUPOU IV
and QUEEN HALAEVALU MATA'AHO

19

The Mass for Mercy served Mom's purpose: well-meaning people stopped telling her not to worry, that Mercy would turn up. If some members of the family at large privately still held out hope, they could not dismiss what Mom and Dad had been going through for the last four months. "It's a tragedy!" Joan Challinor, Mom's sister-in-law, announced dramatically. "A tragedy!" Tragedy or trauma, the Mass declared Mercy's loss and marked the absorption of it into the consciousness of family and friends. Outside this circle, however, disbelief and denial were still in force. When Tommy, the youngest of us and closest to Mercy, told the headmaster of his school that his sister had been lost at sea, there were no condolences, no expressions of sympathy from teachers, no announcement to the student body. The same was true of Mercy's school Darrow: when the headmaster heard about Mercy's loss from her friends, he wrote Mom expressing his hope that she was safe.

Two weeks after the Mass, on the other side of the world, the New Zealand Herald ran a feature story with a 48 point headline: WHERE IS MERCY EWING? At the top of the story was a head shot of Mercy looking sullen and annoyed. Under a dark cloud of short curly hair, her eyebrows are beginning to frown. She is glancing impatiently away from the camera and her mouth is pouty. I think it must have been one of the many photos of her Jessie had taken during their trip to Scotland. "She was bugged at me for taking her picture all the time," Jessie remembered.

The caption under the photo read: "Mercy Ewing. . .Rich, Pretty, and Loved." Mom mailed

It is hard to use either present or past tense to talk about Mercedes Ewing; few people believe she is still alive. In fact, a requiem was said for her two weeks ago in Connecticut. SUSAN MAXWELL *asks ...*

SECTION 2 ★ NZ Herald, Saturday, April 15, 1978

WHERE IS MERCY EWING?

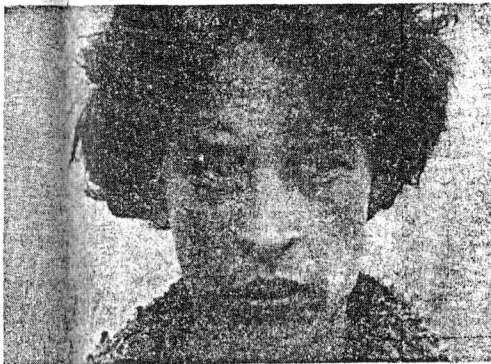

● Mercy Ewing . . . rich, pretty and loved.

AT this moment, a lone yachtsman called Steve Abney is heading for isolated Pacific outcrops, making what will probably be a last search for the girl he called Mercy, or any trace of the yacht on which she and three companions left Tonga last November and sailed into mysterious oblivion.

The yacht was a 57ft catamaran called I Love You II and its estimated date of arrival in New Zealand was December 1, more than four months ago. The yacht sailed from the Vava'u group of northern Tonga and there has since been no confirmed sighting in spite of

mentioned Abney in her last letters. They had become close friends.

But their relationship had a time limit. Steve Abney had to reach New Zealand by December, and Mercy wanted to go with him in the Brita. Like any serious solo sailor, however, Abney firmly ruled out passengers on long voyages.

He had his own rugged survival standards and did not involve anyone else in his risks. He tried to find her passage on another yacht.

Towards the end of October, the big catamaran ILU2 berthed at Neiafu. Abney knew the yacht and its crew from other ports and introduced Mercy to the skipper, a retired airline pilot, Donald Glidden, aged about 50.

ILU2's crew was Tiare McMillan, a 27-year-old

checked out by the police, the marine division of the Ministry of Transport assumed ILU2 had been lost between Tonga and New Zealand. As a routine measure, ships were alerted to watch for the yacht or its wreckage. RNZAF flights were instructed to do the same.

Search and rescue workers from Tonga, Fiji, French Polynesia and Samoa were also involved. Ham radio operators were alerted.

FROM high in the Waitakere Hills in Auckland, Noel Curtis operates an amateur radio network by which he keeps track of yachts in the Pacific, alert for distress calls or to provide any assistance yachties might need.

On December 11, he broadcast information

on its way to New Zealand from Tonga should have been.

Wreckage does drift, but Captain Frank Hunt, who has headed inquiries from the marine division headquarters in Wellington, says that the drifting hull's position was inconsistent with the planned voyage of the ILU2.

It was thousands of miles too far south-west of where prevailing currents would take the wreckage of a vessel that foundered between Tonga and New Zealand.

With his knowledge of marine drift, Captain Hunt says that if the ILU2 was wrecked on its way to New Zealand, the remains would by now be back in the Tonga or the Lau Island groups or practically at Cape Horn and stated the Mercy

region of the Kermadecs. Mr Ewing hired a private plane and flew around the pendulum area for about five hours.

That hope thwarted, he rang radio operator Noel Curtis in Titirangi. By this time, Curtis and his wife, Marion, had a thick wad of information that had filtered in over the radio waves about the missing yacht — some fact, some rumour, mostly hearsay.

"Buck Ewing told me he'd been to Samoa, Tonga and was now in Paihia. He was just desperate to get information about his daughter," said Mr Curtis.

Days later, the weary banker — a man in his 60s — arrived in Titirangi. Noel and Marion Curtis warmed to him at once and they spent the afternoon pooling their facts and examining the rumours.

ado. She knew how to live off the land.

Little is known of the fourth passenger, young Steven Wolf.

Abney considers it is his responsibility to explore several parts of the map where he thinks the crew might have drifted.

Mrs Curtis remembers Abney's morose sentiment that Mercy would have been safely in New Zealand if he had relented and carried a passenger.

Although Abney was determined to test his theory on survival chances with or without financial assistance, Mr Curtis arranged for Mr Ewing to remit a modest sum of

$US500 to cover the yachtsman's fuel and supplies.

★ ★ ★

WILL Abney find anything other searches have missed?

"No," says Captain Hunt, of the marine division. Nevertheless, he lent his marine drift expertise to suggest several places where Abney might look.

The determined lone sailor left New Zealand at Easter, bound for Tonga via the uninhabited Hunter and Matthew islands.

He will also take a look at Minerva Reef, the scene of a dramatic survival epic in 1962 when a Tongan captain and 11 of his crew lived for three months off their wits and fish.

Abney, no doubt, has personal theories on what happened to the yacht and crew. Noel Curtis expects to hear from him when he reaches Tonga.

"I'm not expecting him to find Mercy in a grass skirt," he says. "I just feel that if anyone can find one piece of information that might put us in the picture about what happened, it will be Steve."

★ ★ ★

FROM Connecticut, Buck Ewing is still making hopeful calls to Noel Curtis and Captain Hunt several times a week, even after the requiem for Mercy.

Does he think Steve Abney's search will find his daughter?

"I don't really think so. But I don't like to leave any stone unturned."

me a Xeroxed copy and when I saw caption and photo, I wanted to hide it. Never mind the unpretty photo. The caption made me cringe. How much money one had was unmentionable. It was against the rules, like fighting dirty or showing off. Moreover, despite the privileges of our background, neither Mom, nor any of us children felt rich. We had no access to family money. Dad controlled it all, even the inheritance Mom had received from her mother Mercedes. To all of us, including Mom, he doled out a monthly allowance. In college, my allowance was $300 a month for books and clothes. After I graduated in June 1964, I was expected to earn my own keep—my allowance was for extras. Mercy, like the rest of us, had gone to private schools, had enjoyed sailing on the *Maria* in Long Island Sound, and vacations in Bermuda. Certainly, her allowance from Dad permitted her to save up enough money for her trip—without it, she would have had to work a lot longer to buy her travel tickets. Nonetheless, given her hand-to-mouth existence in Jackson, the description of her as "rich" jarred.

Inserted into the body of the article's text, the Herald had provided its readers with an artist's sketch of a catamaran adrift on an ocean map. Tonga was located in the upper right hand corner and Australia in the lower left. The catamaran was crewless, hatches battened down, sails sagging bereft of wind—a picture that evoked the doomed ship of Coleridge's "Ancient Mariner" becalmed on a "painted sea" rather than a boat lost in a cyclone. Below the illustration, in a large, black box, was a blown-up quote from Dad: "Just tell me, is Mercy dead or alive?" This sounded more like a line from a soap opera than something he would have said. Maybe it was a misquote. Maybe he'd said: "I just want to know if Mercy is dead." I could hear him saying that in his flat, sad, matter-of-fact voice. But not the pumped-up quote in the black box.

The article unsettled me. Mom guarded her privacy closely and having Mercy's disappearance exposed to the world must have gone against her grain. She was not about to fight it, however. "They think it might flush out some new information," she explained to me on the phone and her voice sounded wearily resigned.

"They" turned out to be Noel Curtis. The story was his idea. With Dad's permission, he had contacted a reporter named Susan Maxwell. Given the complexity of the story, she did a masterful job of weaving its myriad threads into a coherent narrative. There are a few minor errors. Dad is said to have eight children and in fact we were nine. Mercy is described as "tall and blond" but she was 5'6" with light brown hair. But what struck me most about the article was Maxwell's focus—the "handle" she had used to make the story newsworthy. Despite the headline and photo, the piece was not really about Mercy being lost at sea. It was about Dad's search for her.

"The single extraordinary element," Maxwell wrote, "in what might otherwise be a not uncommon tale of "lost in the Pacific" is that every day since the search began, Mercedes Ewing's father has been in touch with search and rescue headquarters of the marine division in Wellington." Lost yachts commonplace? The notion was a shock to me. How many yachts disappeared each year into the vastness of the Pacific? It also was shocking to think that my father was a rarity: did no one else come looking for lost sailors?

In Maxwell's story, Mercy is a secondary character—the privileged, outdoorsy daughter who wanted to see the Pacific "without the rosy spectacles that wealth usually provides." Dad is the main character. He is the devoted father, anguished over Mercy's loss, obsessive in his search. Nothing unfactual there—but it's not entirely true, either. The implication is that they were close, that they had a tender, loving relationship. Even the conflict he had with Mercy sounded benign— as if he were Father Knows Best dealing out kindly advice:

> From Connecticut, her father told the Herald: "To be honest, I tried to persuade her not to go off by herself. But she was very strong willed. She wanted to see the world and I couldn't influence her."

Noel Curtis is cast as the sympathetic rescuer and impresario:

> "From high in the Waitakere Hills in Auckland, Noel Curtis operates an amateur radio network by which he keeps track of yachts in the Pacific, alert for distress calls or to provide any assistance yachties might need."

And for love interest, there was Steve Abney, sailing off on a futile search, guilt-ridden at having refused Mercy passage on his own boat:

> Abney considers it is his responsibility to explore several parts of the map where he thinks the crew might have drifted.

Mrs. Curtis remembers Abney's morose sentiment that Mercy would have been in New Zealand if he had relented and carried a passenger.

Of Abney's search, Noel Curtis stated, "I'm not expecting him to find Mercy in a grass skirt. I just feel that if anyone can find one piece of information that might put us in the picture about what happened, it will be Steve."

Maxwell ends the article with her question to Dad: Does he believe Steve Abney will find Mercy?

Dad: "I don't really think so. But I don't like to leave any stone unturned."

I suppose I let Andy read the clipping, but I don't remember discussing it with any of my brothers and sisters and I did not show it to any of my friends. I tucked it away in a shoebox of saved letters.

In 2007, I found it again. I also found Susan Maxwell via the web and we talked on the phone. She told me she had been twenty-five when she wrote her "Where is Mercy Ewing?" story and she had already risen through the Herald's ranks and established herself as a popular columnist and feature writer. In 1981, she was part of the royal press corps that covered the wedding of Prince Charles and Diana. Maxwell went on to write three admiring books about Diana. While on vacation in Hawaii, she met and married an airline pilot who also was a bandleader. They settled in California. Maxwell became a singer in her husband's band. At the time we talked, she was still performing with her husband. She also volunteered as a photojournalist for her community newspaper and gave inspirational talks on "the People's Princess." Not surprisingly, she did not remember details of the story she had written almost thirty years before. Nonetheless, I was disappointed that she could give me no picture of Noel Curtis. (Was he Dad's generation? From the tone and diction of his letters, I thought he probably was.) On the other hand, she did recall talking on the phone to Dad. "I had to get permission from the editor to make an international phone call," she said. "Your father did not believe she was alive."

Our conversation whetted Susan's investigative appetite: she urged me to contact the New Zealand police and obtain the report that determined the *I Love You II* had made landfall in Manugonai. She also suggested searching for Steve Abney or even Scott Glidden, the son of the *I Love You II*'s captain. Both might still be alive and might inform my story. But after weeks of Internet searches, emails and international phone calls, I was no closer to new information. Thirty-year-old records had been lost as bureaucracies had morphed. When I managed to track down an eighty year old man in American Samoa who had been aboard the *I Love You II* on the voyage before Mercy's, I was told he had died two weeks before and had been buried at sea. I searched on line for obituaries in New Zealand but neither Captain Hunt's name, nor Noel Curtis' came up. I called Glidden families across the country without finding Scott. I

"On the Brink." From my 2016 "Discovering Inanna" woodcut series.

felt I was at the edge of a compulsive vortex; that I might sucked into an endless drama of futile searching and lose the story in front of me. That I might get lost—the way Dad had been lost. So I called it quits.

October 9, 1977
Naku'alofa, Tonga

10/9

Dear Ma,

Thanks for your letter...drizzling, overcast day...good for sitting around the guest house, writing letters & listening to the guitars being played...

Tonga tapu is the main island of Tonga and i've been here about a week...riding bikes (the island is absolutely flat, not one hill) flying kites & swimming... been very nice, a lot of contact with other Americans, New Zealanders & Australians...soon i want to get out to some of the other islands...they're supposed to be very beautiful...cliffs, hills, fjords. i'll probably go over with some German people staying here...lots of Germans around Tonga...

The people here are much more westernized than Fiji. It surprised me, cuz Tonga is much more out of the way & not so many tourists.....every one living in wooden houses with tables & chairs... that they use! Fijians sometimes have tables & chairs but they never use them.

i went out to live with a family...and only stayed for

235

one nite...really young couple with a child...The husband came home really drunk...bad vibes...Tongas drink a lot...seems like so many are "suffering in the land"... Many go to New Zealand to make money & get kicked out for some reason or other & now are stuck back in Tonga....i'm hoping it will be different on the outer islands...But money's important every where (except in the backs of Fiji)

Learning about people, you say? i find at this point i'm learning so much more about myself... i mean, everything always comes back to ME. i think more about how i acted in a situation than about the other person. Just my ego-centric way...but i am learning about my self, positively & negatively. i consciously try to learn about others but i usually come back to how i acted & reacted...Maybe it will change...i guess & hope the more i move (or just live) the more i'll be able to absorb..

I'm having a problem of being able to trust people (friends or foe?) so its hard to learn about them.

Letters are becoming a drag...i wrote so many at first cuz i was so incredibly homesick...But it's starting to pass at last! i could feel myself wishing time would speed up and I could be on my way back to the States...But its different now...i realize that the

236

things & people who really matter will still be there when I get back...whenever i get back. Letters now seem an empty & futile attempt to explain what going on... no one will ever understand what's happening here around me & within me ...its kind of nice sometimes... it makes the voyage very intimate.

i guess i'm planning on being in New Zealand in November sometime. It will be well into summer by then...lots of work picking fruit...I guess I don't need to work, with that bundle of money at home...but i like working too...ya know?

The more i think about it the more logical it seems to come home through Asia instead of back across the Pacific. Around the world!!! I don't know if I could handle it by myself. Woman alone in the streets of Asia. What do you do when you can't trust any one? i'd have to latch on to some one else if i was going to go through with it.

It could delay my return home some what...If i'm gonna go around the world i'd take my time maybe 2, 2 1/2 years. I don't think i could handle traveling that long....but i'm meeting so many people who have been going around the world for 4 years!!!!! & some are still so enthused & have such fresh feelings about seeing new

Figi Elitias family

<u>places and people</u>! I've been sending home some packages along the way. A small one from Fiji has slides in it. Maybe you've already gotten it. The big one has some film and one from Tonga has some baskets and tapa cloth.

Well, the kettle's boiling-time for tea.. the Kiwis & Aussies think i'm most uncivilized cuz i don't have milk in my tea....only the female mosquito will bite you, cuz she needs the blood to feed her babies. There are 2,750 different kinds of mosquitoes, some only bite in the day, some only bite at dusk & some can fly in the rain -- dodging rain drops. Their wings beat 250-600 times a second... i quit smoking again..back in Fiji. & my boils have finally fled...went to another doctor in Suva & he said i was allergic to the hepro & that mosquitoes are causing my infections...some mosquitoes bite turtles through their shells...some bite on ants...And did you know that mosquitoes where responsible for the Louisiana Purchase?

The above information on mosquitoes was taken from a reader digest article. bzzzzzzzzzzz.

Well i'm running out of thoughts...i'd like to see your new sitting room...nice windows... right next to your room.. hope all goes well through out the winter...doubt if i'll be home for Christmas, but send me the names of who i give presents too, and i'll try and do something- Much love.

Jessie's photo of Mercy between Fritz and Billy on the sofa at Christmas.

20

Jessie's photo of Mom at Firwood's seawall, after Mercy was lost.

By the end of May, two months after Steve Abney sailed from New Zealand, and six weeks after the New Zealand Herald ran Susan Maxwell's article, Dad had heard nothing from Abney. True to form, Dad made repeated calls to Noel Curtis. No doubt he asked the same question over and over: "What sort of fella is Steve Abney?"

On May 28 1978, Curtis wrote Dad another long typed letter, this one four single-spaced pages in response to "our last two telephone talks." He stands firm on his original position that Abney was "right man to look for traces of ILU2 and Mercedes". He assures Dad that he is certain that "in my long talks" with Abney, the sailor told the truth "as he saw it" regarding the background and history of the *I Love You II* before she left Tonga. Curtis then launches into full disclosure:

> At the same time, I am just as certain that there were some aspects of that history he withheld. . .in many respects he is something of an enigma. Of the many cruising yachtsmen/women we spoke to about the ILU2 (all of whom had met Abney) very, very few spoke well of him. . .
>
> The women, in particular, as a rule said little but indicated their dislike of him by gesture or facial expression. These women, all of them, were no longer young.
>
> Younger women were undoubted attracted to Steve by sheer animal magnetism. For example, Susan Maxwell the journalist was impressed by Steve in her somewhat fleeting contact with him. Mercedes would have been, too, I am sure. . .
>
> [He is] physically as strong as a horse and nimble as a cat. 6'4" or so and weighs about 220. Trim in build, moved quickly and quietly. He knows how to live simply and cheaply from land and sea.

Later in his letter, Curtis submits that even his wife Marney was not immune to Abney's charm and that she had "friendly feelings" for him.

Curtis reports that he had heard no criticism of Abney's seamanship, and he admits that dislike from older yachting crowd didn't necessarily mean much: "As a class, the very yachtsmen interviewed would be regarded as screw-balls or nuts themselves by most people just because of their way of life. We have heard it said many times that to be a long distance ocean voyager in a yacht, you have to be a nut!"

During talks with Curtis, Steve Abney had evaded questions about his personal life so Curtis knew nothing of his background other than he had lived in California and had served in the US Navy—presumably during the Vietnam War. When Curtis asked him what his plans for the future were, he replied, "I'm just going to keep sailing."

The fact that Abney refused to "tell all" was not only irritating to Curtis. It made him suspicious. He wondered aloud to Dad where Abney had gotten the money to own a yacht "in the higher price bracket".

The main complaint that Curtis heard about Abney was that, in Captain Frank Hunt's words, "he spends too much of his time in poor company." Curtis does not speculate on what "poor company" meant. Was Captain Hunt referring to pot-smoking hippies—kids like Mercy? Or was "poor company" an understatement for criminal elements—for drug runners? I should think that if Hunt knew for certain that Abney was involved in criminal activities, he would have warned both Curtis and Dad. In any case, as Curtis points out to Dad, although Captain Hunt and his colleague Captain Collins made "disparaging remarks" about Abney, "neither of them had ever set eyes on him."

Moreover, as Curtis reminds Dad, the crew of *Pegasus*, the yacht on which Abney had found work, were "high in their praise" of him. "The implication is that they got to know Steve," he points out. He concludes the discussion with: "Whatever the pros and cons, whatever the likes and dislikes, I am sure Steve is very fond of Mercedes. . .both Marney and I sincerely believe that Steve became deeply attached to Mercy because she was one of the few nice and honorable companions he had ever known." By pouring oil on troubled waters of Steve Abney's reticence and his"poor company", Curtis is not only reassuring Dad, but justifying his own decision to spend Dad's money on Abney's search.

During these phone conversations with Curtis about Abney, Dad mentioned that he had heard from Silivia and Lautami Nasilai, the Tongan family on the remote northern island of Kava with whom Mercy had stayed and whom he had visited during his search. Silivia Nasilai had written Dad asking for money "to help keep my family." In his next letter, Curtis speculated that perhaps the reason there was no word from Abney, was that he was visiting the Nasilai's to quiz them about the *I Love You II* before he officially entered Tonga at Neiafu. (Curtis misses their names—he calls them the "Lautimes".) Ever the sleuth, he deduced "something must have influenced these people to have written when they did. It could have been a visit by Steve. . .it could have been that someone told them about Susan Maxwell's article. I just cannot help feeling that the timing of the [Nasilai's] begging letter is significant."

Tongan Siliva & Lautaimi

In fact, Silivia's request for money was not "significant". Her letter to Dad was dated April 17, two days after Maxwell's article appeared, so it is possible someone brought the piece to their attention, just as it is possible Steve Abney had visited them and was taking his time reporting back to Noel Curtis. But it was Dad himself who prompted Silivia's letter. In the week after Mercy's Mass, he wrote the family a letter and enclosed a photo of Mercy. Silivia responded by thanking him "for writing, and remembering us here in our island." She told him that his letter and the photo arrived "in April 9th".

I imagine that Silivia's letter with its declarations of her love for Mercy and her own family's poverty had moved Dad and that he mentioned it to Curtis looking for some insight or sympathy. Curtis, however, responded not to the letter's pathos, but by trying to fit it into the "mystery." He was determined to connect all the dots in the case, even Silivia's plea for financial help. There is no further mention of Silivia and Lautaimi in Curtis' missives, so perhaps Dad set him straight in another one of his phone calls.

Of more importance than the Nasilai's letter, and even of Abney's search, was the rumor that the *I Love You II* had made landfall at Mangonui, near the northern tip of New Zealand's North Island. It was Abney who alerted Curtis to the rumor: Abney had called Curtis from a payphone on the day he set sail on his search for Mercy. Technically, since Abney had already cleared customs when he came ashore to make the call, he was on New Zealand soil illegally. He then set sail on his solo voyage. While he was at sea, the New Zealand police investigated the rumor. After interviewing witnesses in Manugoni, they concluded that the catamaran had, in fact, entered New Zealand at Mangonui—not in January as the rumor had it, but at the end of November, 1977.

In his May letter, Curtis tells Dad:

> That ILU2 was there [in Mangonui] I am in no doubt whatsoever. Our police on such an inquiry really do a thorough job. The local policeman is well known in the district. Local folk will talk freely to him, especially when he is asking about something which cannot get them into trouble in any way.
>
> The people mentioned in the police report are those who always know what is happening in the small place. The name ILU2 could not be dreamed up or imagined by anyone in passing contact with the craft.

The police report convinced not only Noel Curtis, but also Captain Hunt and on the basis of the report, he closed the case. He told Curtis that "the purpose of our inquiry was to establish if the *I Love You II* had reached New Zealand. We now know she did." Because the boat's entry was "unofficial", Hunt had no documentation of when she had departed from New Zealand, but his task had been to find the missing yacht, and, given the official police report, he felt justified in saying that he had done so. His involvement was over. I have to wonder if the police report had come as a relief. Perhaps it provided a welcome excuse to end Dad's ever-persistent calls. In any case, the New Zealand Ministry of Transport, Marine Division, declared the case complete. Curtis commented:

> So another gap in the mystery has been closed, Buck. ILU2 did reach NZ. This means that Abney's quest to visit Matthew, Hunter, Minerva Reef was to be fruitless from the outset.
>
> I do not blame Steve. . .it was [his phone call] which eventually enabled ILU2's Mangonui visit to be established. That is to Steve's credit and justifies our confidence in him. He is responsible for the major development that ILU2 did reach NZ.

Curtis was disappointed in Hunt's decision but "quite prepared to keep my inquires on the move if that is OK by you."

It was indeed OK with Dad. Now that Hunt had dropped out, Curtis was Dad's sole remaining comrade-in-arms. He was not ready give up and had nothing to lose except whatever money he gave Curtis for expenses—a small price to pay for the hope of solid information on Mercy's fate. So Curtis kept the case alive on his radio network. The owner of a yacht called *Mascopal* contacted him from Papeete, the capitol of Tahiti which lies some 3,000 miles west of New Zealand. The yachtsman, "a retired senior US Army officer" said that the disappearance of the *I Love You II* was topic of "great interest' in Pepeete since Donald Glidden's girlfriend Taire McMillan and her mother had once lived there. According to the Tahitain rumor mill, the *I Love You II* had been seen "on the coastline of Queensland, Australia." This lead did not pan out—nor did any of the other leads Curtis received via his radio network. Nonetheless, Dad persisted in his phone calls to other side of the world.

In addition to Noel Curtis, he was in touch with a man named Mike Morehart who had known Mercy in Tonga and who, when he heard she was missing, had instigated the air search. Morehart was skeptical of the police report that the *I Love You II* had made landfall in Mangonui, so he went to talk to people there and came away believing, along with Captain Hunt and with Noel Curtis, that the catamaran had been there in November 1977.

In terms of trying to connect the dots of the case, the Mangonui landfall was a very large dot that raised more questions than it answered, but it did offer a possible connecting line to two other dots: the ore carrier *Jeprait's* sighting of an unidentified catamaran under sail 150 miles northwest of New Zealand in December, and the orange hull spotted by the *Tasmanian Enterprise* in the Tasman sea in early February. If, as Captain Hunt originally believed, the *I Love You II* had been lost before she reached New Zealand, the positions of these two sightings made no sense. But if the catamaran actually had reached New Zealand in late November, both the December sighting and the February wreckage, fit on a line drawn between New Zealand and Australia.

Had the *I Love You II* been on her way to Australia when she was lost? If this was the case, it still doesn't explain why Mercy had not contacted home in November from Mangonui. Even when Mercy was stoned, she wrote. The journal she kept at school was evidence of that: pages on pages of stream-of-consciousness musings. And however much cannabis or other mind-altering substances she used on this trip, they did not deter her from writing regularly to Mom. So I don't think it's reasonable to think that, in a dopey haze, she and Steve Wolff and Tiara McMillan all neglected to write home. In October Mercy confided to Mom that "Letters are becoming a drag… an empty and futile attempt to explain what's going on… no one will ever understand what's happening around me and within me…" But in the context of her letter she was referring to letters to her stateside friends.

The witnesses interviewed by the New Zealand police at Mangonui claimed that people from the catamaran had shopped at a local store and returned to the boat laden with paper bags full of groceries. According to Noel Curtis, the local post office at Mangonui had a telephone and it was only a short walk from dockside to the Post Office. Why had Mercy not called home to let Mom know she was safe after a long, stormy passage?

The owner of a local aquarium told the police that he had supplied the *I Love You II* with water. Had the catamaran pulled anchor and moved dockside so that a hose could fill her tanks? If so, how did the boat manage to maneuver in the confined waters of what Curtis described as a tiny harbor? When she left Tonga, she was without propeller drive due to a problem with their hydraulic system. Did she sail off anchor to dockside? And if she had been at dockside, wouldn't the dogs, which according to Abney were housed on deck, have been noticed?

Even more puzzling, the police reported that a young American male had left the boat and "gone to Auckland"—some 120 miles away. He was said to have sped away on a motorcycle with a native carving under his arm. Where did the motorcycle come from? Who did it belong to? And, if the rider was Steve Wolff, or even Mercy mistaken for a boy, why had neither mother had no word from them? By January, Steve Wolff's mother—like Mom— was consumed with worry.

What is more logical, and more painful to think about, is the possibility that they were not on board when the *I Love You II* (allegedly) came into Mangonui. If they were not on board, the only explanation is that boat had been taken over by someone else. A crew of drug-runners, perhaps, who had killed the four of them and the two dogs, made a Mangonui delivery or pick-up, then scuttled the boat in the Tasman Sea. This scenario was in Dad's mind. He and Noel Curtis went over and over it in their phone conversations and it must have haunted Dad.

It haunts me now. Somehow it seems worse to be murdered than to perish in a storm or be run down by a freighter at night. I am not sure why. In a way, all three death scenarios are accidental—a matter of being in the wrong place at the wrong time—and when I try to put myself in Mercy's place aboard the *I Love You II*, being shot seems preferable to drowning.

Unless I wasn't dead when I went overboard—then it would have a kind of double whammy, with anger at the take-over compounded by fear and despair. It is not easy to imagine. It took me months of reading and rereading Noel Curtis' correspondence to give the piracy scenario any credence at all. He took a barely concealed relish in having "solved" the mystery, and this made it easy for me to dismiss his argument. Subsequent research made it even easier to dismiss: neither in the 1970s nor today is there any evidence of piracy being a problem in New Zealand waters of the Tasman Sea. Piracy was and still is rife in the South China Sea and in Indonesian waters, but Susan Maxwell, who wrote the story on Mercy for her paper was surprised that the notion of piracy was even considered as a factor. "If piracy had been a problem, I would have known about it," she said.

Nonetheless, in 1978, the idea of piracy excited Curtis. It allowed him to connect more dots. If the *I Love You II* had gone down innocently in passage to New Zealand, if she had been run down in the night by a Japanese fishing boat as Hunt initially hypothesized, then all the other sightings—the unidentified yacht seen from the *Jeprait*, the wrecked orange hull, the supposedly police-proven landfall at Mangonui were irrelevant and had to be dismissed from consideration. Moreover, all the time and energy Curtis had invested in the case was meaningless.

Mal lele lehi fefine palangiOkatopa va-va

Took a copra frieghter from Nuku'alofa to VauVau-
about hundred miles north of Nakoaplota on the same
latitude as Fiji. The boat ride was an experience...over
crowded and loaded with Tongans and lumber, 3 horses,
5 pigs and a couple of hens here and there tied to
some ones basket. The trip took 3 days and 2 nites...
It was really hard to sleep at nite cuz every one was
crowded on the same deck...bodies piled on top of each
other, big production if you wanted to turn over and
not worth the trouble if you had to go to the bathroom.
But you didn't want to sleep during the day cuz
we were passing beautiful islands, and i saw whales
2 times, flapping their fins and blowing their noses...
incredible first time i've ever seen whales. Saw lots of
Dolphin too.

It was a good boat ride but lasted a little too
long for my comfort.

Pulled in Neiafu (main town of VaVa'u around
9:00 at nite. The moon was out and we were sailing

down a fiord...steep cliffs on either side of us..every one was singing.

Didn't know what i was going to do when i got off the boat. Was still tossing around from the boat ride, and getting mad at the drunk boys trying to get money off of me... i tried to get a room in the government guest house but, the caretaker was off on some other island attending the funeral of some noble who just died, but the caretaker's daughter invited me to spend the nite with her and the next morning took me to her aunt's house which had an indoor shower and toilet. Where i'm staying now. it's a nice arrangement. i've got a nice bed with sheets in my own part of the house. i'm paying $1.50 and get 3 meals a day. Valu is the woman I'm staying with. She's pretty old, but has tons of little kids staying in her house. Can't really figure out the situation, she doesn't speak English too well, but we manage to communicate. She's making me a mat to take home to my mother...it's a nice one, hope you like it. She makes me uneasy at times. i keep thinking she can read my mind..little things just happen to make me think so. She probably can...Tuesday she's taking me to the tail end of the funeral that's been going on for the noble (for a week now.. these are the last two days of feasting and dancing...mourning's all over with after that). i was wondering whether to bring my camara, and before i even asked her, she told me not to...i don't even know how she knew I had a camara...I guess most people (white people) have one.

Haven't been enjoying myself lately. Things are going my way it seems but i never really feel happy (except when i saw the whales). Every thing seems to revolve around myself too much...other people don't seem to be playing as big a part in my traveling as they should...i think i turn people off. i don't really mean to but it just happens. Oh well, i keep thinking things will change when i get to New Zealand...but i don't see how.

Trying to to get to New Zealand by November. Want to get a ride on a Yacht.

i'll try once again. i think i might have a ride on one going back to Fiji and then on to New Zealand. Sounds like i'm going in circles? Could be.

It would be really nice if i could get a ride on a Yacht, cuz then i could cash in my airplane ticket. Starting to run low on money. Don't understand how i could have spent so much...$2,000.00 in 5 months. Money goes. Guess i better learn how to conserve. Think i'm starting to get the gist.

Soon i'm going to send home a check for $900 dollars...could you cash it and send the lump to some bank in Auckland (Bank of New Zealand?) and then write Gen. Del. And tell me which bank to pick it up at?

That would be really good. So now, when you get my check you'll know what to do with it.

10/23 Sunday..went to church with Valu and her numerous children...Free Tongan Church..It reminded me of something out of the 3 rascals. The altar was made of boxes and crates arranged like a temple and pieces of fancy cloth and lace draped around the corners...flowers and tinsel here and there...everything was old and aged so it didn't look cheap. It really had class.

Lots of singing...Tongan style and then one hymn that sounded like Bach or some kind of chamber music.

The priest kept disappearing behind the altar and popping back into the scene with a grunt. All the children sat in the front rows!

On either side of the altar stood a man with a stick, who went around and hit the children who were restless and moving around and also grown-ups who were nodding off. When ever that happened the whole house broke out into a stifled laughing fit.

It was really something to see... After church we went to a feast..a real feast...no more room on this to write...take care and I'll probably be awaiting in Auckland for money..Fuka Otaota Mercy.

At the end of February 1974, when Mercy was a junior at Darrow,
she wrote Mom a letter on the back of this sketch torn from a notebook.
She made no comment on the sketch but told Mom that she was thinking
about dropping out and taking a high school equivalency test. "I could
find something that I wanted to work at and that would be acceptable (?)
to you and Dad. . . My diploma from this place isn't going to mean a
thing to me," she wrote. "It's so very secure in here. I know what's
expected of me and everything is done for me. I'm confused so
I still don't really know what I want to do. Just thought I'd write.

254

21

Even if Dad had turned up proof positive that Mercy had died a violent death, I'm not sure he would have told Mom. I think he saw it as his duty to shield her from a scenario that was far grimmer than being lost at sea. Today, a father might be more likely to share his darkest thoughts with his family—or at least unload them in therapy. But Dad was brought up with the gentlemanly code of "women and children first." His instinct would have been to protect his family. Just as he was secretive about money "for our own good," he was secretive about his suspicion of murder.

From Mom's album: "Mercy at the [our cousins] Childs'. We had a sort of pre-Christmas party because Bill & Sue, Christie and Andy, Fritz and Bonnie were going to be away for Christmas."

That June, Mom and Dad took the house in Bermuda out of the rental pool for two weeks and we children and all the grandchildren came down to visit. The house wasn't big enough for everyone at one time, so we came in shifts. I remember it was crowded, perhaps with Tommy, the youngest, sleeping on the sofa in the living room, and there was the usual big family beachy chaos with sandy feet and wet towels and knees scraped on coral. The kids had fights over Monopoly in the living room while the adults tried to read or drank Planters Punches on the deck which overlooked a turquoise blue cove. And I remember Dad sitting at a small desk in the living room with earplugs in his ears filling page after page with what looked like math problems. He was completely out of it. At meals he didn't speak. We were used to him tuning out. But this was extreme. For the whole week, he simply wasn't present.

Back at home, Sheila and I talked on the phone. She told me that Dad was driving Mom up the walls, that things were very bad between them. "He's still on the phone to New Zealand all the time. He just won't let it go," Sheila declared angrily. "I think Mother should get a divorce."

Never in a million years would the idea of divorce have occurred to me. I was shocked. One of them moving out of Firwood? It was unimaginable. But the fact that Sheila could imagine it as a solution pointed to the severity of the situation. Dad, I diagnosed, had become unhinged by guilt—guilt that he had not been able to save Mercy. I had no clue that he was trying to find out if she had been murdered. In any case, divorce seemed a draconian solution. He needed professional help, I decided. I told Sheila I'd write him a letter asking him to see a shrink. Neither of us imagined that he would. But I couldn't think of anything else to do.

It took me days to write it. I felt angry on Mom's behalf and some pity for Dad—along with dashes of superiority and exasperation. But I didn't want to come across as judgmental, even if I was, and telling him what he should do would get his back up no matter how right my prescription was. When my relationship with him wasn't adversarial, it was at best guarded and

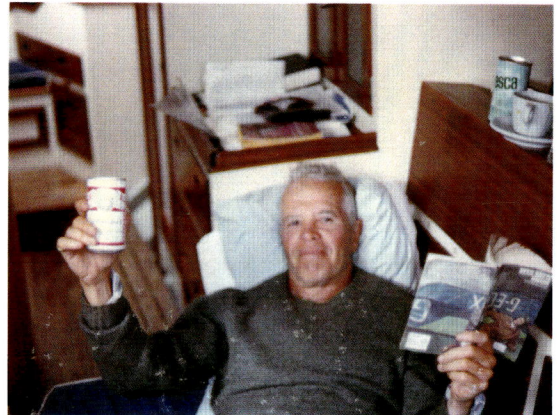

Mom's photo of Dad on the *Maria*

reserved. What I needed, what I felt would work, should be written from the heart and when it came to Dad, my heart felt clenched. So in the end I wrote about a friend I had here in Virginia, a mother whose nine-year old son had died, and how her marriage had ended in divorce. I cited the high divorce rate among couples who had lost a child and told him how much it had helped me to see a psychiatrist during my own crisis after college. I suggested that seeing a therapist might help him work through Mercy's loss. I told him we had all noticed how withdrawn and depressed he'd been in Bermuda. Perhaps I told him we were all worried about him and about Mom. I didn't save a copy of the letter, but I remember that when I finally typed out a clean copy, it was three pages, double-spaced. I gave it to Andy to read, not only for spelling (I've never been a good speller), but to check for lapses in kindness of tone. After he pronounced it okay, with some trepidation I mailed it off. I hoped Dad would go see someone, but knew that would be too good to be true. At worst, I figured, he'd be angry, but I'd weathered his anger enough times before so really, there was nothing to lose by trying.

I told Mom about the letter, and she told me that he had received it, but said that he hadn't discussed it with her. As Sheila had told me on the phone, communication between them had completely broken down. For a couple weeks I heard nothing from him. Then, at a family wedding, Dad and I happened to be sitting at an empty table together. The party was winding down. There were empty champagne glasses on the white linen tablecloth and the band was packing up. He told me he'd gotten my letter but hadn't had time to answer it. He said that he was managing all right and didn't need to see a shrink, but he appreciated my concern. To my surprise, he wasn't angry at all. He just seemed sad and resigned.

Dad was meticulous about answering letters. Even when someone wrote him a thank-you note, he would write back thanking him or her for the thank-you. Ordinary courtesies seemed to move him—as if he felt undeserving in some way. The routine gift of a pair of socks or a packet of golf balls for his birthday could move him to tears. We all shrugged this off as one of his idiosyncrasies—a slightly pathetic one, in my own view. So I wasn't particularly surprised when, in July, he thanked me again in a letter dictated to his secretary and typed on his cream-colored letterhead. He was back in his office after a few days off with Mom on the *Maria*.

Many thanks for your nice letter worrying about me and the fact that I have taken

257

Mercy's death hard. I guess I have been affected by it perhaps more than I know but I am getting over it. Part of my problem in Bermuda was my shoulder [injury] and also the fact that I was trying to figure out an accounting problem which made me appear quite withdrawn.

We had a very nice sail down the Sound when we brought the boat back from Providence. We talked about Mercy on the way down and it really has hit your mother a lot harder than it has me. Part of the problem is that it has really affected your mother very badly but she is getting over it and is much better.

I guess Mercy's death has put a real strain on me but really, Chrissy, I'm all right and I think your mother is too. Again, many thanks for your thoughtfulness in writing me such a nice long letter. I am really all right and your mother is much better. Time will take care of this situation and while we never forget her it will ease the pain.

He signed it "Dad" with a fountain pen and, in his bold, looping handwriting, thanked me yet again.

So he's putting it all on Mom, I thought. I felt a little disappointed. I had hoped, albeit remotely, that my letter might trigger some kind of breakthrough for him. At the same time, I was embarrassed by his gratitude and felt slightly fraudulent. Really, I had written out of concern for my mother, not for him. But I counted the letter a success at least on one point: I had managed to bypass my negative feelings for him. Reading his letter now, I think my letter may have been more successful than I thought at the time. Perhaps, it prompted him—and Mom—to talk over their loss and what each of them had been going through.

By December 1978, Mercy, along with Donald Glidden, Tiare McMillan, and Steven Wolff, had been missing for a year. Steve Abney had completed his six-month solo voyage to Tonga and was back in New Zealand. When he called Noel Curtis from Whangarei to check in, he was angry.

Here is Noel's account of the exchange:

> I asked Abney, specifically, if there was anything to report and he said 'No'. He said that in his opinion it was not ILU2 which visited Mangonui and the police report was all wrong and crazy. Abney then criticized us (you and me) for Susan Maxwell's article in NZ Herald of April 15th last. He ranted about his information having been given in confidence; that he did not want and did not like his name appearing in any newspaper. He said he was angry and upset that he had been given publicity.
>
> Buck, I did not let it go very much further. . .I gave it to him without sparing my language. I was, in fact, rough. That quieted him and he made some stupid remark about not wanting to become bad friends. I then broke it off and hung up. . .
>
> It is so sad that this twist has occurred in what is such a tragic affair. I was obviously misguided in putting any trust whatsoever in Abney and I apologize to you for having done so. . To be taken to task by a beach-combing salt-water bum, who obviously has something to hide in his past, just sticks in my craw. I thought it wise to inform you of this latest development. I will close now.

Steve Abney was now a bad guy in Curtis' book. Curtis began plugging Abney into the piracy theory, casting him as a co-conspirator. To Curtis, the fact that Abney objected to being quoted in the newspaper meant that he had something criminal to hide.

But Abney had a right to be angry—and on two counts. One, Noel Curtis' portrayal of him as the sorrowful lover was inaccurate. In her last letter to Mom, Mercy wrote that they had both been relieved to part ways. They had not had a great romance. Secondly, Curtis had betrayed his confidence. Abney, a private man who had named his boat *Incognito*, had been disbelieving and shocked by news of Mercy's loss. He had opened himself up to the Curtises and had talked freely about his sense of remorse, his hope that she might yet be found. He certainly did not expect that Curtis, without even asking permission, would expose his intimate feelings in the press.

November 9, 1977
Tonga
aerogramme

11/9

Dear Mama,

Moved out of Angi & Valas house about 2 weeks ago & have been living on a boat. Nice boat made in Norway & reminds me of the Maria. Its owner [Steve Abney] is from California and has been sailing around South America & Tahiti, for the last 3 years. On his way from Tahiti he ripped off his main sail and arrived in Vava'u under one small jib...Main sail totaled, he was going to get some Tongan woman to weave him a mat sail, like in the old days...we sailed out to one of the outer islands and found a friendly village that was willing to help us but when they saw the size that the sail had to be, they lost enthusiasm. One woman told us it would take 2 months, but she'd do it if we wanted her to for 2 big cooking pots and some Jerry Jugs. Steve wasn't willing to wait around for 2 months cuz hurricane season was coming up and he wants to get down to New Zealand... We brought in the old main to show the woman and with every one working on it, 2 women, 1 old man, Steve and me, it took 3 full days to sew together. It's pretty strong now, and has been blessed by the Tongan women so it will probably get him there.

Its nice being on this boat, but we don't get along to well, not really fighting but a lot of disagreements. Every thing i do is wrong and i'm getting sick of it, and Steve is too. i think.

i've got a ride to New Zealand on a 65 foot Tahitian Catamaran...beautiful red boat, 2 masts, owned by a retired airline pilot who's been sailing around for 5 years with his girl friend, Tahitian to match the boat, and a cowboy from Wyo... Really nice people, and lots of room on board, so it should really be a nice trip.

It's really interesting listening to people talk about the States who have been away for a couple of years in islands like these. All seem to have a sure feeling of some Atomic or natural disaster happening, and are glad they're safe in the South Pacific but sad to see every friend and their families in the path of demolition. You can really see how one would start feeling like that. Looking at the way people live around here...love and respect in a religious way for the sea and land...small communities, every one having a place and purpose, old and young and middle medium... There's no generation gap. I never understood what a generation gap was...I knew there was a communication gap between young and old but just thought that's how it always has been, nothing unhealthy or abnormal about it. Here, though, everyone's together, any activity, dance, feast, any gathering and the whole town's there. Once I saw this old man and 3 yr old girl carry on a really intent conversation for 1/2 day under a mango tree. Don't know what they were talking about, but it wasn't a lecture or telling stories, probably just talking about happening around the village. The people are so united. Then you think of New York City or even at home, every one's so alone and confused and frustrated about money, love, jobs and the future!!!! Everyone tells me the longer you stay away the less you're gonna want to go back. And it scares me cuz i think its true. i can feel myself rubbing out all the pulls that make me wanna go home.

Today we're on our way back to Kapa... the island where we got the sail sewn. We're going to help the village build a fence to keep the pigs inside so they won't eat all the crops. i've never seen so many pigs in one place. They got enough money for the fence by having this crazy concert...Tongan band, guitars and drums, then people, anyone, would rub themselves coconut oil and go out and dance in front of every one...just letting lose...& people would come up and stick money to the dancer's body. Everyone in the village had to give 10

$ during the nite... some gave more, & at the end of the nite they collected $900.00. So now we're going to help them build the fence & afterwards we're having a feast...hmmm sounds good, yeah.

Well I don't really know when I'll be in New Zealand probably before the end of November.

i'm having problems with immigration here...when i came here i got stamped for a month. i let it run overdue cuz i was out at an island and didn't get back until a week after the visa expired...stupid, i know, but i didn't think there would be any problem. But there was. The customs commissioner really got perturbed and wanted me off the island the next day. i told him O.K. but am planning to stay another 2 weeks at least. Well, i'll just stay out-a-sight, less-profile. it'll be OK i think and if not I'll just be in New Zealand a little earlier than expected. Hope every thing is well in the U.S.A and no bombs have been dropped. If you ever need a hideaway come to Vava'u, Tonga, and go out to Kapa island and look for Lautaimi and Salevi. They'll take care of you. much,
♡ Mercy

22

Sunday lunch on the terrace at Firwood, 1975

In March 1979, almost a year after Mercy's Mass, I received a letter from Dad. Letters from him were rare. Thanks to his secretary's reminders, on birthdays I would receive a dictated note on his business letterhead in which he enclosed a check and remarked on how fast the years were flying by. He always sounded surprised. Once or twice a year, I'd get a postcard from him when he was on vacation with Mom in Bermuda telling me they had played golf and were enjoying the warm weather. And there was the letter of the previous summer thanking me for telling him to go see a shrink. This letter, however, was in his own hand. It was warm and affectionate and more open than any I can recall. Perhaps because of the concern I expressed in my "shrink letter", he felt a connection with me that hadn't been there before and wanted to reassure me that he was still doing okay. Reading that letter now I feel the loss of a father I never really knew as an individual.

It was written with a blue ballpoint on yellow lined paper during a spring trip to the Virgin Islands. As in previous years, he and Mom flew down to St. Thomas and picked up a bare boat charter on Tortola. Sailing together had always been a way of renewing their connection and they both looked forward to their cruises together. It was time away from the high-stress of Wall Street and from Mom's endless rounds of domestic demands at Firwood. "It was always good when we were off on a boat," Mom remembered. The British Virgins were a patch of sunlight in the fog of grief. The waters were blue and clear and dotted with islands, all within easy sails of each other. There were snug harbors, empty palm-lined beaches and yachtie watering holes where you could refuel dockside or drink rum punches on a hillside terrace dripping with bougainvillea. Mom usually packed a small suitcase full of books—history for Dad, novels for herself. They slept late, drank brandy with their morning coffee on deck, swam naked when they could find isolated anchorages, drank martinis in the evening, read by lantern light in their bunks and presumably rekindled their sex life. (Mom and Dad had no qualms about letting us know they enjoyed sex.) "We have had a very pleasant and relaxing cruise," Dad wrote. "Tomorrow is the last day and I hate to see it come to and end. We are at Hurricane Hole all by ourselves. Hurricane Hole is at the eastern end of St. Johns."

Earlier in the cruise, he reported, they had sailed to Virgin Gorda, stopped off at The Bitter End

Summer 1975: Lunch on the *Maria*. Vodka and caviar for two. Mom's photo. She notes that the photo's colors "were not as good as I hoped"

for a drink, then sailed to Jost Van Dyke when they went ashore to have a drink at Foxy's Bar. Foxy, a native of the islands, was a celebrated party-man. They had met him some years earlier—he had been part of the crew on a cruise they had taken along the coast of Turkey and they had enjoyed his high spirits and fun-loving antics. This visit, however, over drinks at his bar, Dad observed a change in him.

> Foxy seems a bit subdued and has lost some of his sparkle and joie de vivre. I guess we all get old and Foxy is no exception but he looks the same. I felt a little depressed after seeing him. . . This cruise has been fine for both of us and your mother is much more relaxed and is beginning to get over Mercy's loss which hit her very hard. I hope we see you, Andy and the boys soon. A great deal of love to you, Dad.

Mom's letters to me that spring were, as usual, cheerful and supportive. She encouraged my writing (feature articles for the now defunct *Virginia Country Magazine*) and my teaching (a seminar on "Images of Women in Literature" at our local community college). She said she was seeing a chiropractor for back pain that she attributed to "a build up of tension from that dreadful last winter". She wrote about teaching herself to type and her work on John D.'s diary.

In April, when she and Dad returned from the islands, she asked Andy to help her design a garden in Mercy's memory. It was to be a water garden, a place for water lilies which she had always wanted to try her hand at. She had picked out a site near the house where it could be seen from the front terrace where in summer we had cocktails and family cookouts. Like the terrace, the new garden would offer a view of the Sound: in the foreground, framed by the branches of the massive copper beech trees John D. had planted a hundred years before, a rough expanse of lawn running down to the seawall; then the stony beach. At low tide, reefs of barnacled black rock. In the blue distance, the Greens Ledge lighthouse, pretty as a toy.

A central feature of the garden was to be an enormous bronze bell. It measured three feet high and its mouth was as wide. It weighed hundreds of pounds. When Andy tried to lift it in attempt to estimate its weight, he broke two ribs. The surface of the bell was weather-streaked with verdigris, like the monumental statues of war heroes and deities cast a century before. This was the bell from the Convent at the end of Long Neck Point. Every day it rang morning

From Mom's album: "During the Thanksgiving vacations while Andy and Tom were here, we hung the bell in the garden. It was not as difficult as we had expected." Tommy Daley on crosspiece. Tommy Ewing, left; Andy and me on right.

mass, the Angelus at noon, evening Benediction. The regular peals of the Convent bell were as much a part of Firwood as the fog horn from the lighthouse.

In 1979, however, the Convent no longer existed. In the Age of Aquarius, a rigorously religious, expensive, single-sex school was no longer a draw. The enrollment, which had been small to begin with (seventy-five girls), kept dwindling. Although teacher salaries were no drain since the nuns were not paid, many of the older nuns were retiring to the Mother House in upstate New York while younger nuns were leaving the order to work in Harlem among the poor. So the Madames of the Sacred Heart of Jesus closed the school and sold the property to a developer who turned it into a gated community. The old mansion with its chapel was split into two "mansionettes". Incongruous new ranch houses were raised on the lawns around them and the school's other buildings—including the gym (formerly a carriage house), and new brick classroom building—were converted into more residences. All the convent's furnishings were sold at auction and Mom's cousins, Sheila Parsons and Dora Rawle, bought the bell and gave it to her. She stored it in our garage.

In Andy's design for the garden, the bell was suspended from a simple staple-shaped frame made of redwood. The mounting which allowed it to be rung as well as seen, had a Japanese simplicity to its design—as did the rest of the garden. The new pond curved around the bell and its frame. At its widest end, water trickled into the pond over an arrangement of rocks. Around the pond, there was an earth berm (to be planted with azaleas, dogwood and a Japanese maple) that sheltered the garden from the road and from a neighbor's tennis court.

When Mom saw the plan—Andy's birdseye drawing of the garden—she was startled. "It's Mercy's footprint!" she exclaimed, her voice at once incredulous and delighted. "Look at it, it's her footprint!" The resemblance she saw amazed her. Tears welled up in her blue eyes—and she quickly blinked them back. I looked at the drawing again. The pond did look like a footprint. The bell sat in the "instep" between the heel and the ball of the foot and the rocks, indicated on the plan by five circles, could have been toes. Andy had not intended a visual pun but he was pleased that Mom was pleased.

What surprised me more than the serendipity of the design was Dad's acceptance of the garden. Generally he resisted any "home improvements" that weren't absolutely necessary. The easy chairs in the living room were worn threadbare but since they were still comfortable, he would not allow Mom the money to have them recovered. But she seemed to have had no problem getting money for a memorial garden, so perhaps it was a measure of his sympathy for her—an acknowledgement of what she had been going through or a peace offering made in the Virgin Islands. When I asked her where she'd gotten the idea to make a garden, she said she thought it had been his idea.

While the garden was under construction, Mom arranged to have Mercy's possessions in

Wyoming sent home. She contacted a young woman named Betsey Bernfield who lived with her husband in Wilson, Wyoming—a town on the outskirts of Jackson. Mercy had met the Bernfields two years before when she had worked at the Teton Science School. In a sympathy letter to Mom, Betsey Bernfield described Mercy as "a wonderful girl to work with" at the school and went on to say that they became friends:

> We grew to love her very much. She had the habit of popping in on us just when we needed help the most—and always pitched right in. When our little baby was born, my husband was working several jobs keeping incredible hours. I was alone and petrified and don't know what I would have done if Mercy hadn't come over and held the baby for me while I got my work done.

Betsey packed up Mercy's things and mailed them to Mom at Firwood. Mom wrote to me that, along with Mercy's wooden backcountry skis and her snowshoes strung with rawhide, there were "four boxes of mismatched socks and holey sweaters and odd shoes. But mostly books and drawings and that is all—it doesn't seem like much in the way of possessions—which of course— is the way it should be." In the same letter, she wondered how long Mercy had been interested in the South Seas:

> Before she left she said I could use her stereo—she bought it herself while she was at Darrow & there on the corner of the cover is a picture of some people in a Polynesian hut—it is surprising the amount of very intricate fine drawings she did and left around in the most surprising places—some on sheets by the pillow—one on the cover of the table in the laundry—inside the closet in the kitchen.

So from my perspective in the woods of Virginia, everything seemed to be on an even keel at Firwood. The terrible rift between Mom and Dad seemed to be healing. But when Andy and I and Morgan and Tim (then seven and five) went up to visit over the Fourth of July weekend, at lunch on the terrace, it became clear that everything wasn't okay after all. Mom had improvised a long table using doors on trestles covered with a bright floral tablecloth. Running down the center was a line of wine bottles and condiments: French Beaujolais, Heinz Catsup, Dijon mustard, wooden pepper grinders, saki cups filled with salt. Dad sat at one end, Mom at the other, and about eight or ten of us sat on each side eating hotdogs and hamburgers from a grill under the magnolia at the edge of the terrace. We washed them down with red wine. I was sitting in the middle, but could hear snatches of what Dad was saying to my brothers Bill and Fritz. He was talking as if Mercy might still be alive. Was I hearing correctly? He was going on about how she might have been sold into white slavery. I looked at Mom. Her neck stiffened; her mouth compressed into a hard line. I felt a stab of alarm. Had my father completely lost it? After lunch he and Billy and Fritz, their faces solemn, retired to the study.

"What's going on?" I asked Sheila as we helped clear the table.

She let out a snort of exasperation. "There was some kind of crank call. Dad thinks Mercy might have been captured by Japanese pirates and sold as a sex slave."

A sex slave? My sister? "That's insane!" I protested vehemently.

There was a ruckus among the kids. "Mom! Mommy!" they called.

"What?" we both answered. I lowered my voice. "She'd die first," I said to Sheila. "She'd have fought—she'd have died fighting!"

Or would she? Today, thanks to coverage in the news, human trafficking is less unthinkable—a hellish reality for hundreds of young girls who are sold and subdued by drugs. Imagining Mercy as a captive, I hope she actually was drowned at sea.

23

Memorial Garden

That Fourth of July weekend, a year and four months after Mercy's disappearance, Mom's memorial garden had just been completed. At Sunday lunch on the terrace, Dad, in defiance of his cholesterol count, was enjoying a hot dog like a little boy eating a stolen cookie. The leaves of great copper beeches had darkened to purple, the sun sparkled on the Sound, and the small white sails of weekend racers tacked back and forth on the blue water. But here was Dad talking about Mercy being trafficked by the Japanese. It was so shocking that I wondered if he was having some kind of psychotic break. Had the trauma of her disappearance in the Pacific gotten mixed up with leftover animosities from World War II?

What set him off, I later learned, was a mysterious phone call. I imagine that when he returned to Firwood after the Virgin Islands, he could not resist the phone in his study and decided to check in with his New Zealand sources. Or perhaps someone had left a message for him at his office while he was away. In any case, in early April, someone had alerted him to a strange bit of news concerning Steve Wolff—Mercy's fellow passenger on the *I Love You II*. Or to be more accurate, a bit of news concerning Steve Wolff's mother—a Mrs. Shaw—in Portland. In the middle of the night she had been woken by a call from a long-distance operator in Japan. The operator asked her to accept a person-to-person collect call for "Linda" from "Jack Ewing".

Mrs. Shaw did not accept the call. She wrote it off as a crank call. But it nagged at her. "Linda" was the name of a girl her son Steve had known. Why would someone call her number asking for Linda? Someone from Japan, no less. And who was "Jack Ewing"? Had someone trying to reach Buck Ewing gotten his name wrong? Did Buck have a son over in Japan? Several days later she mentioned it to someone who passed it onto Dad and, bingo, he was back in his obsessive mode, turning and twisting the phone call over and over in his mind. Whatever acceptance and peace he and Mom had found together in the Virgin Islands suddenly vanished. He was beset with questions. What if the call had been in code? What if it was actually a call for help from someone who had been in contact with either Steve Wolff or Mercy? What if the caller, due to the language barrier, had mixed up the names? The alleged Mangonui landfall might point to their murder. But what if they had not been killed? What if they had been kidnapped for ransom? What if Mercy was still alive somewhere in Japan?

Dad resumed conversations with his contacts in New Zealand. He had two long talks with Noel Curtis, and afterwards, in a letter dated April 9, 1979, Curtis lays out three possible explanations:

> 1. It was a cruel hoax and "there is nothing anyone can do about it . . .the hoaxer SOB

will eventually stop his tricks."

2. "Someone at the Wolfe-Shaw residence is a nut and liar and has made it all up."

3. Someone in Japan is "trying hard to tell you and Linda something which might be of great significance as a key to the ILU2 mystery."

Curtis himself favored the third hypothesis. Clearly the possibility of solving the case excited him. Perhaps in their phone conversations, Dad was resistant, refused to buy in, because Curtis asked him to "bear with me and to at least read what follows. . .and not throw this into the wpb [waste paper basket] without some study." He and Marney, he assures Dad, have spent a lot of time "conning over the puzzling and perplexing Japanese telephone affair."

What he came up with was the kind of solution a mystery writer supplies in the final chapter—a solution that ties all the loose ends of the story into a tidy package. In Curtis' story, Mercy is the victim, the innocent adventurer who falls prey to bad guys who are running drugs, not for fun, but for profit. Steve Abney is one of the bad guys. Another is the owner and skipper of the *I Love You II*, Donald Glidden. Glidden and Abney are in cahoots to make it rich running cannabis. In late November, after all the "good" cruising boats had already left Tonga, Glidden sets sail for New Zealand loaded with cannabis, which Curtis implies, he had picked up in French Polynesia where his girlfriend, Tiara, had connections. At some point underway, Curtis declares, the *I Love You II* had a rendezvous with a "mother ship." During this hook-up, the catamaran's crew was "removed", the cannabis transferred to the "mother ship," and a new crew of bad guys took possession of the catamaran. Then, as Curtis writes it:

> After the 'drug drop' ILU2 was deliberately and cunningly sailed to Mangonui for an illegal visit of two or three days as part of a master plan. She was then sailed out to sea where by prearrangement, she was run down as part of the scheme, torn apart and abandoned. The second crew, of course, went aboard the 'mother ship' before the 'run down'. Making the visit to Mangonui was a key part of the plan, as the crooks wanted the movements to be checked out as they were and the final outcome of the inquiries to be as they now are.

I have to wonder, as I'm sure Dad must have, at Curtis's logic. If the 'crooks' had made a successful delivery to the mother ship, why would they risk an illegal visit to Mangonui? Why not scuttle the boat immediately afterwards? Their "cunning" ploy of wanting authorities to discover their landfall doesn't make sense.

The scenario would work better if *I Love You II* were intercepted by the "mother ship" mid-passage to New Zealand, the crew members (and the dogs?) murdered and tossed overboard, and the cannabis loaded onto the catamaran for delivery to Mangonui. But there are problems with this plot turn as well. The witnesses interviewed by the police in Mangonui mentioned no off-loading of suspicious-looking bales. The only thing mentioned was a native carving that left the harbor under the arm of a young American male on a motorcycle. Would the quantity of cannabis required to turn a profit—a profit that warranted murder—fit inside a portable carving?

I suppose it could have been something more compact and more profitable than cannabis—heroin or cocaine, perhaps. But even allowing for a successful drug drop, casting Donald Glidden as a bad guy doesn't work. Why on earth would he scuttle his own boat? A boat that his son had helped him refit. Yes, there was the wreckage of an orange hull in the Tasman Sea—a hull that may or may not have belonged to the *I Love You II*—but that doesn't make Glidden a drug dealer who helped murder his own crew. Or sold them off to Japanese slavers.

To support his theory of Glidden-as-criminal, Curtis tells Dad that recently he heard from visiting yachties that Glidden had offered them reefer in Tonga. As further damning evidence, Curtis reminds Dad that the *I Love You II* was thoroughly searched by customs authorities in French Polynesia and in the Cook Islands.

And here again, I have to wonder: why *wouldn't* his boat have been searched? What customs official in the 1970s would NOT search a less-than-ship-shape, orange catamaran with the name *I Love You II* and skipper who, it seems safe to assume, probably looked like an aging flower child? What customs officials in that day (or this one) would waive inspection of a hippie boat?

Curtis ignores the fact that during both searches, no drugs were found. He also is vague about what happened to Glidden after the hypothetical "drug drop". Was Glidden "removed" in a double-cross? What about Tiara, his girlfriend? Did they survive, boatless, but rich? Steve Abney, however, Curtis keeps in his sights. Four months after Abney's "attempt to jack me up for the Maxwell story" in the New Zealand Herald, Curtis is still smarting. "That dead-beat has something to hide and never forget it," he warns. He passes on an "extraordinary" rumor that Steve Abney is the heir to share of a large fortune:

> The story goes that Steve is one of three children. When the youngest reaches a certain age some six million is to be shared three ways.
>
> Buck, what better cover up could there be for a man without visible means of support "just sailing around the Pacific" in his small (but high quality) yacht which has no name, to explain sudden wealth . . .
>
> All this, combined with Abney's outrage and even anger when I mentioned the possibility of drugs being involved in the ILU2 disappearance, is enough to convince anyone that the key to the vessel's fate is drug trafficking.

That settled, Curtis moves onto the unsettling phone call from Japan.

"Buck," he urges, "this clue must be followed up." He instructs Dad to advertise in Japanese newspapers and offer a reward "to appeal to greed and avarice and to establish the genuineness of your purpose." He allows that "all kinds of crooks, beggars and nuts are likely to respond," and suggests that Dad employ the "best lawyer you know" to help arrange the ads.

> The drug pushers are a dangerous pack of bastards who play it rough and for keeps. For the safety of us all concerned it is essential that you step very, very carefully . . .
>
> Apparently you have done nothing to trace the origin of the Japanese phone calls. I think you should do this using your consular service on the spot. Somewhere there has to be records of the calls and with the right leverage the information should be available to you. . .

Having warned and scolded Dad, as well as having inflated Dad's "leverage", Curtis ends on an elegiac note:

> I, personally, am convinced that had Mercy not been in the company of Glidden and Abney during that time, one or more of the cruising yachts would have had her join them for the voyage to BoI [Bay of Islands, NZ]. Without exception these vessels all arrived safely in spite of the hazards of storms and heavy going of which they all had their share. I repeat, this adds to our sadness because it was only a cruel twist of fate which places such a fine and inexperienced person as Mercy in that situation.

Another wondering—this one small and a bit mean: How did he know Mercy was "such a fine" person? Was he stroking Dad or was it simply a romantic projection onto a missing girl?

```
I am now certain that my earlier suspicions that there has been a
deliberate 'cover up' in the ILU2 affair designed to conceal the
facts from those trying to unravel the details surrounding ILU2's
disappearance are strengthhened. This goes for Abney; Gary E. Daniel-
son (convicted junkie); the mystery man 'Blackie' in Papeete; to
name but a few. Abney's attempt last December to criticise me for
the publication of Susan Maxwell's article only serves to harden my
opinion.

It may be that some day the truth will out.

Nothing could make me sadder than to write in this manner but every-
thing points to our having been "conned".

Sincerely and with all good wishes from Marney and self.
```

Noël

May 25th 1979.

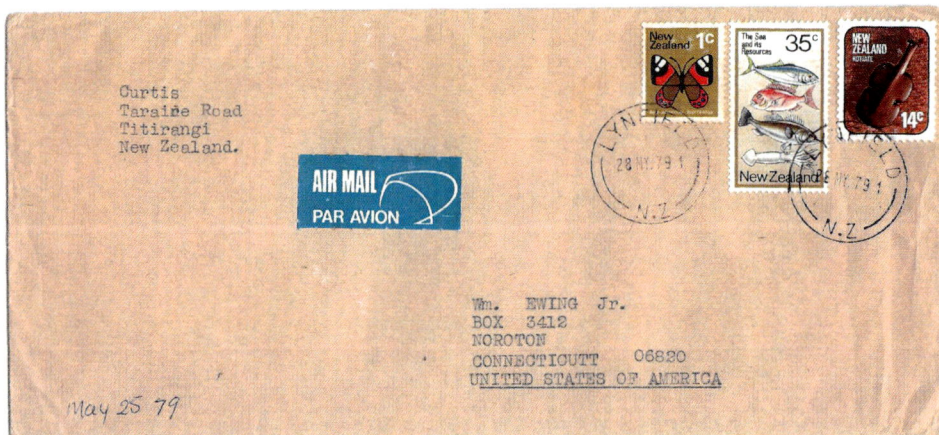

There is nothing in the manila file of notes, Western Union cables, and letters that Dad saved from his search to indicate he pursued the matter of the phone call. But in the spring of 2008, my sister Jessie told me that she also had had a mysterious call from Japan. Early in 1979 she had been working as a photographer for the Quad City Times in Davenport, Iowa and living in nearby Moline, Illinois. An overseas person-to-person call came to her home. Operator said the call was from somebody with the last name of "Ewing" and a first initial Jessie didn't recognize. Moreover, whoever was calling also had the wrong first name for Jessie so the operator did not put the call through. Jessie told Dad about the call and he told her that he had been in contact with the Morgan Stanley Bank in Tokyo and had hired a private investigator.

Three months after the phone calls, when we visited Firwood in early July, Dad was still tormented by the possibility that Japanese pirates had captured Mercy. I'm pretty sure that in his rational mind, he still believed Mercy was dead. But he couldn't help running the sold-into-slavery scenario by his oldest sons. When Dad got an idea in his head, he often would test and retest it against the reaction of others and I think on that July day, he was testing his own take to the phone calls by seeing what Billy and Fritz thought of them.

I remember hearing from my sisters-in-law, that when my brothers retired with Dad into his study after lunch on the terrace, they told him very firmly that, what ever else he did, he had to stop talking about Mercy. Even if he believed there was the remotest possibility that she was alive somewhere in Japan, he had to stop talking about it in Mom's presence and he had to stop talking about it at family gatherings.

So he did. He stopped talking about it—at least to us. He may have kept on talking about it to male friends, or to his trusted secretary Grace Manson who had worked for him as long as I could remember. I'm guessing that his communications with the investigator he hired in Japan took place at his Wall Street office and that if detective reports or bills had once existed, they were lost when his office was closed seventeen years later after his death from heart failure in 1996.

The last letter in the manila folder from Curtis is a kind of I-told-you-so. It is a short one—a single typed page—dated May 25, 1979, and encloses a photocopy of a page from the April issue of a magazine called *Pacific Islands Monthly*. The page is a gossip column under the heading "Cruising Yachts". One of the items is about Steve Abney and his sloop, the *Incognito*. It reads:

> INCOGNITO, an 11.6-m sloop from Santa Barbara, California, built in Finland 31 years ago. Steve and Ruth Abney left home in 1974 for an open-ended cruise that first took them to Panama and Costa Rica, where they spent two years working. In 1976 they spent nine months in French Polynesia before pushing on to the Cooks, Nuie, Tonga before spending the 1977-1978 cyclone season in New Zealand. Now they are back in New Zealand after spending most of 1978 cruising to the Kermadecs, Tonga, Fiji, New Hebrides and New Caledonia. Their plans now are to sail to Papua New Guinea.

At the top of the column, there's a photo of the Abneys sitting together on deck smiling at the camera—an attractive looking couple. He is barefoot, wearing shorts and a T-shirt. He has a full dark beard and an unruly head of hair that looks sunbleached on top. He sits with his long shins tucked up and pulled in under a forearm—a self-contained posture. The knobs of knee, the length of forearm shield his heart, as if he were ready to ward off any advance. His other arm is around Ruth's waist, pulling her into his protective circle. Her shoulder-length hair is loose and against her white shirt, she is cradling a small black cat whose name, according to the caption, is Porthole. They look happy.

In his letter, Curtis assures Dad that the man in the photo is Abney: "There is no doubt of that." But, Curtis complains, in all his talks with Abney, the man never said he was married. Moreover, "of the many cruising folk we have had visit us here"—yachties who had crossed paths with Abney in previous travels—"not one mentioned Abney being accompanied by his wife." This leads Curtis to conclude that Abney is not married and that the item in the Pacific Islands Monthly was part of a cover up "designed to conceal the facts from those trying to unravel the details surrounding the ILU2's disappearance."

But there are many other, less farfetched, reasons why Steve Abney might not have mentioned a wife to Noel Curtis. To begin with, as Curtis himself observed after his initial meeting with Abney, Steve Abney set a high value on his privacy. Would he have wanted to share with the Curtis' that he had committed adultery (if that was the case) with Mercy? He might well have felt that his marital situation had nothing to do with accepting Buck Ewing's commission to look for her. There's also the possibility that he and Ruth were not married but had a long-term relationship unblessed by church or state. Perhaps to avoid hassle, they let the Pacific Island Monthly columnist assume that they were a married couple. Thirdly, there's the possibility that they had an open marriage—an agreement that that each was free to connect sexually with whoever attracted them. Perhaps Ruth had sailed off on someone else's boat, leaving Steve free to invite Mercy aboard in his own boat.

None of these possibilities seem to have occurred to Curtis. He is sold on the idea of a cover-up. His cast of co-conspirators include "Gary E. Danielson (convicted junkie)" and "the mystery man 'Blackie' in Papeete". Who these people are, I have no idea. There is no other mention of them in Curtis' letters, so presumably he had talked about them to Dad on the phone.

Curtis last letter ends:

> Abney's attempt last December to criticize me for the publication of Susan Maxwell's article only serves to harden my opinion.
>
> It may be that some day the truth will out.
>
> Nothing could make me sadder than to write in this manner but everything points to our having been "conned.
>
> Sincerely and with all good wishes from Marney and self.

When I read the item in the *Pacific Island Monthly*, and saw the photo, I was surprised and also relieved. It was as close as I'd come to a happy ending to at least one of the threads in my sister's story. Here is my scenario: as not uncommon sailing couples who cruise full-time together, Steve and Ruth's relationship took a hit from the continual stress of being at sea: cramped spaces, no privacy, social deprivation, unpredictable winds, foul weather, and the need for constant vigilance in order to survive. I imagine that when Steve met Mercy in Tonga in October 1977, he and Ruth had separated. After a few weeks with Mercy on his boat, it became clear to both Mercy and Steve that they were not soul mates. Mercy, I'm guessing, was too combative for Steve. Perhaps she made the absent Ruth look good to him. Perhaps Ruth was in New Zealand and Steve planned to meet her there after his solo passage—good enough reason for not taking Mercy along with him.

When he reached New Zealand in November, he realized that Mercy and the *I Love You II* were missing and had a hard time with it. He didn't want to believe it. He felt guilty for not having taken her with him.

He turns to Ruth for reassurance. I doubt he tells her that Mercy was more than a casual acquaintance. Perhaps he simply says that her father, Buck Ewing from Connecticut, asked him to "check out" some remote islands where castaways might have been able to survive. So they sail off to Tonga with the goal of looking for signs of the *I Love You II* on the way.

A few days after they set sail from New Zealand, Susan Maxwell's story runs in the *New Zealand Herald*. And at one port or another, they hear of it, maybe even read a clipping someone has saved. There is a big blow up, anger, tears, accusations on both sides, but they manage to get through it more or less intact. In fact, the storm is cleansing.

Steve, however, can not forgive Noel Curtis for betraying his confidences, for violating his privacy, for causing Ruth pain and public humiliation. Some eight months later, they return to New Zealand, and Steve still harbors a silent fury. When he calls Curtis to report on his voyage, his anger erupts. Curtis does not take it well.

But—and here's my happy ending—six months later, in April 1979, Steve and Ruth are smiling at the camera. Their heads incline slightly towards each other. They are young and healthy and full of adventure. They will sail to new islands in new waters. In the future, a fortune may await them. In the meantime, they enjoy lots of sex, an occasional joint, and fair winds in the mainsail that Mercy helped sew up.

CRUISING YACHTS

PIM's roving correspondent, Jimmy Cornell, has been 'cycloning' with wife Gwenda and children Doina and Ivan in New Zealand, their ketch **AVENTURA** resting up in Whangarei while they have been looking the country over. He recently returned to Whangarei to check out the international mix which headed there to avoid the South Pacific cyclone season:

● **DUEN**, a traditional Norwegian fishing vessel registered in the American Virgin Islands, on its second Pacific voyage which started in May last year. Duen (meaning

Duen . . . on second Pacific cruise

'dove'), before reaching Whangarei, visited ports in French Polynesia, Suvorov in American Samoa, and Vavau and Tongatapu in Tonga. Plans are to head either for Fiji or Micronesia, perhaps both. On board are three generations: owners Albert and Dotty Fletcher, their son Toby, and daughter Vicky with husband Jim Camp and son James. Built of pitch pine in 1942, Duen is a topsail ketch measuring 15.5 m on deck with a 6 m bowsprit.

● **INCOGNITO**, an 11.6 m sloop from Santa Barbara, California, built in Finland 31 years ago. Steve and Ruth Abney left home in 1974 for an open-ended cruise that first took them to Panama and

The Abneys and Porthole . . . PNG next

Costa Rica, where they spent two years working. In 1976 they spent nine months in French Polynesia before pushing on to the Cooks, Niue, Tonga before spending the 1977-78 cyclone season in New Zealand. Now they are back in New Zealand after spending most of 1978 cruising to the Kermadecs, Tonga, Fiji, New Hebrides and New Caledonia. Their plans now are to sail to Papua New Guinea. Forwarding: Marsh, 5 Bellevue Rd., Mt Eden, Auckland, NZ.

● **GALATEA IV**, a 14.5 m cutter from Vancouver, BC, Canada, which retired couple Bob and Marg Miller left in May last year bound for the Marquesas, Tuamotus, Society and Cook Islands, then Tonga, Fiji and New Zealand. This year they intend to sail to Fiji, then on to the New Hebrides, Solomon Islands and Papua New Guinea. Mostly Bob and Marg sail their large yacht all alone but for the first part of this year's cruise daughters Nancy and Beth will be with them.

● **CHANTALAIN**, a 10.3 m French cutter registered in Noumea with Patrick and Kay Ifrah on board. A Morocco-born Frenchman, Patrick worked for a while in New

Chantalain's crew . . . working trip

Caledonia as a teacher while New Zealand-born Kay worked as a nurse. Last year they cruised in the New Hebrides, Chesterfield and Loyalty Islands. Now they plan to sail to Fiji, back to New Caledonia, then north to the New Hebrides, Solomon Islands, Papua New Guinea and eventually to Japan.

● **MARUFFA**, a 20 m yawl from Boothbay, Maine, US, on a world cruise with owner Katherine Greene, skipper Stephen Sewall, Michael and Stephen McDonnel, Sheila Viele, David Batchelder, Alex Logan and Michael Gilming as crew. Built in 1935, it was

Maruffa . . . Australia bound

rather neglected for a while until its present owner took over in 1977, bringing the Maruffa back to its original splendour. After transiting the Panama canal, Maruffa sailed to the Galapagos Islands, French Polynesia, Samoa, Fiji and New Zealand. Australia and Papua New Guinea are on this year's programme. Forwarding: Mark Sewall, Boothbay, Maine, 04537, US

● **MACUSHLAH**, a 9.3 m gaff ketch from Honolulu, in the Kittywake class, designed by Charley Davies. Owners Dave and Kay Malseed left California in 1970, cruising down the Central American coast to Panama, where they spent two years working in the Canal Zone. In 1977 they set off again, calling at the Galapagos Islands, Marquesas, Tuamotus, Society and Northern Cook Islands, American Samoa, Tonga and New Zealand. This year they plan to sail to Fiji, after which their plans are somewhat fluid.

● **TARRAWARRA**, an 11.6 m sloop from Melbourne. It spent 1978 cruising from Australia to Fiji, New Hebrides, New Caledonia and finally New Zealand and plans a return to the tropics soon. Four enthusiasts built the steel boat over a period of 4½ years but two of them were left behind because of family commitments. The other two, Kim Proud and Tony Robinson have promised to see the world on behalf of those left behind. Steve Dunn is crewing.

● **RISING SUN**, a 10.7 m sloop from Sidona, Arizona, which left Los Angeles in July 1977 bound for Hawaii where Dan and Denny Bache-Wiig spent a year replenishing the kitty before carrying on to both Samoas, Tonga, Fiji and New Zealand. This year they intend to sail to New Caledonia, New Hebrides, Solomon Islands, Papua New Guinea and possibly Japan.

Rising Sun crew . . . maybe Japan

● **ENDEAVOUR**, a 12.5-metre fibreglass sloop from San Diego, owned by Doug and Sandy Thompson, arrived at Tubuai in the Austral Islands writes Don Travers. The Thompsons had brought a gravely ill baby, accompanied by a nurse and the infant's mother, from Raivavae. From Tubuai the baby was flown to Tahiti where it recovered. An almost identical incident occurred about a year before with a Belgian yacht, **KALAIS** (PIM March 1978). After leaving San Diego in May last year the Thompsons visited the Marquesas, Tuamotu and Society Islands before reaching the Austral Islands. The Endeavour was the first yacht to call at Tubuai since June 1978. It returned to Tahiti in January.

Russell, New Zealand
January 25, 1978

Dear Mrs. Ewing...

I was so excited to get a letter w/Ewing return address, I didn't click that it wasn't Mercy's familiar scrawl-

I've been living in Russell, sort of a yachtie sanctuary in New Zealand and found out about 2 weeks ago that Mercy was aboard this catamaran I'd been hearing discussed the past month or so—suddenly a yacht missing took on much greater significance, concern, fear (I'm sure you know the gamut of emotions)...since then, I have discovered that Mercy met and almost sailed with 3 boats that I have met while here...each time I can't help wondering what twist of fate led her to go on "I love you two" and not on one of the ones here which are safe and sound.

But it's wasting energy to ponder the "ifs"...it's a terribly helpless feeling to know someone you love is lost at sea....and I keep trying to find comfort in the old adage no new is good news...and optimistically picture the boat and crew safe on some lush and plentiful and hospitable island...but without communication—and-

for the comfort it gives me—I put in a request with the powers that reign for their safety and welfare whenever thoughts of Mercy cross my mind...It must be an incredibly difficult thing for a parent to cope with.... I can only imagine the heights of worry my own parents would be going through if I were out of touch— your letter held calm and strong words...and I hope both of us will hear news soon.

Mercy's photo from Fiji of her friend Carol on their bilibili.

I'm leaving Russell in a few days, and will be out of touch with my yachtie friends and their ham radios for the next couple of months—please do send word when you hear something, as the newspaper will be my only possible source of information—it's a rare occasion that I look at one.

My concern is deep...and for all of us—I hope the tension of waiting is soon broken...Thanks for your letter—keep in touch...Carol

MONEY ORDER
135 0156549

TRAVELERS EXPRESS COMPANY, INC

FINANCIAL SERVICES

A SUBSIDIARY OF THE GREYHOUND CORPORATION

PAYABLE THRU
FIRST NORTHWESTERN NATIONAL BANK
FARIBAULT, MINNESOTA

75-53
919

DATE 10-14-77

PAY TO THE ORDER OF _Mercedes Ewing_ SEE NOTICE ON BACK

CAMDEN NORTHWESTERN 37 AND 00 CTS DOLLARS
DO NOT PAY OVER ONE THOUSAND DOLLARS

AMOUNT _2647 Penn No._ _Minneapolis MN USA_ _Amy Crawford_
PURCHASER'S ADDRESS   CITY AND STATE   PURCHASER, AS DRAWER'S AGENT

⑆0919⑈0053⑆135 0156549⑈ 90

Mercy,
I just received this letter back again Feb. 1 - 1978.
Are you in New Zealand? or where —
I'd like to repay my debt.
Thanks again
Amy Crawford

Although Mercy wrote to Mom that she was "running out of money," she lent money to a girl named Amy. After Amy got home to Minnesota, she wrote to thank Mercy "for being such a friendly, trusting banker" and enclosed a money order.

24

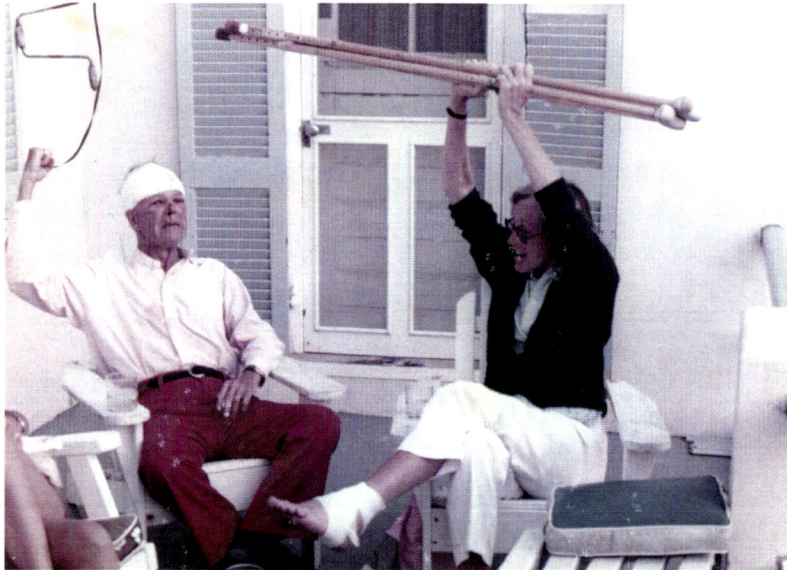

After Mercy was lost, Mom and Dad both suffered severe accidents. Dad ran over Mom's foot. As she was recuperating in Bermuda, he dove head first into shallow water and hit poison coral. Mom clowned for this photo and Dad kept it on display in his study, the "command central" of his search.

A year or so before his death in 1996, Dad and Mom came down to visit us in Virginia. He was 83, frail, suffering from heart failure, still as stubborn as ever, still as tuned out as ever, but diminished. Not the father I had grown up fearing. One evening after supper, the subject of Mercy came up. I remember he was sitting on our sofa. A shadow of pain came into his eyes and he looked down at his hands in his lap and rubbed his knuckles with a thumb. "That was a terrible thing," he said, as much to himself as to us.

"Do you still blame yourself for letting her go?" I asked, ready to argue with him if he did.

There was a heavy pause, and I could feel Mom listening intently. Then he shook his head. "No," he said simply. He let out a breath and compressed his lips into a grim line of resignation.

In real life endings are rarely tidy. The many questions raised by his search never were answered, and the conflict between Mom and Dad was never truly resolved. As Mom remarked more than once, "That really was the end of our marriage." Or at least, the end of a marriage in which Dad was her protector, the husbandly umbrella over her head.

Although there is no natural ending to Mercy's story, Mom gave us the benefit of an artificial one—artificial not in the sense of fake, but in the sense of something made. On the same Fourth of July weekend that Dad was testing, testing, testing the notion of Mercy as a sex slave held by the Japanese, Mom presided over a dedication ceremony for the garden constructed in Mercy's memory. She gathered everyone inside the newly planted berms. We crossed the stepping-stone bridge to the pond's small island of grass and tried to keep the little ones out of the water while we waited for stragglers. The water in the pond was black. There were goldfish in it, and lily pads, and the reflection of clouds. A gentle wash of water ran over the stone boulders at the "toe" end of the footprint. Then Mom came out of the house, barefoot and wearing a striped butler's apron over her wrap-around skirt. She was carrying a tray full of glasses and a bottle of champagne. She asked Dad to read the inscription he had written and had been etched into the small bronze plaque fixed to the crossbeam that supported the bell. He took his glasses out of the breast pocket of his jacket, put them on, and went up to the bell. The glasses were horn-rimmed and gave him an owlish, professorial look. He peered at the plaque.

"This bell," he read aloud, "was placed here in memory of Mercedes C. Ewing, a bold and loving girl, high-spirited and full of adventure, lost at sea in November 1977 in the South Pacific and greatly missed by her family."

Mom gave the bottle to one of my brothers to uncork. There was a loud pop, and an overflow of white fizz. The glasses were filled and passed around and we lifted them and drank to Mercy. Mom's smile looked watery. Then she stepped up to the convent bell, took the rope attached to its bronze clabber, and gave it a hard pull. A very loud, very pure note rang in our ears. It was so loud it was dizzying. It must have carried all the way to the lighthouse, all the way across the Sound. The little ones stopped running and looked up in surprise. As if on a dare, Mom gave it a series of staccato rings, then laughed. "Go ahead," she instructed. "Every one gets a turn." And one hard on another, we rang and rang the bell for Mercy. It sounded like a coronation.

At the bell, 1980
Left to right, sitting: Pat, Jessie, Maria Daley, Sue and Billy Ewing with Tracey, Will, and Rory.
Kids standing: Tim and Morgan Andreae, Bill and Chris Daley
Adults standing: Fritz and Bonnie Ewing, Annette and David Ewing,
Buck and Mary, Tommy Ewing, Andy and Christie Andreae, Tom and Sheila Daley.
(When Mom posed for a photo with Dad, she would bend her knees so as not to appear as tall as she was.)

REFLECTIONS

During the long, sporadic effort of writing this account, from time to time I would have a dream that seemed to describe or inform my process. It was as if my unconscious mind were saying, "Pay attention!" Or: "This is where you are." I remember a dream I had as I was beginning work on Dad's folder: our long-dead dog, a beautiful and valiant little Jack Russell, was diving into dark waters and surfaced with a bright copper penny (A penny for your thoughts?). The date under the head of Lincoln was my father's birthdate. (Dad as the President of a private "Civil War"?). I enjoyed the surprise of these visual puzzles. I wrote them down in a series of notebooks and tried to solve them. Now, like old messages from forgotten phone calls, their significance escapes me.

However, as I neared completion of a later draft, I had a kind of vision that has stayed with me. In that twilight state between waking and sleeping, I saw—and felt—a tear-shaped glass ball slip out of my throat. The surface of the glass was silvered and inside it, a child floated in the Sound under a pale blue summer sky. There was salt water in her ears. She heard nothing. She was weightless and utterly self-contained.

The child, I decided, could be Mercy. The glass ball that contained her was her story. Turning this image around in differing lights, I began to understand that the reality of her life had its own existence—an existence apart from my telling of it. I also realized that when any of us recall her story, our reflections are cast on its mirrored curve surface. Peering at my own reflection on the curve of this narrative, I gradually began to see distortions—distortions of my own making and closely-held for more than thirty years.

One skewed reflection was my image of the *I Love You II*'s owner and captain, Donald Glidden. When Mercy was lost in 1979, I, along with Dad and Mom and the rest of the family, had envisioned Glidden as a bad guy—a sloppy sailor, someone willing to bend the law, a half-stoned hippie, an escapist, an irresponsible pleasure-seeker. Here was a man who reputedly had faked an inner ear problem to get early retirement, a fifty-year old ex-pilot whose girlfriend was a flight attendant half his age. A man who set sail on an ocean passage in cyclone season with a broken engine and a radio that didn't work. A man who allowed Mercy to hide below deck to avoid immigration authorities. Yes, we all admitted, Mercy had been stupid. She had made "poor choices," as Mom put it. And if Dad blamed Mom for "letting Mercy go" on her trip, below the murky surface of loss, intuitively, unthinkingly, we all cast a measure of blame on Glidden.

But my picture of Glidden as a reckless sailor changed when, out of the blue, a pair of experienced sailors from Tasmania arrived in our Virginia woods to visit our friend and neighbor Anne Holliday. At the time, I was wrestling with the piracy/murder scenario, so their unexpected appearance seemed an eerie example of synchronicity. Caroline Langley and Rhonda Haldane owned a 35-foot steel ketch designed by the late American designer Charles Wittholz. They had been cruising for years in Tasmanian coastal waters and also had sailed across the Bass Strait between Tasmania and Australia and up along the west coast of Australia as far as Queensland. Over a jug of wine, late into night, I went over the details of Dad's search with them. They told stories of their own close calls, named other yachts that had been lost, described forty-foot high waves and hurricane force winds. The sea, they assured me, was a far more real danger than the drug-running pirates of Noel Curtis' imagination. When I showed them Dad's snapshots of Donald Glidden's boat with its rakish lines and twin orange hulls, they immediately pronounced it a "Wharram cat", a catamaran designed by an Englishman named James Wharram. Caroline and I went upstairs to my study and she found his web site for me.

Wharram was an early pioneer and innovator of multihull design. Back in the 1950s, when he was in his twenties, he became intrigued by ancient Polynesian rafts and built an experimental twenty-three foot, double-canoe sailing craft. Skeptics described it as "two coffins lashed together". Nonetheless, along with two German girls as crew, he successfully sailed the boat from Falmouth, England, to the West Indies. In Martinique, he and the girls built a second, larger catamaran and sailed it home across the North Atlantic. He described both voyages in a book he wrote in the late nineteen sixties, *Two Girls, Two Catamarans*.

On the assumption that Donald Glidden would have read a book by his boat's designer, I ordered an original copy from a used book site. When it arrived, I opened up the package and found a 192-page paperback whose plain, cream-colored cover and black lettering gave it a self-published look. There were lots of photographs, and of course I looked at those first. Some, in vivid 1950's Kodacolor, were of seascapes at sunset, of "friendly conversing whales" swimming beside the boat in "the moon path", or of "Jim" Wharram in his oversized glasses and yellow foul-weather gear huddled at the helm looking like a young Woody Allen. The black-and-white photos showed Wharram's boat on a tropic beach being built and at sea breasting cliff high waves. They also showed Wharram and his two-girl crew, often happily naked as they sailed, navigated, prepared meals, wove coconut fronds into mats.

If the photos are seductive, so is Wharram's story. It is a tale of adventure on the high seas, in turn uncomfortable, sunnily serene, or darkly fearful. But each near-catastrophe taught him more about the capabilities of his craft and the parameters of its design. They weathered storms, a near demasting, broken rudders. Their fresh water supply became tainted with bitumen paint. The feared terero worms, whose damage caused Christopher Columbus' vessel to go down in a storm, ate holes in Wharram's twin hulls. Fortunately, Wharram had a talent for improvised fixes, so his story is not only a story of lucky near misses; it also is a tale of a man's learning curve, of self-reliance and ingenuity at sea. "The sea fosters individuals," Wharram writes at the end of his book, "who can be in tune with nature, sometimes somnolent, easily relaxed, at other times charged with energy, like a storm."

It is easy to see how Wharram's book might have hooked Donald Glidden—on several levels. It held out a dream of sailing with naked women in tropical waters and offered a way to test manly mettle. It also meshed with counter-cultural attitudes of that era: Wharram disdained "our bureaucrat dominated, machine-operated society" and saw life at sea as a healing choice. Perhaps this stance resonated with Donald Glidden. Certainly it had resonated with Mercy.

But there is more than romance and philosophy in Wharram's book. He made a convincing argument for the safety of his designs. He discussed sail to hull ratios, the difficulty of speeds above the square root of the waterline, how to avoid the multi-hull "leap", "V" hulls versus centerboards. He scorned the experimental saucer-shaped float which one multi-hull designer had placed at the top of the mast as a safety measure: the designer had believed the Styrofoam float would prevent the boat from capsizing. Mom and Dad had read about this and Mom had speculated that if Donald Glidden had had such a device on his mast, they all might have survived. The implication was that Glidden wasn't up-to-date on the latest safety measures; that he was a lackadaisical sailor. But Wharram maintained that the device was not only ridiculous looking; it was useless because the design of the boat itself was flawed. He predicted that the platform between the two hulls was "too close to the sea and would smash in" and the large cockpit at the rear would flood. Wharram complained:

> Why the designer had turned his back on the principles of the Polynesians was not made clear in the yacht magazine, though in another journal, a prospective catamaran designer described the ancient Polynesians as a "bunch of naked natives riding log canoes lashed together with bamboos." Perhaps this racial superiority, particularly against men who went naked, was the unconscious motive for the lack of interest in the Polynesian voyages of the past, or even in mine.

In the 1980s, James Wharram introduced a line of professionally built multi-hulledboats. But before that, all his boats were do-it-yourself. He was not interested in supplying yachts to an elite group of rich sailors. His mission, he declared, was to enable "the urban man" to create an object of beauty with his own hands and then set to sea and "directly and intimately interact with the beauty and power of nature." In the 1970s, the only thing James Wharram sold was plans. Which means that Donald Glidden built the *I Love You II* with his own hands, and perhaps the hands of his son Scott.

Wharram's web site estimates a 3500 hour building time for a catamaran the size of the *I Love You II*. Whatever plans had cost back in the seventies, even adding in time and materials, Donald Glidden had built his boat for considerably less than a conventional yacht of the

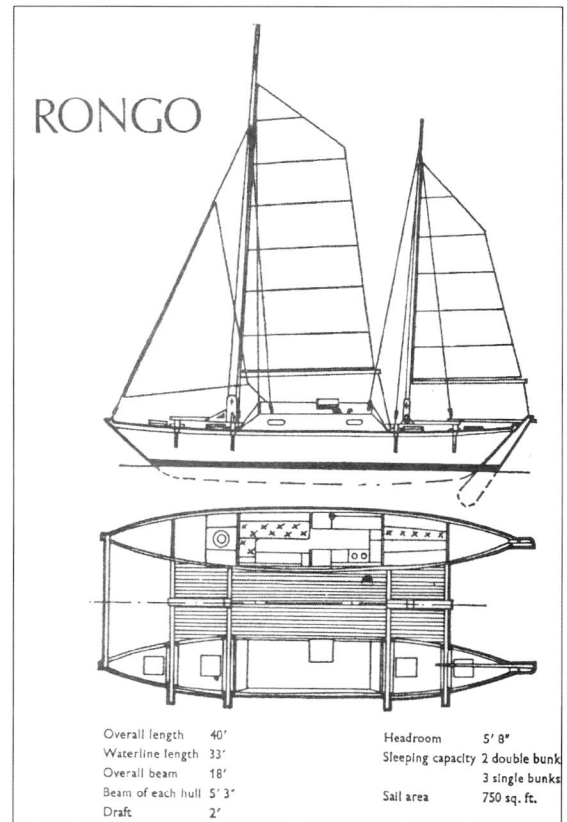

RONGO

Overall length	40'	Headroom	5' 8"
Waterline length	33'	Sleeping capacity	2 double bunks
Overall beam	18'		3 single bunks
Beam of each hull	5' 3"	Sail area	750 sq. ft.
Draft	2'		

Wharram's sketch of his self-built, ocean-going catamaran, *Rongo*. The *I Love You II* was approximately 15 feet longer.

same size. Had he spent two or three or four years of weekends and evenings building a 50-plus foot catamaran in his garage? Or had he worked full-time on it? What if his inner-ear problem was real? What if it grounded him?

A self-built boat of any type suggests commitment and self-discipline, mechanical skills and craftsmanship and a large investment of time and patience. A self-built Wharram cat suggests that Glidden had an imagination, that he was intrigued by the idea of a modern boat designed according to ancient principles. Clearly Glidden had been more capable and more creative than I had imagined. I had interpreted the *I Love You II*'s broken radio and a malfunctioning engine as a sin of negligence. But there may have been no place in Neifu, or even in the capitol city of Nukuualofa, that could repair a maritime radio. There may have been no place in Tonga to buy the necessary parts to fix a foreign diesel engine.

After Mercy was lost, and Mom had settled on Captain Hunt's theory that the *I Love You II* had been run down by a trawler, she declared bitterly that "if only" Glidden's engine had been working properly, they would have running lights at night and might have avoided being hit. In a 2007 conversation, however, she conceded that they might have used oil lanterns on deck at night.

I remember mornings on the *Maria*, after the breakfast dishes were done, we washed the black soot off the glass shades of the cabin lanterns that we lit after dark. In order to save the boat's batteries for an emergency, we rarely used the cabin's electric lights. For Glidden, oil lanterns were certainly an option and he might have used them not only as a way to save battery power, but also as an aesthetic enhancement, an evocation of ancient Polynesian sailors. So the lack of electricity was not necessarily unsafe. With oil lanterns they could have been seen at night. IF their lights had not been obscured by towering seas. And IF there had been someone on the trawler's bridge.

An October 2007 article in the *Washington Post* featured a sailor from Maryland named John Atkisson who had just completed a single-handed circuit across the Atlantic and back in a 32-foot sloop. Atkisson told the story of how, 100 miles off Ireland, he was sailing a compass course on autopilot and was down below cooking breakfast when he heard "what every solo sailor most dreads—the sound of diesel engines nearby." He sprang to the cockpit, but was unable to disengage his autopilot in time and the resulting collision crumpled his bow and pulpit railing and almost dislodged the steel headstay that supported his mast. Miraclously, the sloop's fiberglass hull was undamaged—there was no gaping hole, no gush of cold sea filling the cabin. He limped into Crosshaven, Ireland for repairs. He figured that had he been 100 yards farther along on his course, the trawler would have sheared him in half. Thereafter, he saw trawlers in his dreams. He also rigged an alarm on his radar that would wake him if another ship approached. None did.

Shortly after I finished reading *Two Girls, Two Catamarans,* I was cleaning out a file drawer and found a letter from Noel Curtis that Mom must have sent separately from the letters in Dad's folder. It was dated March 7, 1978. Curtis had just interviewed Abney aboard the *Pegasus,* the yacht Abney had been hired to help repair. Curtis had quizzed Abney about the condition of the *I Love You II's* engine and Abney had repeated what he had told Curtis in an earlier interview: that "on or about Nov. 15, 1977 the hydraulic transmission unit to the propeller burst and was unserviceable." Rather disparagingly, Curtis reports that Abney's knowledge of the catamaran's "means of mechanical propulsion was so poor as to be almost useless." But, Curtis tells Dad, "even with a transmission unit undamaged, the craft's propeller would give it a speed of only about one knot." This means that Glidden only used his engine for maneuvering inside a harbor. At sea it would have been useless.

In keeping with Wharram's low-tech philosophy, his early catamarans were intended to be propelled by wind only. Presumably, the *I Love You II's* engine was Glidden's own add-on—an American-type convenience, useful in port, but not essential for sailing. Curtis informs Dad:

> The engine, a diesel, was a good one mounted on the main platform and cased in wood. It appears that the unit (hydraulic) transmitting the engine power to the propeller never did work satisfactorily.

The fact that the propeller was out of commission doesn't necessarily mean that the engine didn't work. Its alternator might still have been able to charge batteries and provide electricity. I remember times, when sailing on the *Maria,* our rather iffy diesel would die and we would drop anchor under sail or, trickier yet, sail onto a mooring. We were rather smug about our seamanship—when we pulled it off. But even on the rare and embarrassing occasions when we

From Mom's 1958 album: "a beautiful warm sunny sail" on the *Maria*. Dad had two weeks summer vacation and he and Mom would get off on the boat for a week by themselves. Then we kids would join them for the second week. Top: Mom at helm. Center: David in life jacket and Jessie in sunglasses; Fritz. Bottom: me with book; Billy at helm and Mom with a morning beer. Mercy would have been two and left at home with Patrick in the care of our nurse Marie Burns.

ran aground in port, we usually could kedge off using our dingy, a spare anchor, and muscle power at the oars. Or we could wait for the incoming tide to lift us off. There seemed nothing unsafe about the lack of an engine.

Mom was disdainful about motorboats in general—she called them "stinkpots". When we sailed on Long Island Sound, big Chris-Crafts would roar past us trailing diesel fumes. "Hold on," she would yell to us kids, as the *Maria* heaved in their wakes. She didn't like the *Maria*'s inboard diesel much better than stinkpots. It seemed to always give trouble and Dad was constantly tinkering with it—down in the bilge instead up in the cockpit with her. It was his engine, not hers. Even in heavy weather, if given a choice (though Dad often didn't give her one) she would prefer to sail under a storm jib—trailing a sea anchor if necessary—rather than crash through the seas under power. The same was true with the *Maria*'s ship-to-shore radio. It was Dad's, not Mom's. She liked being out of touch. She resented the intrusion of the outside world into her vacation. She saw it as important for Dad, at least when they were on the boat together, to forget about ups and downs of the stock market and the stress of office politics at Morgan Stanley.

So, after all these years, I realize that in fact, Mom shared more with Donald Glidden than the anger of loss could allow: both preferred wind power to motors, both were unconcerned at being out of touch with civilization, both found respite and healing at sea. The big difference is this: my mother's vacation was Donald Glidden's life. He had made a bid for personal freedom and, by all appearances, attained it. On the *I Love You II*, he had escaped the world of conventional duties and negotiations. Mom, on the other hand, never realized personal freedom. Her escapes from her nine children were few and far between and even when she and Dad were off alone on the *Maria*, she felt duty-bound to support his decisions. She knew she was the better sailor, but he was the Captain.

If my image of Donald Glidden shifted as I wrote Mercy's story, so did my perception of

Dad and Mom. At the time, it was clear to us all that Mercy's loss had divided them, split their marriage apart. Out of this division, I formed a judgement as two-dimensional as one of Mercy's doodles: I saw my mother as a hero and my father as crazy.

Mom, to my mind, did everything right. She had cried alone and with us. Over boozy lunches with her close friend Adele Edgerton, she had confided fears for Mercy, her frustrations with Dad. By the sheer strength of her will, she had managed to let go of all the appalling uncertainties of Mercy's disappearance. She had walked and prayed her way to acceptance of the fact that Mercy was never coming home again, then pulled the rest of us along with her and initiated our grieving with an Easter Monday Mass.

The only time I saw her give vent to her anger and sorrow was after the Mass, after the reception Sheila had held at her house. I was upstairs at Firwood on the third floor, napping off too much of Sheila's good Chardonnay, when I was woken by the sound of breaking glass. CRASH, tinkle, tinkle, CRASH, over and over. The noise echoed loudly up the back stairwell. I ran down two flights to the kitchen and found Mom throwing glasses into the trashcan. On the kitchen table, there was a tray of bar glasses, gifts that my father had received over the years. Some had violets painted on them. Some were black with gold oil wells on them. Some had Christmas wreaths on them. And one by one, she was hurling them into the trashcan. She looked defiant, determined. I thought she had lost it.

"What are you doing?!" I cried.

She turned and there was an odd look of satisfaction on her face. "Life is too short to live with glasses you hate," she announced.

Her statement struck me as profound: the wisdom of a heroic mom.

Last, but certainly not least, as much as she loved Mercy, Mom did not elevate her in death to sainthood. I remember her once talking critically about the way her Aunt Evelyn, her mother Mercedes' sister, had mourned her oldest son John who had died at age 17. Evelyn set up a kind of shrine to him on the mantle piece of the living room at Firwood. I imagine his photograph in a silver frame, a vase of white flowers. Every time one of her younger sons, aged 16, 14, and 12, misbehaved, Evelyn would declare that her "dear John" never would have done such-and-such a thing. Mom herself remembered her departed cousin John as a bully with a mean streak. Perhaps her Aunt Evelyn provided Mom with a negative example, an example she was determined to avoid.

It is only now that can I see that the strength I so admired in Mom also had a downside. With the same resoluteness, with the same unflinching will that got her through Mercy's death, she held onto her anger at Dad. She could not forgive his accusation that she was at fault for "letting Mercy go." The very cold shoulder she often turned to him must have deepened the depression he suffered at the end of his life.

Perhaps forgiveness is a state of grace that one cannot attain by sheer force of will. Perhaps her drinking, which was heavy to begin with and became even heavier after Dad's death, had trapped her in an angry loop. Not until the end of her own life, was she able to let go of it.

"Do you still feel angry at Dad?" I asked her during one of my last visits with her.

"Oh," she said wearily, "it was just a case of the office boy kicking the cat." She didn't want to talk about it anymore, didn't want to remember. At that point she was in her eighties, immobilized by pain and suffering cognitive impairment. She could no longer read, though she always kept John LeCarre's *The Night Manager* within reach—a kind of security blanket. I felt a little guilty for bringing up the losses of the past. Although she was often frustrated by her increasing loss of independence, she seemed content in the present. Often she would declare how fortunate she had been in life.

This statement always made me want to object. As a mother, she had suffered through more traumas than Mercy's loss. My sister Sheila became permanently crippled after complications from brain surgery. In the same week, our developmentally handicapped brother, Patrick, was hit over the head with a chair by his roommate and ended up as a quadripelegic. Mom buried Patrick in 1995 after he succumbed to pneumonia at age 41 and she buried our brother David in 2008 after he was felled in an instant by a heart attack at age 56. But if I did object to Mom's "good fortune", she would remind me that she was not the only woman in the world who had lost children, that she had spent her life in a beautiful place, had never known poverty nor been victimized by war. "I've been very lucky," she would insist. I had to admit she was right. Her perspective was broader and truer than mine.

As for distortions in my view of Dad, I saw his blaming Mom as part of the craziness I had diagnosed. I didn't believe he was being intentionally cruel. He was just crazy. Somehow in searching for Mercy, he'd gone off the deep end. Drawing on a quick mix of pop-psychology and Sophoclean drama, I theorized that his obsessiveness was rooted in guilt. He himself, openly and repeatedly, expressed guilt over not having been able to stop her from going to Tonga. But I preferred to believe that his conflicted, occasionally violent, relationship with Mercy was closer to the core of his guilt.

Not until after his death in 1996 did I understand that he was no more deranged than anyone else in the throes of grief. I was a hospice patient care volunteer at the time and, as part of an in-service training session, I attended a talk on gender differences in grieving. Gender differences? I wondered. Don't we all grieve the same way? But the speaker, a bereavement counselor named Thomas B. Golden, quickly disabused me of this notion. Venus and Mars mourn differently.

Golden, after a loss of his own, found himself uncomfortable with the "talk it out" mode of grieving expected by his fellow therapists, most of whom happened to be women. So he began to study male grieving rituals in primitive societies and eventually wrote a book on his findings called *Swallowed by a Snake*. His thesis is that the grief model in our culture is a feminine model that often does not meet the needs of a man. While the "feminine" mode of grief is inclusive (we want to connect with loved ones) and emotional (we talk about our feelings of loss), the natural "masculine" mode tends to be solitary. A little ding! went off in my brain. Solitary: Dad had refused to take any one with him on his trip. Masculine grieving, Golden observes, tends to be cognitive. Another ding! Dad's need to solve the puzzle. And there was more: Men find relief from the pain of loss in action (ding!) and in rituals that help them connect with their loss. (Ding, ding! Dad's endless evening phone calls!) My brain was ringing and all the dings made one big dong. Or rather, a Duh. Suddenly it all seemed so obvious. Just as the bell Mom had rung for Mercy had cleared the air for our family, the ringing in my head cleared my view of Dad.

I even began to suspect that my own grief mode was more masculine than feminine—hence the solitary, cognitive explorations of this story. Still, I felt little sense of connection to him. Due to World War II, he was absent during my babyhood, and then after the war, Wall Street claimed him, and he was virtually absent during my childhood. When he came home from work in the evenings, he was unavailable behind a newspaper. Sometimes, to help mother out—perhaps on Marie's days off—he would give us a bath. And sometimes he would come home with candy in his suit pocket for us—a pack of Chuckles, a sugary gum-drop type candy that came in five colors, and we would vie to see who got "the black one", liquorice being our favorite. In general, however, like his mother, Maria, Buck Ewing had little interest in young children. While he was proud of the family he had sired, being with us was more of a duty than a natural pleasure.

During my teenage years, I went out of my way to avoid him. He was controlling and when disobeyed or disrespected could become violent. My primary emotion in his presence was a stomach-turning fear. Perhaps by the time Mercy was an adolescent—some fifteen years after my own adolescence—he had mellowed. But by all accounts Mercy had not been afraid of challenging him. Tommy Ewing, two years younger, remembers her as "brazen". She stood up to Dad and fought back. Perhaps she had a model in Jessie, who was six years older: when Dad hit Jessie, she would yell, "Go ahead, hit me again if it makes you feel better!"

It wasn't until I began working on Mercy's story, that my picture of him began to shift. As

I read the correspondence in his manila folder, I recognized him as the father I had known: obsessive, stubborn, single-minded, irritatingly persistent. But there was a positive side to Dad's one-track tenacity. I found a healing irony in the fact that while these traits made him a less than an ideal father, they were desirable, even indispensable, in someone trying to cut through government bureaucracies and a maze of rumors.

As I pieced together the path of his search, I became less judgmental towards him. I recognized in him my own tendency toward obsessiveness. Perhaps all writers and artists have this bent and I had to wonder what he might have been if his father had not ordained a career in finance for him. Given the freedom to follow his own natural inclinations, would he have been a writer, a spinner of tales? Certainly he had the curiosity and imagination: as a venture capitalist, he was always looking for the magical unturned stone.

The new shadings in my picture of Dad were intellectually satisfying, but they didn't really soften the casing around my heart. What did that was another story, a "Dad story" that my brother-in-law Tom Daley told me as I was finishing an early draft of this account. According to Tom, when Dad was in New Zealand, he experienced what he believed was an attempt on his life. Dad did not tell this to any of us children or to Mom. But he told it to Tom not long after his return from New Zealand. He and Tom happened to be sitting together on the evening commuter train out of New York, and Dad, instead of burying himself in his paper as was his wont, told Tom the following story.

He said he had been driving at night in an isolated rural area of New Zealand when the headlights of a car had appeared in his rearview mirror. They came closer and closer until they were right on his tail. He was driving faster than he had ever driven before and it was in the dark on an unknown road. Tom doesn't recall how Dad escaped. Presumably, he drove into a town, a lighted, populated area, and the vehicle had disappeared. The point of Dad's story—what he'd confided to Tom—was that he'd been badly frightened. He believed he had come close to being murdered for his money.

Certainly, with his rumpled, and sometimes threadbare, clothes, he didn't look the part of a rich man. My brother Fritz recalls walking past him in an airport lounge. Dad was asleep in a corner and Fritz mistook him for a bum—what we now call a "homeless" person. Another time, on a business trip with Dad, Fritz pulled out a gold American Express card to pay for a car rental and Dad frowned in disapproval. "You shouldn't have a gold card," he said.

Dad and me 1942

"Why not?" Fritz said. "They sent it to me in mail."

"People will know you have money," he replied. His own American Express card was the standard green one.

Dad was secretive about money in his own family as well. Mom had no idea how much money she had of her own—how much she had inherited from her parents. Nor did any of us daughters have a clue as to what our "expectations" might be. He obtained power-of-attorney from all of us children, had his accountant prepare our tax forms, and refused to give us copies of what had been filed. When Andy and I made wills after the births of our children, Dad's lawyer refused to work with our attorney. Like John D. Crimmins before him, and like his own father, Buck Ewing attempted to control his children with purse strings—a strategy that proved unsuccessful in all three generations.

When I studied Dad's Shell Road Maps of New Zealand, I guessed that the chase most likely happened on the way back to Auckland from Kawakawa where he had met with the psychic and flown over the ocean for five hours in a rented plane. In Kawakawa, Dad had spent a good deal of money—if not in payment to the psychic, then to the pilot. I'm sure he had with him a shockingly large cash supply of dollars—a five-hour flyover of the ocean probably didn't make a big dent in it. It's reasonable to assume that the pilot didn't take American Express: use of plastic was in its infancy then. Moreover, Dad's father, whom he idolized, used to walk around with two thousand dollars in his pocket as a matter of course—this, of course, was in the pre-credit card days. And like his father, Dad himself always carried an untold number of hundred dollar bills in the money clip in his pocket. So he had enough money on him to kill for.

Moreover, Dad was what Mom calls "a trusting soul". I suppose the negative word is "gullible" but that implies stupidity, and he was by no means stupid. He simply lacked the discerning intuition that some people claim to have when they meet a stranger—the self-protective, gut feeling that discriminates between the trustworthy and the untrustworthy. He assumed that everyone was decent and honorable (as he himself was), and a number of times in his business career, he had been cheated and betrayed by people he counted as loyal friends. So it's also possible, that instead of being a random target, he was set up by someone he met in Kawakawa.

It's also possible, of course, that there was no malice in the car behind him. The driver could simply have been an impatient local who was familiar with the road and wanted to pass. Perhaps numbing fatigue, a strange road at night, and a sense of failure had suddenly blossomed into acute paranoia—a kind of panic attack that might have killed him in a car crash as surely as any highjacker.

I turned Tom's story over and over in my mind. I imagined my father driving alone at night, periodically shaking his head to shake off his fatigue. Perhaps, at the approaching glare in his rear view mirror, he first felt a prickle of annoyance. Then a flash of anger at the persistent rudeness of it. Maybe he slowed to allow the vehicle to pass and when it didn't, he felt a sudden stab of fright and stepped on it, flooring the accelerator till the speedometer's needle wavered over 100. Never mind that it was kilometers-per-hour, not miles per hour. He felt he was driving faster than he had ever driven before, and it was in the dark, on an unknown winding road, in the left-hand lane. It was the kind of chase scene that his hero Steve McQueen might have relished, but for Dad, at that moment, it had all of the cold terror of a bad dream.

This incident, heard second-hand from his fellow Wall Street warrior, was a gift for me—a private measure of mercy, as it were. Never before had I imagined my father as fearful. For the first time in my life, I saw him as powerless and vulnerable. I was able to think of him in a more whole-some way, as an individual who was actually rather like myself. I no longer had to keep his ghost at arm's length. I realized that for a relationship to be healed, a person does not have to be alive.

Finally, I also realized that although I found no answers to Mercy's disappearance, I no longer felt the need for them. Now her story seems complete to me. Like the child floating face to the sky inside the silvered teardrop, I am weightless. The salt water of Long Island Sound is in my ears. The noises of discord are muffled. For a measureless moment, I am one with the movement of the rippling tide.

—

ACKNOWLEDGEMENTS

September, 1985. Mom's birthday at Jessie's in Chicago. Jessie set her camera up on a tripod and put it on timer as we toasted Mom. Left to right: Jessie, me, Sheila, Mom.

I am beholden to my sisters and brothers for sharing their memories of Mercy with me. Thank you, Sheila, Jessie, Bill, Fritz, and Tom. Special thanks to Sheila for digitizing hundreds of photos from our mother's albums and to Jessie for lending her telling photos to this account. Thanks also to Joan R. Challinor for her cover photo of Mom and Mercy on the beach at Firwood and to my cousin Mary Challinor for her portrait of her father. Both Mary and her sister Sarah contributed

their "Mercy stories". I am grateful to many dear friends who over the years have read or listened to and given supportive input on my many drafts: Suzanne Kilgore, Harry Papagan, Larry Gilg, Tiffany Rousculp, Theresa Curry, Janet Brome, Nan Hathaway. I am also grateful to graphic designers Lindsey Dengel and Pam Owens. Lindsey helped me dig into this project and get a grasp on the very complicated task of orchestrating images into my text. Pam's meticulous eye and design talent brought the book's layout to completion. Finally, and with much love, thanks to Andy who lived through Mercy's loss with me and has accompanied and encouraged me through the long, sporadic process of writing about it.

Overall, Virginia. 2017